DOS PASSOS AND THE FICTION OF DESPAIR

ROWMAN AND LITTLEFIELD
TOTOWA, NEW JERSEY

DOS PASSOS AND THE FICTION OF DESPAIR

IAIN COLLEY

ROWMAN AND LITTLEFIELD
TOTOWA, NEW JERSEY

© Iain Colley 1978

All rights reserved. No part of this publication may be
reproduced or transmitted, in any form, or by any means,
without permission

First published in the United States 1978
by ROWMAN AND LITTLEFIELD, Totowa, N.J.

Printed in Hong Kong

Library of Congress Cataloging in Publication Data

Colley, Iain.
Dos Passos and the fiction of despair.

Bibliography: p.
Includes index.
1. Dos Passos, John, 1896–1970 – Criticism and
interpretation.   2. Despair in literature.
I. Title.
PS3507.0743Z56   813′.5′2   77–13428

ISBN 0–8476–6020–6

For Liz, Scott and Marius
and for my Mother

Contents

Acknowledgements

No one but myself is to blame for any errors of fact or oddities of judgement in the following pages. However, I should like to record multi-farious debts of gratitude to the following: Nigel Builder; Keith Carabine; James Epstein; Anita Newton; Shaie Selzer; John Whitley.

Special thanks are due to my wife, who not only gave her energy and patience to the typing of my script but bravely tolerated unpleasant moods into which the researching and writing of this book cast me.

I should also like to record my thanks to Mrs Elizabeth Dos Passos, who has been generous in granting permission to quote from her late husband's works.

I.M.C.

June 1977

Introduction

To define, analyse and judge the meaning of failure in the work of a serious modern novelist is to treat his work as an appreciation of life, enlarging and informing our comprehension not simply of literature but of the intimacies and the public gestures of ourselves and our contemporaries. Failure, or a sense of it, is a fundamental human experience – endemic in our time, if not in all history. The two major writers of his generation most familiar to Dos Passos – F. Scott Fitzgerald and Ernest Hemingway – both saw failure as a dominant theme. In Fitzgerald's writing the disjunction between the world as it is pictured by the romantically enhanced imagination and life as it must be lived in rooms and streets is conveyed in images of extreme grace and sensitivity. Hemingway is the principal creditor of twentieth-century American letters: if he could be conjured away, almost everyone would be out of debt. With the courtesy of an actor, each played his role to the hilt. Their lives and their art invade one another. Both died in a conspicuously fitting manner, a textbook case for the moralist or psychoanalyst. Yet both stood for the tragic view, the belief that an immaterial good survives the ruin of the honest, the brave and the young.

Dos Passos is not a tragedian, and as a man he is so elusive as to be a source of embarrassment. *USA* is known, and widely appreciated – particularly by those who are free from the preconceptions of the literary specialist – but the most generally known fact about Dos Passos is that he switched political sides. True, the facts of his life are known; but they are less vivid than the portrait of Hugo Bamman, in Edmund Wilson's *I Thought of Daisy*:

> . . . Hugo was really on close terms with no one. As soon as he had sampled the conversation and caught the social flavour of a household or group, he would simply go straight away and bottle a specimen for his books, where he would assign it to its proper place in the economic structure. He distrusted his family and his early associates, because he believed that they had sold their souls to capitalist institutions; but though he chose to live exclusively with outlaws . . . he never managed really to be one of them and perhaps never trusted them, either.

So tough remained the insulation between himself and the rest of humanity . . .[1]

Hugo Bamman is a figure in fiction, but he is drawn from Dos Passos and provides a rare clue to the character of Dos Passos in 1929 as observed by the keenest and most intelligent critic of his generation. Above all, Bamman's shyness and detachment help to explain the difficulty of envisaging Dos Passos as a person. Like Bamman, he seems to have swum in and out of people's lives as, according to Carlos Baker,[2] he disastrously swam into Hemingway's. Throughout the following chapters, 'Dos Passos' will signify the novelist and not the person.

From American writers born around the turn of the century there grew up the 'Lost Generation'. The tag now has the air of a faded romantic slogan, yet, as Malcolm Cowley wrote,

> the generation deserved for a long time the adjective that Gertrude Stein had applied to it . . . It was lost because its training had prepared it for another world than existed after the war . . . It was lost because it tried to live in exile . . . The generation belonged to a period of transition from values already fixed to values that had to be created.[3]

But normative insecurity is a stimulant to men of spirit, to iconoclasts, anarchists and poets. Randolph Bourne saw in the decay of the old values their very inadequacy, and called for an upsurge of creative innovation:

> Our intellectuals have failed as value-creators, even as value-emphasizers . . . The allure of fresh and true ideas, of the speculation, of artist vigor, of culture styles, of intelligence suffused by feeling, and feeling given fibre and outline by intelligence . . . can hardly come . . . while our reigning philosophy is an instrumental one.[4]

In the same month, before Fitzgerald had received his commission and while Hemingway was still a cub reporter with the *Kansas City Star*, John Dos Passos was on ambulance duty in the Argonne. In a letter to Rumsey Marvin dated 12 September 1917 he had written of 'the net of slavery'.[5] No excuse of pragmatic expediency justified the war to him: the profound moral sensitivity that was to distinguish the Lost Generation had been tempered in fire.

Dos Passos and Hemingway first met in Italy in 1918, shortly before the latter's 'traumatic wounding' at Fossalta di Piave. They were regular companions after 1924, when Hemingway was living at the sawmill in the Rue Notre Dame des Champs and Dos Passos arrived for what he later described as 'one of my fitful stopovers in Paris'.[6] Dos Passos was to write of the Hemingway of the early days with affection and respect – 'The School of Paris was already full enough of faddism to make a cat

sick, but Hem never fell for the shoddy'.[7] In Hemingway's memoirs of
that time Dos Passos is identified – though not by name – as the 'pilot
fish', and denounced with paranoid vindictiveness:

> He is always going somewhere, or coming from somewhere, and he is
> never around for very long. He enters and leaves politics or the theatre
> in the same way as he enters and leaves people's lives and countries
> in his early days . . . He has the irreplaceable early training of the
> bastard, and a latent and long denied love of money. He ends up rich
> himself, having moved one dollar's width to the right with every dollar
> that he made.[8]

And after the publication of *Chosen Country* Hemingway mentioned in a
letter that 'the Finca Vigia supported a pack of fierce dogs and cats
trained to attack one-eyed Portuguese bastards who wrote lies about
their friends'.[9]

Hemingway's quarrelsome and competitive nature tended to make
trouble even where there was no real cause, though for many years the
two writers were close friends and companions. Their friendship died
owing to the Spanish war, a casualty of the time, and their estrangement
was virtually final; each softened later, and even corresponded, but the
closeness of the 1920s never returned.

As authors, writes Alfred Kazin, 'Hemingway and Dos Passos were as
essentially unlike each other as two contemporaries sharing a common
situation can ever be';[10] yet he also refers to 'the hard and deliberately
plain prose which Hemingway and Dos Passos . . . established as their
own'.[11] Kazin is right both to stress the realistic lineage of Dos Passos
and to suggest the difference between him and Hemingway as artists.
Hemingway is an apostle of heroism, and his archetypal hero is the lone
individual afflicted by the pain and injustice of life yet redeeming all by
his courage. Hemingway's art is mythopoeic; the universe in which his
stricken gladiators suffer 'timeless' and 'perennial'; his range of effects
narrow but intensely concentrated. The short story was his natural
medium, and his comparative neglect of the historical dimension handi-
capped him as a novelist.

But in his stories Hemingway showed creative vigour of an exceptional
kind. He rendered a fantastically simple philosophy in terms of the
utmost literary sophistication. Perhaps no critic could admire Hemingway
as much as he admired himself – with the progressive degeneration of his
talent he became a supremely obnoxious character – but even the sneering
Fiedler is obliged to admit that 'His authentic work has a single subject:
the flirtation with death, the approach to the void. And this subject he
managed to treat in a kind of language which betrays neither the bitterness of death nor the terror of the void.'[12] Hemingway had to believe in

heroism and tragedy because he also believed in some immanent hostile principle: the mysterious They who kill you the first time they catch you off base, who send fatal thunderbolts, who load the dice and fix the odds so that man, necessarily a loser, can only prove his worth, to himself or to God, by foredoomed acts of self-assertion or endurance. Such an outlook has its contingent weaknesses – the self-pity that Fiedler mentions, and the Job-like sanctity surrounding Hemingway's heroes in books such as *A Farewell to Arms* in which there is a frequent failure to objectify. But above all it paradoxically restores human significance to the post-1918 disaster area, and it does so by taking man outside history. Though the Nobel Prize citation justly praised Hemingway for reproducing 'the genuine features of the hard countenance of the age', his lack of historical awareness is a severe restriction; when he stretches the narrative line to produce a longer work he produces a succession of linked sketches rather than an organic book.

The individual depicted by Hemingway struggles against fate, and although he cannot win outright the author insists that 'a man can be destroyed but not defeated'.[13] The circumstances of his destruction may be set in a historical context – war, revolution, *après-guerre* dislocation – but these tend to be local definitions of an eternal human destiny. Hemingway does not picture a golden past. Even the stories from *In Our Time* which have a pre-war setting concentrate on pain and loss, and the power and freshness of the best ones still communicate the sickening shock of innocence blenching before necessary horrors. Hemingway's art strains to picture the big existential moments as they occur, vivid and traumatic; he rejected 'timeliness', and he could not have written, as Dos Passos did in 1934: 'the business of a novelist is, in my opinion, to create characters first and foremost, and then to set them in the snarl of the human currents of his time, so that there results an accurate permanent record of a phase of history.'[14]

Yet Dos Passos, by creating characters who are intended to chart the currents of their time, is often charged with neglecting the inner dynamism of human relationships, and it is true that at his weakest he has the air of beachcombing, of turning over every object in his path without considering its essential value. Hemingway found a totem and a style very early in his career, and the peak of his development, reached so early, left him only a long decline. Hemingway's superb professional discipline eventually tightened so fiercely on his art that it distorted it; there was no room for natural growth. In the early books, one can see how exactly his observation and technique correspond to his understanding of a tragic fate:

Once in camp I put a log on top of the fire and it was full of ants. As it commenced to burn, the ants swarmed out and went first towards the centre where the fire was; then turned back and ran towards the end. When there were enough on the end they fell off into the fire. Some got out, their bodies burnt and flattened, and went off not knowing where they were going. But most of them went toward the fire and back toward the end and swarmed on the cool end and finally fell off into the fire.[15]

Here is the 'delusive simplicity' of Hemingway's writing. The third sentence, with its understated irony distilled in the word 'enough', transforms description into comment and prepares the reader for the significance of the next two sentences, relating the memory to the panicky retreat from Caporetto and to Henry's impending loss of Catherine in childbirth. It is a model of artistic detachment. In comparison, a representative passage of early Dos Passos collapses because the writer lacks the confidence to let his situations speak for themselves:

There were tiny green frogs in one of the putty-colored puddles by the roadside. John Andrews fell out of the slowly advancing column a moment to look at them. The frog's triangular heads stuck out of the water in the middle of the puddle. He leaned over, his hands on his knees, easing the weight of the equipment on his back. That way he could see their tiny jewelled eyes, topaz-colored. His eyes felt as if tears were coming to them with tenderness towards the minute lithe bodies of the frogs.[16]

And when he glimpses his own militarised reflection in the water he concludes – redundantly – 'So this was what they had made of him'. The temptation to press his hero's claims in explicit terms that enfeeble the impersonal imagery has overcome Dos Passos.

But Hemingway's early adoption of a settled logos created stresses which are never satisfactorily solved: they result in the disappointing non-fiction (*Death in the Afternoon* and *Green Hills of Africa*) published during the years when Dos Passos was at his most creative; the degeneration of tragedy into stylised brutality; the fatal flirtation with politics; the supersession of the young genius by a messiah of the *ex cathedra* judgement, suspicious, vain and boastful; the lapse of a memorable style into ludicrous self-parody. The lack of personal direction and the over-receptivity to influences one finds in the youthful work of Dos Passos become a positive virtue once his maturing consciousness and his agnostic, enquiring attitude of mind have formed themselves in a coherent relationship with his subject-matter and treatment. *A Farewell to Arms* had been Hemingway's farewell to society, and its demands upon the individual; when he returned to society – in *To Have and Have Not* – his manner proved too inflexible to accommodate the fluidity of his material.

Social relationships resist the simple imperatives of tragedy, and Henry Morgan, the crippled machismo-hero, articulates in his death-ravings a message of solidarity that is hopelessly incongruent with the fundamental persuasions out of which Hemingway writes: 'No matter how a man alone ain't got no bloody chance'.[17]

Though Dos Passos shares with Hemingway a pessimistic outlook, his pessimism is of a radically different kind. He does not deny nobility, but he accepts that it is largely vitiated by a host of countervailing forces. While Hemingway 'is most successful when he starts from his hero's private sense of experience and moves outwards towards general . . . judgement',[18] Dos Passos, after the conventional wistful romanticism of *Streets of Night* and *Three Soldiers*, reaches for objectivity by focusing on the aspects of experience that are never quite private. In *Manhattan Transfer* one encounters a method and a viewpoint that remind one curiously of James's description of Maupassant:

> If he is inveterately synthetic, he is never more so than in the way he brings this hard, short, intelligent gaze to bear. His vision of the world is for the most part a vision of ugliness, and even when it is not, there is in his easy power to generalise a certain absence of love, a sort of bird's-eye-view contempt. If he glances into a railway carriage . . . a dozen dreary lives map themselves out in a flash.[19]

What unites Dos Passos and Hemingway is a respect for craftsmanship. Dos Passos wrote of *A Farewell to Arms* that it was 'a firstrate piece of craftsmanship by a man who knows his job. It gives you the sort of pleasure line by line that you get from handling a piece of well-finished carpenter's work'.[20] Similarly, Hemingway referred to the 'instrument he wrote with', which he would rather have 'bent and dulled and know that I had put it on the grindstone again and hammer it into shape and put a whetstone to it and know that I had something to write about, than to have it bright and shiny and nothing to say, or smooth and well oiled in the closet, but unused.'[21] And Dos Passos frankly stated that 'a novel is a commodity that fulfils a certain need'. Their seriousness is well illustrated by their consideration of literature as an object with a use-value. Hemingway underlines the possibility of action, Dos Passos the institutional restrictions on action. Dos Passos' characters are experts on working up an enthusiasm only to deflate it, Hemingway's mute figures who husband their resources for the testing moment. Hemingway brings to life those unforgettable flashes of intensity when man, in contact with elemental themes, transcends his own mortality in the depths of pain. Dos Passos, always more interested in the non-exceptional person, follows with a detached sympathy 'This strange disease of modern life / With its sick hurry, its divided aims'.

Of Scott Fitzgerald Dos Passos wrote, in an acute obituary essay:

> The establishment of a frame of reference for common humanity has been the main achievement and the main utility of writing which in other times and places has come to be called great. It requires, as well as the necessary skill with the tools of the trade, standards of judgement that can only be called ethical . . . The fact that at the end of a life of brilliant worldly successes and crushing disasters Scott Fitzgerald was engaged so ably in a work of such importance proves him to have been the first-rate novelist his friends believed him to be.[22]

This was a typically magnanimous tribute to a writer who had been slighted by his inferiors. Yet it is no more than Fitzgerald deserves. Of all the writers of his generation, not excepting Faulkner, he is the most complete. From his own divided nature he created the 'dual vision' that permitted him to objectify his situations while at the same time sharing in the sense of romantic enchantment that he communicated to his readers. Dos Passos never joined in the game of disparaging the Fitzgeralds, whom he first met in 1922; 'They were celebrities in the Sunday supplement sense of the word . . . and they loved it'.[23]

Unlike the retiring Dos Passos, Fitzgerald did enjoy the limelight; yet he never grew to be a grand old man like the venerable Papa Hemingway – he was cast as revel-master to the roaring twenties. Only since his death has it been recognised that an egoistic and tiresome hedonist can co-exist with the mature, responsible and serious writer that Fitzgerald was, while his letters have revealed his personal development – through failure and bitterness – into a concerned, intelligent man and father. Henry Dan Piper has spoken of the 'new disillusion'[24] for which Fitzgerald's sensitivity made him a spokesman: the adoption of a critical, pessimistic and indignant attitude towards America. In Fitzgerald's case this is most evident in *The Beautiful and Damned*, which echoes the spirit of Stearns's *Civilisation in the United States*. But Fitzgerald's topicality was the least of his strengths as a writer.

John William Ward observes that 'Both *The Great Gatsby* and *USA* are sad books, books of defeat'.[25] It is true of all the most accomplished works of both writers. Gatsby is certainly a romantic failure, but not as Jimmy Herf, Dos Passos' hero of 1925, is. For Gatsby represents a concentrated and fanatical form of romantic desire, while Herf disintegrates as a hypnotised victim of the various impulses that fascinate and repel him. Gatsby is a man who made a fortune so he could get the girl he fell in love with when he was younger; he is also a prodigy of selfless love who almost achieves an impossible feat of time-redemption and who casts away the world's glory with a quixotic gesture. Fitzgerald was able to portray both Gatsbies through his superlative use of the narrator, Nick Carraway, and through his capacity for charging the public events of his stories with a current of personal intimacy. 'Fitzgerald's work is full of precisely observed external detail, for which he had a formidable memory, and it is this gift of observation which has led to the superficial opinion that he was nothing but a chronicler of the social surface, particularly of the twenties. Yet, for all its concrete external detail, his work is very personal.[26]

As death is the central value for Hemingway, the incontrovertible fact that gives meaning to life, so love is with Fitzgerald; the touchstone of his art is spiritual fulfilment through romantic love. But he recognises that love is not an independent value; it is extensively modified by the operations of society, and Fitzgerald's keen sense of society enabled him to observe and portray this fact with the wary eye of an 'outsider'.

> The man with the jingle of money his his pocket who married the girl a year later would always cherish an abiding distrust, an animosity, towards the leisure class – not the conviction of a revolutionist but the smouldering hatred of the peasant. In the years since then I have never been able to stop wondering where my friends' money came from, nor to stop thinking that at one time a sort of droit de seigneur might have been exercised to give one of them my girl.[27]

The plot af Gatsby derives from this very possibility, and from Gatsby's prodigious plan to reverse the facts of history by harnessing the success-dream to the ends of his Utopian imagination. Nick Carraway knows that Gatsby represents 'everything for which I have an unaffected scorn',[28] yet despite his prudence and conventionality he is impelled to be Gatsby's champion. Gatsby's essential innocence – the quality of heart that redeems the shoddiness of the crooked bootlegger – expands into a vision of the verdant American past: 'Gatsby's story and the meaning of his failure are somehow linked to the meaning of the American experience . . . If Jay Gatsby has failed in the pursuit of some ideal vision, so (we are made to feel) has America',[29]

Yet so complete is Fitzgerald's view of his subject, and so positive his clear-eyed respect for the ideal Gatsby represents, that the story, in the rhythms of its beautiful closing sentences, makes the reader understand the worthiness of a struggle against the chains of time and corruption, even at the cost of wholesale and repeated failure. Dos Passos' America, on the evidence of *Manhattan Transfer*, is a graveyard of ideals. Instead of the utterly dedicated passion of Jay Gatsby, there is a bone-deep weariness and discontent, and Fitzgerald's one vivid metaphor for modern urban desolation – the valley of ashes, over which

are suspended the eyes of Dr T. J. Eckleburg – is replaced by the hectic
tawdry glitter of New York City:

> . . . bruised notes of foxtrots go limping out of doors, blues, waltzes
> (We'd Danced the Whole Night Through) trail gyrating tinsel memor-
> ies. . . . So Sixth Avenue on Fourteenth there are still fly-specked
> stereopticons where for a nickel you can peep at yellowed yesterdays.
> Beside the peppering shooting gallery you stoop into the flicker, A HOT
> TIME, THE BACHELOR'S SURPRISE, THE STOLEN GARTER . . . waste basket
> of torn up day-dreams . . . A nickel before midnight buys our yester-
> days.[30]

The scaling-down of the proposition that money can buy back the vanished past is of a piece with Dos Passos' looser, flatter depiction of New
York in the twenties. Where Fitzgerald imbues his creations with ultimate meanings that lie behind them, Dos Passos takes the viewpoint of
the street spectator who leads his life in separate successive moments.
The thirst for vicarious experience in a rotten civilisation is a kind of
drug; temporarily, it eases the pain, but finally it creates a dependence
more virulent than the original malady.

Dos Passos' treatment of love is not exempted from this rule. Gatsby's
love for Daisy is all-encompassing. Love in *Manhattan Transfer* is another species of trap – like the success-trap, the politics-trap, the art-
trap. In particular, it is not so much a transcendent goal as a means of
exploiting another, equally hapless person. Viewed through the synoptic
perspectives of *Manhattan Transfer*, Ellen Thatcher is both victim and
persecutor. The glamour she radiates is the world's glamour, tarnished
and deceptive. But Daisy Buchanan, as the reader sees her via Nick Carraway's sudden empathetic sharing of Gatsby's consciousness, stands
for something more than a parvenu's fantasy:

> 'She's got an indiscreet voice', I remarked. 'It's full of—' I hesitated.
> 'Her voice is full of money,' he said suddenly. That was it. I'd never
> understood before. It was full of money – that was the inexhaustible
> charm that rose and fell in it, the cymbal's song of it . . . High in a
> white palace the king's daughter, the golden girl.[31]

The effect of Gatsby's intensity, of which Carraway is the sensitive
yet critical conductor, is to make us admit the relevance of his vision.
The impulse to dismiss Daisy as unworthy of Gatsby's emotions and
Gatsby as a childish dreamer is surpassed by a realisation that human
passion itself is a creative instinct. In expressing this truth, the author
is not simply faithful to his role; he is faithful to experience. 'Scott
Fitzgerald was perhaps the only successor to James who did justice to

the attitude of wonder and also moved towards an increasingly profound analysis of it – its shortcomings and frailties, its poetry and its
fate'.[32] Though disillusionment is a major theme of Fitzgerald's, he repudiates 'cynical disillusion', and the tantalising gulf between prosaic
reality and the human aspirations that yearn to transform it appears
as a tragic disparity.

The possibility of bridging the gulf remains; without it, Fitzgerald's
art would much more closely resemble that of Dos Passos. As it is, Fitzgerald's completes the tragic equation. The 'icy, despairing'[33] books of
Dos Passos cancel it. When Fitzgerald examines 'deterioration' in *Tender
Is the Night* he is working slightly closer to Dos Passos' territory. Yet
his writing preserves its essential character. The progressive break-down
of Dick Diver, the lapse of his charm and distinction into a 'trick of the
heart' performed with increasing fatigue until it gives out, is dynamised
by all Fitzgerald's anguished sympathy for the dissipation of a vital
quality. The novel appeared at a time when the bubble of the twenties
had burst, and at a superficial level its subject-matter was unfashionable,
but its insistence that 'splendour is something in the heart'[34] carried
forward Fitzgerald's efforts to show the emotional and moral verities
that lie behind social appearances.

Dick Diver's fall is partly due to his association with the cruder imperatives of the wealthy, but he collaborates in it as a means of setting
Nicole free; he 'uses up the emotional energy which is the source of his
personal discipline and of his power to feed other people'.[35] This energy
he will never recover and the society he leaves closes ranks with something like the relief felt by Baby Warren: its mediocrity has ceased to
be challenged. *Tender Is the Night* is an ambitious novel, and its defects
have been widely noted. Yet to call Dick Diver's story 'less a tragedy
of will than of circumstance'[36] is a curious judgement. Such a description
might be reserved for the characters of Dos Passos, and in *USA* one encounters a man of comparable qualities who degenerates amid vicious
squalor.

Like Dick Diver, Richard Ellsworth Savage has charm and intelligence;
he responds to European civilisation; he is taken up by a group of people
whose interests are conventional and whose motives are self-serving.
However, he does not have Dick Diver's 'lifting trick'. Savage's life is
recounted in great detail throughout *1919* and *The Big Money*, and it
is a record of ascending worldly position bought at the cost of innumerable petty betrayals. Despite his dubious heredity, Savage had seemed
a young man of promise. But he forsakes culture and ethics to become
the hired slave of J. Ward Morehouse. His rottenness is credible, yet it is
registered as the sum total of swarming indignities; he never surrenders
a passionate vision of splendour: 'Blackmail, Oh, Christ. How would it be
when Mother came home from Florida to find her son earning twentyfive

thousand a year, junior partner of J. Ward Morehouse being blackmailed by two nigger whores, male prostitutes receiving males? Christ . . . It would ruin his life.'[37] Scandal, maternal disapproval, exposure are the penalties Savage fears, and they fully express the shallowness of his assumptions. After Dick Diver's nightclub disgrace, one is made to feel how an incident as commonplace as a drunken brawl can imply resonating depths of significance: 'What had happened to him was so awful that nothing could make any difference unless he could choke it to death, and, as this was unlikely, he was hopeless. He would be a different person henceforward, and in his raw state he had bizarre feelings of what the new self would be. The matter had about it the impersonal quality of an act of God.'[38]

Savage's instant of remorse is the respectable man's terror of having his secret vices uncovered; Dick Diver's is much more. The difference lies not purely in the literary treatment, but in the convictions from which each writer proceeds. Dick Diver's actions are those of a man who believes in heightened romantic possibilities. By his charismatic example, he makes others, less perceptive, aware of them, and by untiring artistry Fitzgerald makes the reader aware. There is a sense of life expanding in limitless perspective, whereas Dos Passos pictures the closing-in of squalid necessities and the desperate immediacy of the life-draining convention.

In renouncing affirmative values such as appear in the writing of his contemporaries, Dos Passos approaches the terminal despair of Samuel Beckett. But unlike Beckett, he is an author with a lively sense of historical detail. The slick and easy pessimism towards which his conception of failure can drift – and which can be observed in the stories of a narrowly realistic writer like John O'Hara – is warded off by a synchronism of multiple aspects. He does not, as Joyce did, celebrate the 'whatness' of life in all its teeming manifestations; often, he seems insufficiently assured, and he lacks the great artist's power to dominate reality by the force of strong imperatives. His commitment is to truth, to a common language of ordinary experience. His subjects are failure, alienation and despair. His method – in the four novels that will last – is synthetic. Dos Passos is not simply an authentic member of the Lost Generation but a writer who has been as eloquent as any in our time in expressing what it means to lose and be lost.

1 The Ether Cone: Harvard and *Streets of Night*

Though Dos Passos did not establish his métier as a writer of fiction until his service with the Norton-Harris Ambulance Corps, he had begun his apprenticeship at Harvard, through his contributions to the *Harvard Monthly*. In a review of Dos Passos' university years, Charles Bernardin pictures Dos Passos as a normal intelligent young American of his generation who enjoyed cultured conversation, eagerly satisfied his epicurean tastes, and graduated *cum laude* without exerting himself. But he does note that the author, whose upbringing had been plutocratic-cosmopolitan, was 'eager to lay hold on life'[1] and wanted to 'become a part of the "vulgar herd" '[2] – dominant attributes of the early Dos Passos heroes. Though Bernardin draws attention to the parallels with the undergraduate career of Dick Savage, he does not mention *Streets of Night*, the novel begun at Harvard which exposes such ambivalent emotion about the Harvard experience.

Dos Passos' first story appeared in the *Harvard Monthly* for July 1913. Thereafter he contributed regularly until July 1916. His first four pieces for the magazine are inconsiderable by the canons of mature fiction, but they suggest the themes and conflicts that were to persist in his writing: disillusion, failure, entropy. 'The Almeh' (July 1913) recounts an adventure of two Anglo-Saxon tourists in Cairo, Dick Mansford and Jack Hazen, English and American companions contrasted as to character and outlook, who are touring the native quarter. Dick is attracted by its exotic and colourful atmosphere; Jack is repelled by the dirt and smells. 'He seemed far more interested in the donkeys than in anything else; he complained constantly of the heat and the smells, and did not seem to be very much carried away with the picturesque strangeness of the street along which they were passing.'[3]

Suddenly, during a street fracas, Dick glimpses 'a face exquisitely fair and of great beauty':[4] the face of an Arab girl whose veil has accidentally fallen away. Jock, who has meanwhile been staring at the scarred backside of a donkey, scoffs at his friend's romantic enchantment. Earthbound, sceptical, he insists that the girl is merely a common woman of the bazaar, and in his heavy kidding of Dick he reveals his American preferences for the modern and the material over art, romance and tradition. Dick, who is an artist and a believer in the inner reality, finds that the haunting face of the Almeh interferes with his attempts to paint conventional scenes of the Middle East. 'Finally, giving up in despair, he set to work scrawling with a pencil on an old sheet of paper. He started outlining women's heads, but he seemed to be able to draw nothing but a pair of dark eyes and a pale face under a black hood.'[5]

The face is an obsession, and it becomes the cause and symbol of a growing conflict between the two friends. However, they see the girl again, unexpectedly, at a dancing house at which she gives her performance after a succession of 'over-painted women, loaded with ugly jewellery'. Her distinction is instantly apparent: 'Hers was real dancing. Her steps were different from those of her predecessors, culminating in a wild whirl about the room. She tore the veil from her head as the dance came to a stop, and stood smiling in the center of the floor, amid the applause of the crowd.'[6] Jack drags Dick away before the latter can make a foolish or impulsive gesture; but that night Dick stays up to work with special intensity on a fresh picture. In the morning he proudly shows to the worried American 'a nearly finished oil representing a lovely Almeh dancing in the light of a flaring torch'.[7] Even Jack has to call it a 'masterpiece'; but in the denouement of the story Dick is made to face reality of a kind he has rejected. There is an after-breakfast donkey-ride. They are led by their guide past a mudhut, which he boastfully points out as the house of his father. 'He sheik – rich man. He pay hundred pounds English for wife for me.'[8] And the two visitors are looking at 'a little group of grimy, naked brats . . . playing about a young woman, who sat at the doorway . . . preparing the mid-day meal. Every now and then she would scream at the children in a harsh voice. Flies swarmed about her, and about the food.'[9]

The young woman is, of course, the beautiful object of Dick's nympholeptic desire. She is now portrayed in her day-time habitat, and Dick's dream is destroyed. Yet though the imaginings of the artist have been spoiled, there is little satisfaction for the coarse and practical American. Though cast in the form of a conventional magazine story, 'The Almeh' faithfully mirrors the concerns of its seventeen-year-old author. There is the alien and exotic setting, in which even a donkey-boy may bear the name of Saladin; the brash, 'athletic' American youth and the European artist–idealist. What is striking about the story is the neutrality of its conclusion. It does not attempt to satirise either man at the expense of the other, but it depicts the limitations of both. Dick does not, in the end, have the courage to ignore the repellent details that spoil his vision. Beauty must exist in an acceptably pure and abstract form if he is to acknowledge it. Jack on the other hand, wins a kind of cheap victory: the girl is a bought wife, she lives in squalor with 'naked brats', everything he has hinted to Dick is true. But it is a tasteless triumph for him.

For the work of a very youthful writer, 'The Almeh' is a self-assured sketch. True, there are a number of flat sentences and dead phrases, but there is little embarrassingly purple writing, and Dos Passos has absorbed much of the professionalism of the 'well-made' magazine story. There are signs of technical facility in the description and the pacing of the narrative, and he is learning the difficult art of showing the passage of time – the action is divided into three episodes, spread over three days, and each part is given a suitable dramatic weight relative to the others.

Dos Passos' next contribution was a story set against a background of the Greek War of Independence. 'The Honor of a Klepht' appeared in the *Harvard Monthly* for February 1914. It, too, has an exotic flavour and a much more frankly melodramatic colouring – 'If that really is Ali of Telepen encamped over there, there will be little left of Itea by tomorrow's sunset'[10] – but there is a continuity of theme: in this case the disillusion is both romantic and sexual. A young klepht, preparing to face the Turkish invader, arranges that Louka, his girl, shall join him and his warrior band in the mountains. As the Turkish army launches its attack, chaos engulfs the townspeople. Christos waits in vain for Louka at the mountain rendezvous. Later he sees her, resisting violently, being dragged off by the leader of the Turks. On the following day the klephts counter-attack the enemy, and during the battle Christos fights his way to Ali Pasha's tent. There he finds Louka 'sitting before him on a divan . . . She was dressed in costly silks and leaning against a pile of embroidered cushions. Behind sat a slave girl fanning her.'[11] Christos stays only long enough to pronounce her dead; then he returns to lead his men in a mass suicide jump. 'The Turks took no klephtish heads as trophies from that battle.'[12]

'The Honor of a Klepht' is a slight romantic tale, less well conceived than 'The Almeh', and the central formula – love, death, mystery – is baldly presented. At its heart, however, is the tension between the exceptional man (artist, warrior) and the reality which he attempts to transfigure by the force of his ideals but which resists and disillusions him. No reasons are given for Louka's submission. In the nature of things profound hopes are disappointed. This pessimism awaits experience or practised artistry, but is undeniably present.

Dos Passos' next fiction for the *Harvard Monthly* shows definite advance. The perfumed atmosphere of oriental antiquity is abandoned, and there is a new vein of comedy. The owlishly solemn student with his incense-burner promises to become a contemporary American. 'The little man alighted from his buggy and hurried into the house. He was hot and flustered; for the July night was absolutely airless, and the thought that he was late had made him perspire. He had realized suddenly only a few minutes before that his wife would probably be waiting dinner for him.'[13]

So begins 'The Poet of Cordale' by 'R. Dos Passos' (December 1914), but this could equally well be a paragraph from *Manhattan Transfer*: the precise and dispassionate selection of a single figure or face from the crowd whose life and aspirations are anatomised. But Hardwick the 'grotesque' is still a man who challenges his environment by daring to be more than a drummer; and while the writing pays its homage to the old magazine tale, the content is assuming the character of Dos Passos' adult work.

Hardwick represents the Jack–Dick polarity in a single figure. He is at one and the same time a conforming citizen of the commercial world and the imaginative man who desires to see a higher reality embodied in art. In particular, he loves 'to recite passages, whose meaning he hardly understood, but whose form he loved, from the verses of a certain Persian philosopher.'[14] The Rubaiyat had not yet become, as it did in the post-war period, a transient popular cult of Babbitry; Hardwick sincerely admires it. Invited to perform at a local Independence Day celebration, he (or his wife) decides that 'Barbara Frietchie' would be the most suitable offering. Omar, naturally, would be profane and indecent. 'Barbara Frietchie' is de-sensitised, *acceptable* poetry.

Nervously, Hardwick prepares for the great event. 'He took a long while in dressing and shaving that morning, and Susan had to call him twice before he came to breakfast at table. He found he could eat nothing; his coffee seemed to have no flavour.'[15] Flat, stiff, behaviouristic: the manner is growing familiar. But the reader is also heartily nudged with the information that 'Corby Hardwick . . . like most people, had his share of obstinacy.[16] For his apprehension is not wholly due to stage fright: he is guiltily planning to deliver an encore. Sure enough, 'Barbara Frietchie' is so well received that the audience demands another poem, and Hardwick reels off 'The Rubaiyat of Omar Khayaam' to a gathering of chapel-faced Chautauquans – the very soul and essence of Mencken's rural 'booboisie'. Especially noticeable in the verse's catalogue of earthly delights are urgent supplications for 'wine, wine, wine'. The temperance-minded congregation are scandalised, and amid the growing fury Hardwick rushes out, flings away the text, and sits by the roadside 'hunched up in the middle of the little vehicle, sobbing'.

So once more Dos Passos writes of grief born from the conflict of differing realities. He suggests the incompatibility of art with American puritan ethics and the American success credo. The little man who dares to mix the two is a twofold failure – the boobs despise him, and he lacks the ultimate confidence in art that would permit him happily to forfeit their respect. And this conflict – art versus the world – is a genuine one for Dos Passos, a potentially fatal polarity.

Art, however, was beginning in Dos Passos' mind to cede priority to 'current affairs'. As the war in Europe continued he was drawn more and more to political matters. This side of his interests appears in the fourth *Harvard Monthly* story he published, in March 1915. Titled 'Malbrouck, it is a mood-sketch involving a French war-widow whose child insists that she sing a song which touches, in the words of its refrain, the very theme of her bereavement. It is essentially a sentimental piece, though the record shows that he was awakening to subjects other than art or personal emotions. 'His sixteen contributions before 1916 included ten stories; among his thirteen contributions during 1916 he included only three stories; and his two final publications in the *Monthly* were serious essays about American domestic and foreign policies.'[17] His first paid article, the phillipic 'Against American Literature' appeared in the *New Republic* in the autumn of 1916, calling for a fresh, masculine and vital approach to fiction. But after leaving Harvard he effectively ceased to be a short-story writer: the need he developed for a historical perspective ruled out the tale. 'July' was a dry run for the character of Jimmy Herf in *Manhattan Transfer*, and the later sketches he published in various periodicals were incorporated, with minor changes, into the *USA* trilogy.

The war, and his own material contribution as a member of the Norton-Harjes Ambulance Corps, had the effect of arousing Dos Passos' political sympathies. But they remain sympathies. The romantic pessimism of his student writing alters, but not into a strongly committed acceptance of the revolutionary cause. On the contrary, it becomes a recognition of the global losing streak.

But there is all the difference in the world between an adolescent feeling that the world is hopelessly wrong and an artistically formed pessimism. Dos Passos' 'Harvard novel' is strictly a young man's book – self-pitying, melodramatic, solemn – and was published in 1923, after his success with *Three Soldiers*. The setting is chiefly Boston before the First World War, and the three principal figures – Wenny, Fanshaw, Nan – are perpetually divided between 'art' and 'life'. One major fault in the construction of the novel is evidently due to the time-lag between the book's inception and its final published form, which gave Dos Passos time to reconsider his material and to extend its chronology to take the war into account. The most natural ending would be Wenny's suicide which occurs about two-thirds of the way through, leaving the latter sections dangling.

The exact process of alteration and revision is not clear in detail – even the author seemed to forget[18] – but it appears that *Streets of Night* was begun during his Harvard period, dropped when he left for

Europe, and later resumed. Dos Passos' diary for March 1916 has an entry entitled 'Le Grand Roman' which sketches an outline, but almost eighteen months later it becomes plain that his war service has modified the original idea:

> The great war novel is forming gradually in my mind. I have almost a feeling that the Streets at Night will get encorporated – will be part I. let's for the splendour of God have an outline!
> 1 Streets of Night
>   X and Y friendship
>   Miss Z –
>   The new Egoist –
>   From two points of view first serious
>   Cantabridgian atmosphere – European motif –
>   calling and recalling . . .
>   Death of X
>   Damnation of Z – alma
>   Part II The war . . . the philosophy of scorn
>   De trop de la delicatesse
>   J'ai perdu la vie . . .[19]

The two-line tag from Verlaine certainly expresses Wenny's feelings in *Streets of Night*, while the 'new Egoist' title identifies Dos Passos as a member of the generation raised on Wells and Shaw; Fitzgerald, one remembers, first planned to call *This Side of Paradise* 'The Romantic Egoist'. However, as things turned out, Harvard and the war were not thematically married into one book. *Streets of Night* centres on Harvard and Boston, and it treats its situations with none of Fitzgerald's youthful enthusiasm and wonderment. Its main subject is not so much self-discovery as inadequacy and the impotence of the lonely individual who attempts to found his life on a principled denial of tradition. It is also 'heroic' in the sense that the protagonist chooses death rather than an acceptance of his own helplessness.

Streets of Night begins by introducing Fanshaw McDougan. The picture of Fanshaw as a substitute blind date on a river picnic with his friend Cham and a pair of chorus girls has a satirical promise never quite kept. Fanshaw is of the type of the unpopular, priggish swot, yet he suffers inner conflict – more or less rationalised as the struggle between native sensuality and official Victorian sex-doctrines – and he finds it hard not to offend his partner by keeping an aloof distance. Afterwards, he swings up and down the register of imaginary erotic experience as he confronts an essay on French classical literature. 'Marriage was for ordinary people, but for him, love, two souls pressed each to each, consumed with a single fire.'[20]

The foreshortened syntax of interior monologue heralds Fanshaw's reflections through Poe to a memory of Elise's 'common' perfume. And whether or not the reader is intended to interpret his pen-flicking as symbolic masturbation, Fanshaw remains a prissy, effeminate and life-denying soul who *feels* the pull of life, but will never yield to it. He stands all too evidently for the man who has substituted art for life – and consequently has failed to realise the true significance of either.

But Wenny is the true hero of the book, and his problem is not to scratch away the nagging itch of desire and find a protective illusion, but actively to reject the society that offers him comfort and distinction at the price of his heart's desire. His role in the story is to attempt to solve this problem, while Fanshaw and Nan witness his deterioration and failure. His friends speak of Wenny as being 'alive', or 'too alive', but his case is precisely that he can never feel alive enough in the dead Boston atmosphere, and his first prophetic words are 'I'm about dead'.[21]

Despite the self-conscious erudition of the three young people they never provide a fully analysed definition of the repressive forces in their native culture. The antitheses in which the conflicts are dramatised remain at a metaphysical level, though there are two major sources of imagery that suggest the conditions of their restlessness. Pro-life and anti-life tendencies revolve, in the first place, around indices of class. 'Wenny wore a woolly suit that had been wet, as it had been raining; the smell of it mixed with a tang of tobacco filled her nostrils.'[22] Such is Nan's perception. Wenny is like someone who works outdoors, cannot shelter from the rain, and picks up cigarette fumes – perhaps does not wash or change his clothes as often as a respectable Bostonian should. 'He has the hands of a ditch-digger'[23] – unlike Fanshaw with his neat, effeminate appearance and 'limp hands'[24] – and Nan pictures 'the moulding of the muscles of his arms, the hollow between the shoulders, the hard bulge of the calves'.[25] To her he is akin to a classical sculpture or a manual labourer; the one an approved sublimation of Eros, the other a fearful threat. Wenny's collar has 'a line of grime around it',[26] and Nan's mind flickers between fantasy and truth, guarded longing and maidish disapproval. Warming to Miss Fitzhugh's story of Mabel Worthington and 'the garlic-smelling ruffian',[27] she imagines a serviceable conjunction of the vulgar and the sublime: the girl who played the violin in the Fadettes had run off with 'an Italian who smelt of garlic like a young Greek god'.[28] This idea fits with her shamefaced admiration of Wenny's 'ditch-digger's' hands. The subversive implications of a myth about lower-class sexuality are merged in the safely antique physical perfection of 'Greek gods'. This potentially disturbing mixture – Wenny with his 'shambling walk like an Italian labourer's'[29] and the immigrant who snatched Mabel away from the Fadettes – is further disinfected when Nan adds the ingredient of universal wisdom. The southern European immigrants of the congested Boston slums are transformed into Greek gods who, though they chew garlic, make 'epigrams'. Wenny the agonised seeker disappears under the mask of Wenny the idealised statue, and is therefore easier to reject when he lays his ditch-digger's hands on Nan's body.

While Nan makes a sugar-coated equation of lust with plebeianism, Fanshaw the parvenu professional aesthete bears a reactionary hatred towards the United States, cherishing a lost aristocratic ideal where taste and culture were immune from extinction by democratic levelling. A 'mid-western disciple of Pater',[30] he has a mind filled with evocations of the European past, from the collection of ornaments in his Nebraskan drawing-room cabinet to Titian and Canaletto. In his purple day-dreams the three of them, unshackled from democracy and industrialism, drift along 'in a barge out of a Canaletto carnival, gilt and dull vermilion, beautiful, lean-faced people of the Renaissance'.[31] With a pedant's instinct to annotate his own thoughts, he fills his brain with symbolic equivalents for the sensations he cannot bring himself to experience directly. Even Wenny, for whom he has a protective, platonically homosexual affection, becomes in Fanshaw's mind a literary case-history. 'Verlaine's last absinthe-haunted days; Lord Byron; a puffy-faced Don Juan; the verdict of history.'[32] At Cham's wedding, of which he can snobbishly enjoy the social and epicurean distinctions, he is revolted by the coarse dialogue of the male guests and the earthy carnality underlying the ceremonial. Eternally divided between his sterile vision of a vanished Old World culture and the Boston which gives him a good living but abounds with commercialism and vulgarity, Fanshaw becomes an abject figure for satire whose ultimate ironic destiny is to flee homeward from the bed of an Italian whore to whom he has at last surrendered his virginity.

For Nan and Fanshaw the symbols and fantasies of their inner lives act as drugs. They shrink the universe to manageable proportions. In Wenny's case, the universe expands as he attempts to make an existential fight against spiritual suffocation. The Boston low life of which Nan feels the power in a fantasised way and which to Fanshaw is unspeakably 'common' draws Wenny like a magnet: *nostalgie de la boue*. Protestant uplift has made him wish to de-intellectualise himself. However, in pursuit of his Byronic ideal of living through the senses he finds himself continually frustrated by his background and upbringing. Desperate to grow away from his father, he grows into the likeness of his father's early manhood, sharing what the clergyman has described to him as 'bitter moments of profligacy and despair.'[33] Only misery arises from his efforts to adopt attitudes of revolt which he finds he cannot live with full conviction. ' "That's alright, except he got the profligacy and I got the despair. Go whoring and repent yours is the Kingdom of God. A fine system alright, but he repented so damned hard he spoiled my fun. Like being a eunuch, funny that, a generation of eunuchs." '[34]

This stresses the element of psychological determinism. If your parents have strong beliefs, you will end up reproducing those beliefs, either directly or by straightforward reaction. But Wenny aims to escape from the bonds of *social* determinism by locating the underground culture of America in Boston's brothels and saloons and through his association with Whitey, the first of Dos Passos' 'vags', who can speak from experience of life on the bum. He starts to create a positive to set beside Fanshaw's cultivation of the sensibilities and Nan's violin lessons. 'Whitey loafing on street corners in New Orleans watching the high yallers drive by in barouches. By God, I must live all that.'[35] Yet this too is illusion. Wenny cannot manage to leave Boston, all he can do in the face of a world that casually negates his every spasmodic gesture of protest is to offer it the existential 'No'.

Wenny, feeble and bemused despite his craving to plumb the depths of experience, is a true Dos Passos loser, though the story of his passage to self-extinction is awkwardly told. True, Dos Passos can here produce sentences of the type that appear in later, realistic books:

> They walked beside the water. Along the path were mashed cracker-boxes, orange peel, banana skins. The river was full of canoes now . . .[36]

> Fanshaw found himself staring with a faint internal shudder at the red knuckles as his fingers moved round swiftly in glass after glass under the faucet. They drank orangeade in silence. Wenny paid the girl behind the cash register, who showed two gold teeth in a smile as they went out.[37]

But he can never resist the temptation to create wordy, 'literary' and decadent passages:

> Her white bedroom was full of sunlight that poured through the white window opposite her bed, smouldered hotly on the red and blue of the carpet, glinted on the tall mahogany bedpost and finally struck a warm tingling coverlet over her feet and legs.[38]

The flow between reporting that blends realistic narrative with 'objective epitome' and poetic description that aims to drown the senses with a revelation of platonic properties is too spasmodic to actualise the two worlds of the novel and relate them satirically. There are too many passages in which a phrase chosen to suit the tenor of a fulsomely romantic passage strikes the reader's ear with an arch-counterfeit ring of cliché. 'Drowsy quietude', 'encompassed them about', 'gleaming cascades', and other dead leaves from the herb-garden of romantic rhetoric abound.

The appeal of the archaic to Dos Passos appears to lie in the sense that it represents a culture which, though obsolescent and unserviceable, has given a universal language to artistic genius. But it is because he shares so many of his characters' ambiguities and puzzlements that he fails to make *Streets of Night* a conclusive illustration of the forces which enervate and destroy people. 'We don't fit here. We are like people floating down a stream in a barge out of a Canaletto carnival, gilt and dull vermilion, beautiful lean-faced people of the Renaissance lost in a marsh, in a stagnant canal overhung by black walls and towering steel girders.'[39] So thinks Fanshaw, wildly mistaken, just as Nan is wrong when she fantasises Wenny into the Italian labourer and re-fantasises the labourer image into one of the 'Greeks who made epigrams'. The trouble is that it is generally very difficult to care deeply whether Fanshaw and Nan are right or not, or about their frustrations and sufferings, or even about their failure to suffer and articulate with any kind of conviction. These figures are portrayed either with suffocating closeness, or with the angular outlines of over-intention; the novelist's voice is the voice of a novice.

But auspicious signs abound in this novel, even with its lack of originality. One influence is revealed in the frequent, and sometimes curiously apt, echoes of the early poetry of T. S. Eliot. The distinctive elements of Eliot's style – 'a concise diction, a dry irony, the use of descending cadences'[40] – repeatedly appear. For example: 'Nan was out in the street again. A dusty wind had come up and was making dead leaves and scraps of newspaper dance in the gutters and tearing ragged holes in the clouds through which blue sky shone.'[41] This is by no means direct plagiarism, but the vocabulary and tone are so close to parts of the 'Preludes' that it is hard to believe it could have been written if Dos Passos had not read

> Six o'clock.
> The burnt-out ends of smoky days.
> And now a gusty shower wraps
> The grimy scraps
> Of withered leaves about your feet
> And newspapers from vacant lots . . .

Throughout the novel appears – effectively, much of the time – a persistent image of the Boston fog: cold and insidious, inimical to the rebellious and free life that lurks, pining for self-expression, beneath all the failure and frustration. 'Slowly, the yellow fog, the cold enormous fog that had somehow a rhythm of slow, vague smells out at sea sifted in upon her, blurred the focus of herself that had been for a moment intensely sharp.'[42] Prufrock's 'yellow fog that rubs its back upon the window panes' must spring to mind. Nan herself is so much a female Prufrock, timidly withdrawing from the intense challenges of life; sometimes related suggestively to Prufrock by parallel imagery. 'Nan let the brown croutons slide off the spoon . . . I'm twenty-eight and every seventh day of my life I must have done this. Twenty-eight by fifty-two, what does that make?'[43]

Even Eliot's working-class bogey-man Sweeney is evoked by the appearance of Boston 'muckers' who stimulate in Nan ambivalent feelings of menace and allure. 'A fat man threw away his cigarette and advanced towards a blonde girl who had just crossed the street; with one hand he was straightening his necktie. The smile on his puffy, razor-scraped face kindled in her straight lips.'[44] This man is kin to the Sweeney who 'knows the female temperament. And wipes the suds around his face' and the apish, horrifying lout in stanza one of 'Sweeney Among the Nightingales'. Yet Dos Passos' employment of the Eliot imagery is still a trick. He has not the matured and dedicated purpose of Eliot, whose pessimism has little in common with the pessimism of the adolescent confronted by a world of stuffy inhibitions that blocks his aspirations and saps his energy. Eliot was always prematurely aged. Even so, in seizing on the chronically peevish aspects of Eliot – the mood of cultural disintegration and its contingent imagery – Dos Passos gives to his novel a strong sense of urban loneliness, of weary dog-days and crowds who are all strangers to one another, that partly annuls the weakness of his characterisation.

Nan is a somewhat clinical study of repression leading to hysteria; Fanshaw might almost be a caricature of Eliot himself. Both are woodenly constructed, and came alive only at rare moments, usually when they are animated by their concern for Wenny. Wenny is the central subject. Though he is insufficiently objectified, he commands special attention by his foreground position and because he speaks with the essential voice of the author. At least one critic has chosen to treat Wenny as an almost pure reduction of the writer's adolescent self.

In *Streets of Night* the hero's wish to change places with a double is unrealized, and therefore the explorations of the relationship between hero and Vag remains [*sic*] tentative. The two come together at a moment when Wenny faces the collapse of his dreams of love, adventure, and 'reality'; he has failed to 'burst through the stagnant film of dreams' into 'head-long adventure' (p. 116), he has been humiliated in his confession of love to Nancibel; he has lost his chance for recognition, personal contact, marriage – his one chance 'to live like a human being.'[45]

It has to be agreed that the encounter with Whitey is of vital importance to Wenny, yet the conclusion that Whitey represents an acceptable father-image from the 'real' side of life is to make a false reduction. Wenny's problems are never exclusively psychological. He never simply rebels against his father, but against an environment and a value system – Harvard, puritanism, intellectual orthodoxy, a genteel tradition in decline. Alas, this system is engrained in his soul, and it inevitably kills each of his sincerest impulses. Fanshaw and Nan implicitly accept Harvard standards, but to Wenny they signify an indulgence of the sensibility that cuts out 'real life'. 'Culture, you mean, God, I'd rather rot in Child's Dairy Lunches.'[46]

In fact, the novel principally comes alive in the pages where Dos Passos touches the nerve-centre of Wenny's unease. The satirical tableaux of Bostonian refined society are thoroughly feeble, the drawing-room conversations painfully and tediously thin. Yet when Wenny, in his instants of revelatory self-knowledge, starts to mock his own solemnity, there is a hard pictorial gusto to the writing. It moves and resounds with the right kind of graphic vigour: the later and most typical strength of Dos Passos as a novelist.

> What's the good of dreams? It's hard actually I want, will have. Yama, yama, blare of brass bands, striped flags waving against picture postcard scenery, brown oarsmen with flashing teeth and roses behind their ears, and Nan, both of us rolling on red cushions in the leaping stern. Bay of Naples and musical comedy moonlight and a phonograph in a flat in a smell of baby carriages and cabbage grinding out love songs, 'Funiculi, funicula.'[47]

In this burlesque of Fanshaw's imaginings the comic juxtaposition of grand and vulgar sensations presented through impacted grammar and sensory association permits the reader to follow the author's track into the character's mind. It is never plumbed – it does not need to be – but the freeness of flow reflects Dos Passos' ability to forsake artifice and create a true moment of life. This manner works best at the level of sympathetic irony, and is easily spoiled by an opulence of vocabulary or an excess of highly literary metaphors.

> The men at the table around him were tiny and gesticulating like things seen through the wrong end of a telescope. The cocktail stung his mouth, sent a writhing gold haze all through him. The glass was the centre of a vortex into which were sucked the cutting edges of

light, flickering cones of green and red brightness, the voices and the throbbing, rubber faces of the men in the bar.[48]

An urge to depict the viewpoint of a drunk, fatigued, deeply alienated man will be a staple in Dos Passos' fiction. Here he has not yet learned to avoid clumsy images verging on cliché in conjunction with mystic abstractions and sudden poised shocks. The vagueness of the passage, the uncertainty about whose point of view is being adopted, and the 'writhing gold haze' in all its misleading echoes become mannered and unintentionally comic. Yet Dos Passos was to persevere: the death of Joe Williams in *1919* would show, in its economy and the finely chosen colloquialisms of its narration, how such incidents could be conveyed in all their hallucinatory physical ugliness.

Streets of Night largely fails because it seems unable consistently to use the voice either of experience or innocence, because it has a hasty patchwork air, and the mixture of styles and attitudes is never balanced or synthesised. As a self-image, though, Wenny does live: he carries the weight of the author's contempt for Harvard, and that contempt succeeds partially in animating the character and making his fate credible. Hence one sympathises, even with the ideas of Fanshaw who manages to make of Wenny's suicide a further excuse for hating the vulgarities of a democratic popular press:

The headlines seemed reflected in their ghoulish leering as they read gluttonously every detail of the bullet searing the warm flesh, the warm flesh quenched in the water of the basin, the body that people had loved, talked to, walked with, floating like an old coat among the melting ice-cakes at eight-twenty this morning. Their sallow, flabby-jowled faces as they read greedily like vampires. Youth had been killed.[49]

Wenny, of course, redeemed himself by taking the irrevocable way out. Nan is left with an ouija-board, Fanshaw with his Harvard lectureship in the history of art: pale substitutes. But despite the downbeat and self-pitying mood, the 'romantic sociology' (as Dos Passos called it in a letter from Harvard) of the Boston back streets provides an exciting and flavourful locale for the story.

According to Charles Bernardin, Dos Passos was not as unhappy at Harvard as *Streets of Night* suggests. But it is a familiar discovery in examining Dos Passos' career that his personal life and emotions are not strictly correlated with the attitudes of his fiction. The independence of his art from purely biographical or political facts is too often undervalued. Dos Passos has not the great imaginative gift of Fitzgerald, of transforming public facts so completely by passing them through the prism of his creative sensibility, but neither is he a scissors-and-paste reporter, arranging data that has scarcely been subject to the fictionalising process at all.

Streets of Night, though it draws on Dos Passos' Harvard experience, is not a transliteration of his student career; it uses Harvard and Boston gentility to suggest the stifling, oppressive institutions that deny the hero his freedom. If this device fails, it fails partly because Harvard and Boston will not quite bear the symbolic significance with which the author seeks to freight them. Universities, however trifling in their academic absorptions and inimical to real intellectual growth, are not, except perhaps in the hands of a more developed artist, sufficiently weighty symbols for the cheating and suffering which life inflicts on men. One human institution which can be so used, and which often in its horror and violence stimulates a forced growth even in the very young or insouciant, is war. And war was to be a subject with which Dos Passos quickly found himself at home.

2 'Getting in Bad': *One Man's Initiation: 1917* and *Three Soldiers*

'The overwhelming majority of conscripts went into the army unwillingly and once there were debauched by the twin forces of official propaganda . . . and a harsh, unintelligent discipline. The first made them almost incapable of soldierly thought and conduct; the second converted them into cringing goose-steppers.'[1] In writing his analysis of the effects of the First World War on the drafted American soldier, Mencken naturally stressed what he saw as the craven and ignorant nature of the American people. He added that, although there might come a time when the slaves would revolt against their leaders, the American citizen pitched into a European conflict 'got no farther than academic protests against the brutal usage he had to face in the army'.[2] Mencken does not specify any writers in this charge, but to look at Dos Passos' two novels of the war is to understand how hard he strove to absorb his experiences as part of his non-academic education, to realise the horror he encountered as a means of forming his own view of the world. Though he was never a conscript and saw the war as a member of the celebrated 'finishing school' of the Lost Generation, the Norton-Harjes Ambulance Corps, he was able to share the bewilderment and pain of the common soldier – and though he is exceptional in having the means to render this fact in literature, he does so in *One Man's Initiation: 1917* with a unique freshness.

Such freshness often precludes the technical sophistication that shapes out of the raw material of life a finished and harmonious work. The literary innocence of the young Dos Passos reveals itself in the loose arrangement of *One Man's Initiation* as a series of autobiographical sketches, lacking the later controlling aesthetic and resources of style.

The book begins with an introductory chapter written in the dramatic present. This favourite device is well used: it carries the reader along with Martin Howe's first direct impressions of a country which for him has always denoted high civilisation – a culture rich both in the magnitude of its artistic achievements and in its provisions for sensual gratification. Martin himself is initially presented as a young man totally unscarred by disillusion, ready to inherit what history has prepared for him.

> Martin is stretched on the deck in the bow of the boat with an un-opened book beside him. He has never been so happy in his life. The future is nothing to him, the past is nothing to him. All his life is effaced in the grey languor of the sea, in the soft surge of the water about the ship's bow as she ploughs through the long swell eastward.[3]

In the relaxed, observant lyricism of these sentences lies a true effort to portray the character of a mind preparing itself to receive unimagined experiences. It is drowsy, unafraid and hopeful. What in the Harvard pieces had been strained and derivative is almost unselfconscious. The lyrical colouring is there, but relevantly there, not borrowed from a stagey conception of what literature ought to be. And the whole of this first chapter, which serves as an evocative preface for what is to follow, finely relates the short-lived innocence of the young American who has had no serious emotional training for what he is about to witness and who cannot understand the seemingly bloodthirsty and inhuman prejudices of the French civilians. Howe's first glimpse of France are shown through the lens of a lyrical imagination, yet it is as though the subject-matter itself has imposed on Dos Passos' prose an unstudious authenticity. There are no heated and festering distortions, no lurid or decadent incongruities to screen an essential artifice. In the imagistic colourings of the landscape – quiet, controlled – is evidence of a vision alert for the precise appearance of new sights and reluctant to force on to them any purely literary significance or any ironic, fateful premonitions. 'Through his port-hole in the yet colourless dawn he saw the reddish water of the river with black-hulled sailing-boats on it and a few lanky steamers of a pattern he had never seen before. Again he breathed deep of the new indefinable smell of the land.'[4] Martin's own innocence is thus under-lined, an innocence in its way just as fundamental as that of the other ambulancemen, non-artists with their Western casualness of speech and their native, unreflecting puritanism.

Martin's original lightheartedness of attitude, which is summed up in a song that treats the war as 'the Hamburg show', cannot last and actually begins to fade well before he has seen any military action. The first shock arrives very suddenly, as Martin is seated under the awning of a Paris café, where he can drink in the enchanting unfamiliar colours of the townscape. As he contemplates the dish of wild strawberries in front of him, a woman in mourning and a wounded soldier take seats at the table next to him. 'He found himself staring at a face, a face that still had some of the chubbiness of boyhood. Between the pale-brown frightened eyes, where the nose should have been, was a triangular black patch that ended in some mechanical contrivance with shiny little black metal rods that took the place of the jaw.'[5] The image of the disfigured soldier haunting cafés and pleasure-spots far from the front lines is a central one. It helps define the protected innocence of the Americans; and one remembers that Fitzgerald, who always regretted never getting 'over there', kept to the end of his life a volume of photographs of mutilated combatants. Dos Passos uses the image here with attentiveness and sincerity, exhibiting a serious artistic respect for his material.

But *One Man's Initiation* is not a book thoroughly earmarked by this approach. The author's innocence is partial and intermittent. The style which can legitimately and carefully provoke a reader's sympathies by showing 'the sequence of motion and fact that made the emotion' can lapse into false dramatisation, showiness and a miscalculated sentimentality. 'Martin sat, his chair tilted back, his hands trembling, staring with compressed lips at the men who jolted by on the strident, throbbing camions. A word formed in his mind: tumbrils.'[6] Martin has not yet been to the front, and the concern he feels is the pity of a spectator who can only guess at the suffering of the battlefield. Yet the focus of this paragraph is Martin's sensibility, and the vibrations of that sensibility, far from being graded and objectified, are given a dense weight of feeling, and the subject of that feeling seems not to be the pity of war. It seems to be the self-conscious attitudes of Martin Howe. *One Man's Initiation* is largely a personal report, in the sense that the author and his fictional persons are seldom distinct. For this reason, shock and outrage are felt instantly and vividly by the reader. But for this reason also, there are moments when the exquisite savouring of ideas on the part of the auctorial self-image blocks that vividness. The word that 'formed in his mind' (a typical Dos Passos formulation) is vague and fustian. The troops of a modern democratic army have little in common with the aristocratic victims of revolution – but if they happen to be going to their deaths and if you have been impressed by your reading of Carlyle, it is a tempting allusion.

The absence of a dual vision – a means whereby the hero can be known at first-hand yet effectively placed in some critical setting – makes of *One-Man's Initiation* a 'young man's book'. Yet its immaturity gives it a paradoxical strength. It is the one work by Dos Passos in which passion and hope are not conceived of as thoroughly futile, and in its concentration upon emotions that were fundamental and recent it is genuinely traumatic. The work of the mature Dos Passos is 'engrammatic':[7] it analyses not moments of cataclysmic shock – which leave to man still the possibility of heroism – but the niggling and low-keyed disappointments that pave the way to extinction. *One Man's Initiation* holds a residue of American optimism, and this optimism, as it collides with the brute faces of experience, creates a sombrely tragic resonance in the language.

> Infantry tramped by, the rain spattering with a cold glitter on grey helmets, on gun-barrels, on the straps of equipment. Red sweating faces, drooping under the hard rims of helmets, turned to the ground with the struggle with the weight of the equipment; rows and patches of faces were the only warmth in the desolation of putty-coloured mud and bowed mud-coloured bodies and dripping mud-coloured sky.[8]

The poeticism of the treatment – especially in the final cadences – in no way diminishes the experimental value of the scene. The subject – as in a Käthe Kollwitz sketch – demands a sense of beauty in the drawing, since otherwise there is nothing but a bare statement of human insignificance. But there are no refinements of self-obsession here: one can see how Martin's face is linked to those of the soldiers, without being made privy to Martin's ideas. The next sentence happens to reveal these ideas (doomed youth), but passages such as this have a right to stand by themselves, because they are self-expressive. There is no attempt to milk the scene for extraneous emotions, to reflect pity back from the war to the psyche of the reporter, or to dissolve its essential meaning in a bath of lapidary descriptiveness.

Martin, too, is ultimately not altogether either a receptive node who transmits to the reader a sense of profound horror or a sensitive and introspective projection of the author's inner conflicts. *One Man's Initiation* has something of the shape of a *bildungsroman*, and a crucial part of its meaning is to articulate the changes wrought in Martin Howe's outlook. Unlike the characters of *Streets of Night*, who are virtually incapable of doing anything but talk, Martin has involved himself in a world of action. His motives for doing so are mixed: 'Perhaps it's only curiosity',[9] he tells the woman who is treating him as a defender of civilisation, not without truth. Like Dos Passos, he wants to 'see the show', and though his feelings are against the war it is reasonable for a young man of his type to be attracted to what can easily be made to appear an 'adventure'. At first, the undertaking is not adventurous enough. Caught in an administrative machinery full of muddle and mystification, Martin and a fellow-volunteer confess – in a youthful, literary manner – their disillusion.

> 'What do you think of this anyway?' said the wet man suddenly, lowering his voice stealthily.
> 'I don't know. I never did expect it to be what we were taught to believe . . . Things aren't.'
> 'But you can't have guessed that it was like this. . . . like Alice

in Wonderland, like an ill-intentioned Drury Lane pantomime, like all the dusty futility of Barnum and Bailey's circus.'

'No, I thought it would be hair-raising,' said Martin.[10]

The attitudes struck are false and callow, but they belong to the characters. Moreover, although 'dusty futility' is to remain a central theme in Dos Passos' fiction, Martin does discover that war can be 'hair-raising'. The faintly affected ennui of the bureaucratic mismanagement of affairs is displaced by a 'passionate revolt'. Though this revolt is limited to a turbulence of mind and feeling its causes lie not in theoretical dissatisfaction but in concrete experience.

His eyes followed along the shapeless bundles of blood-flecked uniform till they suddenly turned away. Where the middle of the man had been, where had been the curved belly and the genitals, where the thighs had joined with a strong swerving of muscles to the trunk, was a depression, a hollow pool of blood, that glinted a little in the cold diffusion of grey light from the west.[11]

Only the over-deliberate touch of lyrical sentiment in its conclusion spoils this moment. Otherwise, in its solid simplicity it achieves exactly what has hitherto been missing: the location of a single barbarity compelling and insuppressible in its ghastliness. This is not dusty futility, and there can be no sardonic amusement in the response to it.

The overcoming of hatred – never felt by him personally, but thickly swarming around him – becomes a primary need for Martin. One of the finest pieces of writing in the book is an account of Martin's rescue of an enemy soldier. In dragging the mortally wounded German to a dug-out, Martin suddenly realises that he has justified himself by a single act. 'The effort gave Martin a strange contentment. It was as if his body were taking part in the agony of this man's body. At last they were washed out, all the hatred, all the lies, in blood and sweat. Nothing was left but the quiet friendliness of beings alike in every part, eternally alike.'[12] The language, purified to the degree where it is coterminous with the experience it describes, has the sure and unmistakable feel of authenticity. Dos Passos *was* the man, he suffered, he was there, and in *One Man's Initiation* – itself a relatively minor work – he can energise some of his situations with the tensions of real emotional truth. Certainly when he writes under the pressure of circumstances that bear for him a major personal significance he creates passages of fine intensity. At these points Martin Howe lives as credibly as Nick Adams. But *One Man's Initiation* is never as concentrated as the early Hemingway stories, it attempts to include a polemical vein, and in its gusty political rhetoric – partly offered as Martin's conversion resulting from his war experience – it dilutes the value of that experience. 'America, as you know, is ruled by the press. And the press is ruled by whom? Who shall ever know what dark forces bought and bought until we should be ready to go blind and gagged to war? . . . Now the darkness is using the light for its own purposes . . . we are slaves of bought intellect, willing slaves.'[13]

So Martin orates in the climatic chapter which theatrically relates a debate among ordinary soldiers who have come to see through war propaganda and to understand that they were cheated. In a rather mechanical way, Dos Passos ensures that there is a sufficient variety of opinion to give the discussion some energy of ideas. It notably lacks lifelike characterisation – except in the case of Tom Randolph – but it is a reasonable portrait of the young men forced to think by the intensity of their war-time initiation. In the savagery of nationalistic struggle they have sensed the crisis of a civilisation, and each has his proposal for a juster and more stable future. A 'blonde Norman', Jesuit-educated in Texas, has kept his faith in organised religion, and he argues that once total power is given to the Catholic Church it will have the strength and wisdom to ensure a reign of peace. 'All the evil of the Church . . . comes from her struggles to attain supremacy. Once assured of triumph, established as the rule of the world, it becomes the natural channel through which the wise rule and direct the stupid, not for their own interest, not for ambition for worldly things, but for the love that is in them.'[14] Merrier argues the case for revolutionary socialism – 'organisation from the bottom . . . by the ungreedy, by the human, by the un-cunning'.[15] Lully the anarchist denounces the evil of all government, and insists that 'Overorganisation is death. It is disorganisation, not organisation, that is the aim of life.'[16] André Dubois, frustrated by the recognition that they are talking helplessly in a void, speaks for the 'stupid average working-people' who may achieve, if they can find the levers of action, what the intellectuals are impotent to do.

All four share a passionate disgust with the status quo and an eagerness to redress the wrongs of an oppressive system. Martin feels that 'all his friends were gathered in that room'.[17] Yet in the final chapter all are dead and Martin has to be content with the fact that he has been ' "initiated" in all the circles of hell'.[18] Martin's own contribution to their symposium is the phillipic against American hypocrisy that amply illustrates both the depths of his disillusion and his powerlessness to do more than protest vocally. For unlike Frederic Henry, Martin makes no bid to escape the war and find satisfaction in an ideal private life. Dos Passos himself had recorded in his letters the same sentiments, but despite getting 'in bad' with the Italian authorities he had done no more.

My first letters home were full of hurlyburly about stringing up capitalist warmongers to the lampposts on Fifth Avenue, but by the time

I'd lived through a few months of war, though I hardly admitted it to myself, I had inwardly decided to let others storm the barricades. My business was to tell the tale.[19]

And *One Man's Initiation* does tell the tale – graphically, and without doctrinaire conclusions. However juvenile and incomplete, it relates with admirable fidelity the receptiveness of the adolescent awareness. Martin Howe, a frank self-image of the author, learns that the world outside America and its universities is a violent and terrifying place. He never learns how it may be restored to harmony, but he does have glimpses of a harmony that the imagination can bestow on certain timeless scenes – the abbey among the beech woods, for instance, built over the years in several of the great European architectural styles and surviving into the age of mustard-gas and the machine-gun. This, and the 'salmon-coloured villa' that recurs in Dos Passos' novels, symbolise a beauty and continuity that are threatened not only by war but by the existence of modern industrial society itself and that will prove to be unreachable. Yet Martin's restlessness nags him – a restlessness composed of his intellectuality, his aesthetic responses, and his questioning attitude to a world that will not permit him to be a mere adventurer of the spirit. Martin's alienation, though less explicit, is as profound as that of Nick Adams.

Martin Howe will be a worrier, though. His curiosity and sensitivity compel him to analyse the meaning of the hell he is subjected to, but largely because he implicitly shares the view of Lully that 'disorganisation . . . is the aim of life' he is barred from constructing an outlook that will completely make sense of the suffering he has witnessed and help him prescribe a remedy. The radical rhetoric in which he excoriates those responsible for suffering may be the real Martin, but it is never as real artistically as those moments in which, sick and horrified, he is brought face to face with the fact of death. As a testament of experience, *One Man's Initiation* is still valid. As the art of a novice, it is excusable. As the first step in a career which will attempt to look unflinchingly at the conditions of human failure it has not yet faced the worst horrors of all.

In a larger and far more ambitious work published two years after *One Man's Initiation*, Dos Passos produced a novel in which the essential material of his service with the Ambulance Corps is more fully treated and made to serve general conclusions. *Three Soldiers* has three protagonists but only one hero: John Andrews is its 'focus of sensibility'[20] and the story is principally concerned with his effort – and failure – to discover a means of personal self-realisation that will redeem the impersonal and inhuman mechanism of army existence. Paradoxically, his original motive for enlisting had been to submerge his identity in the mass. 'He was sick of revolt, of thought, of carrying his individuality like a banner above the turmoil. This was much better, to let everything go, to stamp out his maddening desire for music, to humble himself into the mud of common slavery.'[21] *Nostalgie de la boue* is a regular theme in Dos Passos' fiction, but it always acts with a more or less parallel tendency to prove oneself creative or vital. The mass only seems attractive when one is not a part of it and has the leisure for ultimate refinements of one's own world-weariness. Andrews is the Eastern intellectual, crippled by class guilt and an over-indulgence in literature and ideas, who discovers, by a slow and painful process of direct experience, that he must positively strike out against authority if he ever means to achieve freedom to work and create as he wishes. This process involves the realisation that common people are not mysterious and romantic beings and that 'common slavery' is what it says, not an edifying or aesthetically enjoyable principle. Dos Passos is aware of this – necessarily, since the book derives largely from his own experience – and there are anti-lyrical descriptive passages that render with a judicious neutrality the sense-data of communal life. 'At the other side of the wide field long lines of men shuffled slowly into the narrow wooden shanty that was the mess halls. Chins down, chests out, legs twitching and tired from the afternoon's drilling, the company stood at attention.'[22]

Almost a 'khaki demonstration': in its impersonality, its concentration on what can simply be observed and its tacit denial of individual feelings in the assembled group of soldiers, the opening paragraph of *Three Soldiers* prefigures the later, 'objective' Dos Passos. But objectivity is never a consistent value in the novel. Nor is there a disciplined relation, as in *Manhattan Transfer*, between the individual in his own little hell and the social inferno that surrounds him. The novel suffers from digression and from erratic variations of style. What makes it significant from the point of view of the Dos Passos oeuvre is the drawing of the hero. Andrews is a sympathetic hero, unlike Chrisfield and Fuselli who have a restricted and representative meaning, and he is, as Stanley Cooperman writes, 'a development from rather than the parallel to the "half-baked" twenty-two-year-old of *First Encounter*.'[23] Andrews is the most pure and extreme form of the early Dos Passos hero, the man who fails but in his failure creates his own identity and gives an existential meaning to the act of revolt for which he is condemned. In the case of John Andrews, it is art that stands for the fulfilled life. In his composer's vocation he glimpses a purpose that will rescue him from the machine to which he has surrendered himself and from which he increasingly feels the necessity to break free. Music is art in an especially 'pure' form – in the sense that it is largely free of ethical or ideological content – and Andrews is faced with the problem of adapting his almost religious belief in music to the bitterness of reality. Washing windows at his training camp he senses 'a rhythm . . . pushing its way through the hard core of his mind'.[24] This is the rhythm of military life itself, powerful and insistent, and it spurs Andrews to resolve that 'he must fix it in himself, so that he could make it into music and write it down, so that orchestras could play it and make the ears of multitudes feel it.'[25] His original conception had been a 'Queen of Sheba' symphony, music on a theme distant and exotic, as unreal as his belief that he could renounce his own individuality. 'Instead of finding comradeship, he learns that each man is isolated by military routine into his niche within the system.'[26]

His service, therefore, provides for John Andrews a radical education. The academic views he brings with him are subjected to cruel revision in works of the grinding servo-mechanism. At the same time, the hostile forces in *Three Soldiers* are presented quite differently from those in *One Man's Initiation*. The immediacy of a violent confrontation with pain and death is superseded by the slow, dismal and demoralising process of the erosion of vitality. It is in this context that Andrews's initial inspirational heroism has to be modified. Like Anthony Patch, Andrews is the young man of bourgeois background who stays in the ranks, where he is unpopular, cannot accept official views of the war, and finds himself rotting away in a state of acedia and frustration. Up to a point, the remorselessly applied external discipline quells the urge to rebel, or limits it to a nagging introspection. Andrews has begun with more heroic motives than Patch, but even after his wounding, while he is recovering in hospital, his urge to protest wears an abstract and contemplative air. He imagines a roster of self-sacrificing heroes from the past – 'Democritus, Socrates, Epicurus, Christ' – and resolves to strike a positive blow for individuality:

> He felt a crazy desire to join the forlorn ones, to throw himself into inevitable defeat, to live his life as he saw it in spite of everything, to proclaim once more the falseness of the gospels under cover of which greed and fear filled with more and yet more pain the already unbearable agony of human life.
>
> As soon as he got out of hospital he would desert . . . This was his last run with the pack.[27]

The reversal of his earlier idealistic intentions is forced by his discovery of the 'real' world; and even this resolution is not instantly carried out. Made one day before the armistice, it is forgotten once Andrews sees the opportunity of studying music in Paris – ironically under army auspices. Here, in a limbo world, he meets an eccentric *galère* – Walters, Sheffield, Henslave and their ilk – with whom he has in common a cultivated bourgeois background, and he uses their sense of class solidarity to engineer his transfer to Paris of the Schola Cantorum. The fundamental error of this course of action – its purely temporary palliative effect on the disgust that has led him to a position of indignant pacifism – is at first obscured by the patent delights that Paris can offer him. To this extent, Paris is an apt symbol for the very concept of art – as an auto-telic act – that he must ultimately reject. It furnishes a garden of epicurean delights: Jeanne with her snobbish respectability and warmth, and Genevieve Rod, the pedantic refined apostle of drawing-room culture, take the edge off his despair. He falls into a backward-looking romanticism: 'Today everything was congestion, the scurrying crowds; men had become ant-like. Perhaps it was inevitable that the crowds should sink deeper and deeper into slavery. Whichever won, tyranny from above or spontaneous organization from below, there could be no individuals.'[28]

This is a defeatest lament for the disappearance of personal self-responsibility, or of the belief that it can be a sustaining value, subsequently underlined in the picture of 'white marble halls' in which 'his real self . . . his name and number'[29] lie at the mercy of the engulfing machine. Outside Paris, arcadia beckons, and Andrews, absent without leave in order to spend an idyllic day with Genevieve, is arrested by the military police. Here the chips are down. He must choose either to embrace the system or to commit a definitive act of protest. He can no longer waver or dream. In the event, his escape is made on the example of a seventeen-year-old thief, but it is a willed and conscious action, for more so than the casual negligence of rules that led to his punishment. Andrews means it to be absolute and irrevocable; moreover, he has the courage to insist that it shall be so when the gentleman-ranker element in Paris later suggests that he can easily clear himself.

> 'I'm not crazy, you know, I've figured up the balance perfectly sanely. The only thing is, you fellows can't understand. Have you ever been in a labour battalion? . . . Good God, you don't know what you are talking about, you two . . . I've got to be free, now. I don't care at what cost being free's the only thing that matters.'[30]

Andrews falls straight through conventional society, with its ranges and levels of accommodation, to a pit of anarchists, outcasts and renegades in the lower depths. However, his exhilaration at having committed himself so unequivocally – 'It's us against the universe' – does not last, for in that transfigured landscape beyond the machine but also beyond the possibility of easy self-redemption all his newly discovered values are stripped of their romantic, affirmative character. The loneliness of barrack communality gives way to the ache of the fugitive. In an effort to make sense of his experience and to unite his aesthetic aspirations with the lessons of service to the machine he proposes to entitle his symphony 'On the Soul and Body of John Brown'. He contem-

plates the history of the great American fanatic, and the example of
faith he has bequeathed.

> The stockade was built; not one of the sheep would escape. And those
> that were not sheep? They were deserters; every rifle muzzle held death
> for them; they would not live long. And yet other nightmares had
> been thrown off the shoulders of men. Every man who stood up cour-
> ageously to die loosened the grip of the nightmare.[31]

The instinctive horror with which Genevieve repudiates the doctrine of
revolutionary defeatism is no longer an invitation for him to temporise.
The pull of her world has ceased to fascinate; but equally Andrews senses
that he cannot give himself to an organised movement of rebellion.
'Half by accident he had managed to free himself from the treadmill.
Couldn't he have helped others? If only he had his life to live over
again. No: he had not lived up to the name of John Brown.'[32]

This is an end of the road for John Andrews's personal rebellion, yet
the broadening of consciousness and action that would relate his stand
to a more general 'spontaneous organization', such as the May Day
strike in Paris, seems impossible for him to achieve. In one sense, he
has travelled far: yet he cannot see a next step. Although he knows that
his landlady is liable to betray him, he makes no decisive effort to ensure
his freedom. The M.Ps arrive to collect him. He confesses his crime.
The final image of the novel is of the sheets of paper on which he has
been composing being fluttered from the table by a breeze 'until the
floor was littered with them'. Andrews has made a gesture, but it is essentially a gesture of renunciation, a profound, despairing and intransigent
'no'.

Andrews's defeat is conclusive, but it bestows tragic moral credit on
him. He is a true hero.

> If Andrews' method of renunciatory action does appear somewhat
> too precious, too 'arty' and melodramatic, this may well be a com-
> ment on our own moral environment rather than his. For Andrews . . .
> a gesture of renunciation could be both deeply courageous and authen-
> tically moving precisely because of the aesthetic sacrifice involved.[33]

So writes Stanley Cooperman. Yet it is surely not the case that
Andrews's sacrifice is exclusively 'aesthetic'. His defeat as an opponent
of the system entails the defeat of his plans to be a creator, but the
central sacrifice is a sacrifice of human values. These values, though
nessesarily vague, can be recognised in his proposed change of title
for his symphony. They fail to emerge as positive criteria partly because
his only means of registering a protest against the world that mistreats

him is negated by the very conditions which provoke it. It is not 'art' which is the victim in *Three Soldiers* but the individual as a self-willed being; the underlying conflict is between 'organic' life and institutional-ised power forms – between life that is disorganised yet harmonious and the omnivorous 'system'. Unfortunately, Andrews does not fit either of those categories. He is the self-questioning intellectual, who can neither integrate his sensibility with a natural order nor bow to the demands of society. For this reason, the conflict is artistically muddled. Andrews is unmistakably the Dos Passos hero, and in his admirably brave and defiant refusal to serve he commands sympathy. Yet he is one of *three* soldiers; among those three he stands out as a figure conceived in quite different terms. Dos Passos has not yet learnt to gather around his major char-acters lesser characters drawn in relevant proportion.

Some of the difficulty does arise from the fact that 'Andrews all but vanishes beneath the height of adjectives, literary and musical allusions, colour poems, chiaroscuro "moments" and enamelled surfaces which have little to do with the experience to be rendered'.[34] *Three Soldiers* suffers from residual aestheticism and stylistic indecision. Andrews is often hard to identify amid the 'scenic absorption', but even more inimi-cal to the portraiture is his transitional presence between the early Dos Passos romantic heroes who are in some sense their own masters and who fail tragically, and his later characters who are essentially victims, dominated by impersonal circumstances. Of course, this dilemma is pre-cisely Andrews's own; but since it is also the author's, it lacks fully cogent expression.

Part of the background imagery of the novel is 'nature' – but nature is often presented in purely literary contrast with the man-made devas-tation of war. Within three pages, for instance, the following sentences occur: 'The larks filled the wine-tinged air with a constant chiming of bells.'[35] 'They walked on, hearing the constant chirrup of the larks.'[36] 'They stood still in the darkening field, staring up at the sky, where a few larks still hung chirruping'.[37] 'Birds chirped and rustled among the young leaves',[38] Such ironies, perfectly just in themselves, register the incongruities which the author desires to draw from the observable fact that birds still fly above the war-torn countryside. Yet they weaken and lose their meaning with repetition and through the unresourceful lyricism of the style. Rhetoric of this nature slows the dynamism of the book. However, there are signs of a fresh development: appearing not for the first time but now in a definite and insistent pattern come the very characteristic engrammatic reports on feeling, memory, states of mind.

As he worked a rhythm began pushing its way through the hard core of his mind, leavening it, making it fluid.[39]

Memories of movies flickered in his mind.[40]

A vivid picture came to his mind of the puddle with its putty-coloured water and the little triangular heads of the frogs.[41]

These occasions, especially associated with John Andrews, embody the 'detailed recording of sense data' that is to be more completely developed in *Manhattan Transfer*. John Andrews is not so obscured by 'fine writing' that we are not aware of the process by which these sense data impose themselves and mould his disposition. But Andrew is given too much weight to carry in a theoretically 'tripartite' novel and the structure bulges with undigested emotion. Relatively, he effaces and makes almost superfluous the life stories of Chrisfield and Fuselli. He is both a victim – a restless, other directed half-being in the grip of a life-denying organisation – and an existential fighter for a lost cause. *Three Soldiers* illustrates the high-water mark of Dos Passos' taste for self-conscious literary 'art', and hints at the direction which his interests will take in the future. The formal duality of nature and art versus regimentation and ordered chaos never quite works because it is forced in to a historical situation it will not fit. But in tackling the problem Dos Passos has begun to acquire the technical means to express his altering purpose. Nature as a substantial alternative to an increasingly mechanical world becomes implausible. From *Three Soldiers* on, it will appear as little more than a stated or implied quality of the agrarian past, while art as the supreme achievement of the creative individual will also lose its primary significance.

In the final pages of *Three Soldiers* occurs an almost prophetic passage on the encroaching universe of remorseless *things*. John Andrews may not completely understand it, in the still unfaded glow of his sacrifice, but the objects which he piles on his bed, and which symbolise to him his material poverty, are just that aggregate of manufactured objects that signifies the invasion of the dying self-willed cosmos by reification. 'A toothbrush. A shaving set. A piece of soap. A hairbrush and a broken comb. Anything else? He groped in the musette that hung on the foot of the bed. A box of matches. A knife with one blade missing, and a mashed cigarette. Amusement growing on him every minute, he contemplated the pile.'[42]

This method – the list of the tangible – will grow in Dos Passos' hands to be a principal mode of realising his fictive world. John Andrews has finally fallen 'under the wheels' of a machine too powerful for him to fight. There is heroism in his disavowal, but a heroism markedly tempered by hopelessness – the 'dusty futility' of Martin Howe. Andrews's vague feeling of revolt against the senseless waste of life and material' focuses on the army as a specific enemy. But the true enemy is the whole of modern life which denies to Andrews the opportunities for romantic fulfilment on a grand scale, and to which the isolated individual can only offer the responses of negation. Not even mass action can wipe out the trapped echoes of engrammatic despair. The hypersensitive John Andrews, when he tries to explain his desertion, voices fatalistic apathy. 'It seems to me . . . that human society has always been that, and perhaps will be always that: organizations growing and stifling individuals, and individuals revolting hopelessly against them, and at last forming new societies to crush the old societies and becoming slaves again in their turn . . .'[43] To which Gevevieve quite naturally replies, 'I thought you were a socialist'. But in fact there is nothing in Andrews's experience that could possibly give him grounds for belief in socialism, other than as a source of quasi-poetic slogans. The 'system' is not simply the gearing-up for emergency conditions of an exploitative society for which there may be social remedies. The system is life itself, modified by the particular course of social development but always hostile to freedom, justice and hope.

As David Sanders writes '[Andrews's] wound has no effect comparable to the mortar explosion at Fossalta del Piave; it is chiefly a transitional device as the novel suddenly becomes centred about its artistic hero'.[44] In a word, it is not traumatic, and the heroism of John Andrews, though authentic, is in the last analysis unrelated to its context. There is brutality and oppression in the army, but more often than not there is pointlessness, irritation and inefficiency. Heroism becomes a living objective when it is transcendent; when there is nothing to transcend it becomes stagey or comic. It is never quite so in the case of Andrews: with at least one half of his mind he lives the part of the Byronic antinomian so intensely that his destruction is awesome. However, Dos Passos is moving in a different direction from Hemingway. He cannot accept the world as a testing-ground for honour and courage, where a man can be destroyed without being defeated. What he does see is 'a *context* of pain, a context created by hundreds of personal pains – getting sick at the stomach, the morning after, being disillusioned with parents or children, mean family quarrels, ulcers, loneliness, the wasting of a talent, incurable diseases, garbage cans in alleys, the smell of unwashed bodies.'[45]

In this accurate description of the Dos Passos understanding of the engrammatic quality of life can be discerned the basis of his rejection of heroism. How does one overcome such heartaches and natural shocks? If at all, by aspirin, resignation, or oblivion. Certainly not by dramatic triumphs of *machismo*. Andrews is the last Dos Passos protagonist who can reasonably be called heroic, as Hemingway would understand the term. Increasingly, the author's aim will be to register the commonplace **and inevitable assault** on human organisms of numerous small pangs –

not to explain them or offer a cure, but to face them with unflinching realism.

In order to survey his material in this fashion, Dos Passos has to broaden its scope. The individual consciousness as the centre of attention is required by stories of individual prowess, where it deepens and concentrates the effect of the hero's personal contest. In choosing to portray engrammatic despair, Dos Passos introduces the 'common man' – in all his incarnations – into his work. Common people, such as Whitey in *Streets of Night*, the Italian labourers who fascinate Nan, the 'muckers' imagined by young Herf in *Manhattan Transfer*, cease to appear as enigmatic ghosts. In *Three Soldiers* Chrisfield and Fuselli represent the American masses forced to adapt to the demands of the military machine. They are not introspective, 'artistic', or self-torturing like John Andrews and they are not pictured with the same complexity of inner life, but in each case the forces operating against successful adjustment are overwhelming. The army has an overriding will and purpose of its own, inflexibly unresponsive to the needs of the enlisted man. Both Chrisfield and Fuselli are failures by the army's standards, though they have no initial quarrel with it, and given more reasonable chances might even do well.

Their ordeal reveals a social truth: when civil society grants exceptional powers to the military it effectively subordinates itself to the army and abolishes the reality of democratic government while hysterically flourishing the clichés of democratic theory. What this critical measure means in practical terms for the mass of men is told in the histories of Chrisfield and Fuselli. Either they accustom themselves to the absolute loss of their own humanity or they fall and are crushed. In Chrisfield there are elements of the old populist 'man with the hoe', the rural slave who, if his awareness could be adequately aroused, would be the unsung hero of the revolution, as Andrews recognises when he tells Chrisfield that 'It's you that it matters to kill'.[46] But Chrisfield is not the type of man to seek revolutionary answers. Fuselli, the model of the myth-swallowing city underdog Dos Passos was to analyse more closely in *Manhattan Transfer*, complains that the army will never give him a chance to prove himself; but his own personality, so snivellingly concentrated on blunt self-advancement at whatever cost to his dignity as a man, catches on the mechanism. Individualistic in a narrow way, he has no natural place either in the service hierarchy or among the free fellowship of man who accept each other as comrades. Both are statuesque figures, included for their representative value.

Fuselli is most prominent during the book's first two sections, when John Andrews has not yet emerged as the centre of interest. Uneducated and ignorant, his approach to the life of an enlisted man is delusive, since he has always accepted officially propagated attitudes. Indeed, he is made to feel 'important, truculent' by the ritual of the draft board; he is obsessed with the need to be 'careful not to do anything . . . wrong':[47] and he is genuinely shocked by the unconscious protest his mind makes in a dream in which he has assaulted an officer and broken out of jail. Fuselli obsequiously strives to make a rewarding adjustment. Impressionable and stupid, he sinks himself into the group personality, lives the lying fantasies of the anti-German propaganda movies and partly inhabits a fool's paradise of individual opportunity. "Gee", he said to himself, "this war's a lucky thing for me. I might have been in the R.C. Vicker Company's store for five years an' never got a raise. An' here in the army I got a chance to do almost anything." '[48]

Fuselli never sees action, though he certainly knows the fear of death during his voyage to France. Though humiliated almost to revolt by the casual disposition of the officers, he never finds the will or energy to strike back. His fear of getting 'in bad' is deep rooted: at the core of his ingrained feelings of social inferiority lies the willing slave's futile hope of 'getting on'.

> Something of the gesture with which the lieutenant drew on his gloves caught in the mind of Fuselli . . . The president of the company that owned the optical goods store, where he had worked, at home in Frisco, had something of that gesture about him.
>
> And he pictured himself drawing on a pair of gloves that way, importantly, finger by finger, with a little wave of self-satisfaction when the gesture was completed . . .[49]

He has set his mind on a corporalship – a low enough distinction, but one which is constantly to elude him. Meanwhile, there are the intermittent pleasures of the soldier posted abroad – talk, alcohol, women, the foci for adolescent dreams and sensuality. In these matters the great hero of the bistros and apostle of 's'en foutisme' is Dan Cohan. Cohan, like Tom Randolph in *One Man's Initiation*, somehow triumphs over circumstances by being breezily natural and not worrying. He does worry Fuselli, though: Cohan's irreverence strikes Fuselli with the fear that it 'might get him in wrong'. Even to sex Fuselli brings his solemn and illusory expectations of self-improvement. Tragicomically divided between personal ambition and the brute facts of collective discipline, he innocently panders his girl to the top sergeant. Immediately afterwards, his modest aim of making corporal is ruined by the return of the Red Sox outfielder from hospital. Such blows radically change his attitude to military life. Previously a blend of fear, respect, indoctrination and the desire to make good, it now becomes the grudging acquiescence of the broken spirit. 'They had not treated him right. He felt full of hopeless anger against this vast treadmill to which he was bound . . . He felt he couldn't go on, yet he knew that he must and would go on, that there was no stopping, that his feet would go on beating in time to the steps of the treadmill.'⁵⁰

Although his faith is momentarily restored by his transfer to the camp stores when the rest of his company leaves for the front, his disillusion is sealed at the end of section two, 'The Metal Cools'. Made to perform tedious donkey work, he finds himself a witness to the death of the boy soldier Stockton. Fuselli has decided that Stockton, who cannot raise himself from the bed, is 'crazy' for disobeying an order. A lieutenant is called, and orders that court-martial papers be drawn up. But Stockton is dead, and the victory of organised insanity over every kind of human principle is clear.

Fuselli's fate is determined for him: his individualism is powerless against external forces. Chrisfield suffers a parallel victimisation. He is a Hoosier farm boy, unlettered, brave and practical, and his qualities are stressed by the novel's pastoral imagery, such as the 'smells of moist fields and of manure from fresh-sowed patches and of cows and pasture lands coming into flower'.⁵¹ Chrisfield is attuned to a basic rhythm, the flow of agrarian life. In springtime he sows, at harvest-time he reaps, and when his government announces that the killing-time has arrived he puts on his uniform and shoulders a gun. Chrisfield accepts the natural-ness of taking life, but he finally cannot adopt the posture of unques-tioning submission demanded by the military juggernaut. The army corrupts him, by harnessing his killer instinct for purposes that cannot be justified by regular imperatives of survival, and then makes him declare himself an outlaw. Unlike the lumpen-proletarian Fuselli, Chris-field really has exercised self-reliance, and to push him too far is to make him strike back with instinctive savagery.

Stalking through the forest on a reconnaissance mission which he subsequently relates to John Andrews alone, he is filled with terror as his helmet is tweaked off by a branch. ' "Ah'll make them pay for that," he muttered between clenched teeth'.⁵² Shortly afterwards he discovers the corpse of a German soldier whose hideously mutilated body begins to haunt his dreams. This experience is crucial for Chrisfield. A pioneer type, he is not squeamish, but large-scale political murder cannot be justified like the organic struggles of life. The artificial nature of army regulations is highlighted for him by the development of a feud with Anderson, who plays it all by the book others have written for him and whose quarrel is much more real to him than the conflicts of nations. Chrisfield likes to feel solidarity with his fellow men, and he likes to conduct disputes on an informal man-to-man basis; his opportunity comes during an infantry battle in which Anderson is wounded. Ander-son begs a drink of water from Chrisfield, and then reverts to the tone of the bullying officer. Chrisfield pulls a grenade from his pocket and kills his enemy. There is no guilt, no remorse. 'His feet beat the ground in time with other feet. He would not have to think whether to go to the right or to the left. He would do as others did.'[53]

But this assurance is purely temporary. Like most men, Chrisfield seeks both community and identity, but the army denies him both. His need to be part of a group is quite foreign to the jingoistic and bogus fellow-feeling whipped up by the 'Y' men, with their repulsive mixture of soft soap and nationalistic brainwashing. Chrisfield may prefer to match with men who speak his language and share his culture, but he was effectively willing to perform the work of the German army in settling his score with Anderson. He is not 'defeatist', and would never under-stand the political case for pacifism and desertion, but there are limits to his tolerance of authority. Unlike the poor Fuselli, he does 'get on' with his fellows; and unlike Fuselli, he 'gets ahead' by achieving pro-motion – the only one of the protagonists to do so. However, the in-dividual and collective urges working upon him set up a conflict that drives him to desert. Though he feels no personal regret at having killed Anderson, he fears punishment if he is exposed, and the fear of exposure makes up his mind.

Chrisfield is reduced to living in hiding in a huge capital city, unsure of his future, half wishing that he could reinstate himself. But as Andrews points out to Al, the army 'is not the sort of thing a man can make good in'.[54] Chrisfield is the kind of man who might have made a good combat soldier, just as Fuselli might have made an efficient orderly or clerk. Their waste as human material illustrates the blindness of the system. Both are defeated: Chrisfield in his Paris rat-hole, Fuselli in the labour battalion where he has been sent for contracting V.D.

Chrisfield and Fuselli are not existential figures, they are deliberately broad types. Fuseilli is a particular city type, the proletarian victim of 'false consciousness'. Chrisfield, a rural mid-westerner, has lived by the harmonious currents of nature; his thinking is limited by the very simplic-ity that makes him likeable. His mental life is elementary, and he is at a loss when removed from his native environment. In an unaccustomed setting they lose their paths, and, unlike John Andrews, they have no reasoned philosophy to explain their 'getting in wrong' – or to defend it.

Though Chrisfield and Fuselli to some extent throw Andrews into relief, for the most part they appear to be characters in a different kind of book. Their destruction is more schematically portrayed as a revelation of how society has betrayed the small people who cannot cope with change or deception. The realistic detail surrounding them never has the conviction of what is related through John Andrews's sophisticated mind, and as subordinate characters they are not on the same plan as he. What they share with him is the impotence and despair of the hopeless case. Though there is no decent human being in the novel above the rank of corporal, and though Dos Passos concentrates on the experience of the ordinary infantryman, he does not infuse his creations with the invincible heroism of the common man.

For this reason, it is hard to share Hemingway's view that *Three Soldiers* was 'written under the influence of Barbusse'.[55] *Three Soldiers* mingles a realistic treatment of war with lyrical interludes and with explorations of the consciousness of John Andrews, the alienated intellectual. Its major strength lies in its use of the conditions of service life as a metaphor for the ever-present doom of modern existence: the dull heartache and difficulty of forming positive convictions. Andrews's desertion carries no further implications than the expression of his own denial of the forces that have denied him. Even as a non-social act, it has attenuated value. 'A Hemingway character can take matters into his own hands, when he has seen violence and suffering enough, and make a private peace – there is always a Catherine Barkley and a retreat in Switzerland. He has at least retained the power to act . . . Andrews has nothing left but the concentration of his rage.'[56]

Or the thin wine of his despair, for Andrews at the last is apathetic and resigned. His mind wavers or is paralysed: the artist's consciousness, theoretically capable of taking in so much of life and restoring it to harmony, is overcome by the grind of experience. The sentence from Stendhal which Dos Passos chose as the epigraph for his novel stresses the plangency of this opposition: 'Les contemporains qui souffrent de certaines choses ne peuvent s'en souvenir qu'avec une horreur qui paralyse tout autre plaisir, même celui de lire un conte'.[57] Yet Andrews is not just a sensitive soul badly treated by a wicked world: he is an author's self-image, true, but he is likely to be a reader's self-image as well. There are many moments when the presentation of his character is flawed by self-pity or by verbal extravagance, but the pain and humiliation he suffers are authentic, and few could face them heroically. The futility of his desertion matches the futility of the 'machine' he seeks to evade, but there is no reason to believe acquiescence is either preferable or possible.

Dos Passos' two 'war books' display growing talent, but he does not, like Hemingway, become fixated as a novelist of action. Like Cummings, he is an accidental casualty; but he is not a celebrant. The sympathetic neutrality he exhibits towards most of his creations is not informed by a creed of hope, either political or artistic.

> . . . the boy who thought he was going to be a tramp turns out a nearsighted middleclass intellectual (or a tramp; it's as bad either way). Professional deformations set in; the freeswimming young oyster fastens to the rock and grows a shell. What it amounts to is this: our beds have made us and the acutest action we can take is sit up

on the edge of them and look around and think. They are our beds till we die.[58]

Both hindsight and prophecy, this amply confirms the practice of the young novelist. His job *was* to 'tell the tale', and in telling it he fore-sees little promise of regeneration by social change. Nor has he devalued his subject. The immaturity of *One Man's Initiation* and *Three Soldiers* springs largely from technical limitations which, in *Manhattan Transfer*, are to be resourcefully overcome. The vision of despair belongs rightly and naturally to the story, in which the helplessness of the individual twisting in discomfort on the 'bed' that makes him is vividly proved. That this vision is not the product of war-time conditions only it will be the task of other novels to expound.

3 Brownian Motion: *Manhattan Transfer*

In his published fiction up to 1925, Dos Passos seemed still to be a sensitive recorder of experience rather than an artist complete. This is not to say that there was no development. The first book, so bleedingly raw in its depiction of battlefield shock and so rhetorically diffuse in its abstractions from that experience, barely qualifies as a novel. It is more like the diary of a horrified spectator irresistibly forced into rebellion. This rebellion, though, is a rebellion of the mind and sensibility. It cannot be maturely absorbed as a practical conviction which derives from traumatic disillusion the energy and will for a programme of action. Yet the essence of Martin Howe's involvement in the war is a disillusioning personal crisis, of which the true nature is half recognised in the author's prefaces to subsequent editions of *One Man's Initiation*. In 1945 Dos Passos wrote that 'To us, the European war of 1914–18 seemed a horrible monstrosity . . . the boys who are fighting this present war drank in the brutalities of European politics with their breakfast coffee';[1] in 1968, anxious perhaps to disavow his younger self in the light of conversion, he added: 'We were young hotheads. We took to shouting all the war-cries of the Marxist dogma.'[2] The sheer barbarity of warfare, for which the American initiate was unprepared, and the sentimental reaction to it, peer out from the sceptical words of the middle-aged writer. Martin Howe becomes, by the novel's end, neither a case-hardened warrior nor a seriously committed socialist, but a traumatised youth whose emotional resources of pity and indignation have been touched by an encounter with bloodshed, waste and muddle.

The next incarnation of the Dos Passos hero, however, definitely revolts and is definitely defeated. The desertion of John Andrews *is* a volitional act. It is ultimately futile – symbolic and self-sacrificial – but it offers a gesture of defiance to the army machine which has affronted his senses and misused his comrades. It raises the need for an alternative system of justice to the army's degrading and remorseless discipline. What such a system could be is never adequately investigated, chiefly because Andrews has to struggle with parallel conflicts. As a would-be composer of symphonic music he is an eccentric, and he would be so even in peacetime society. He suffers from contrary impulses to submerge himself in the mass of mankind and to shine as a heroic creator. The niggling enforced privations of military life interrupt his epicurean dreams. His intended solution to his manifold difficulties, the composition of a symphony to be titled 'On the Soul and Body of John Brown', borders on the absurd. Yet Andrews does go one step beyond Martin Howe: he does not treat the war itself purely as subject-matter for his artist's instinct, he takes a stand, albeit a confused and unsatisfactory one, and he suffers the penalty. The timeliness of its initial publication meant that *Three Soldiers* was received as a 'war book' rather than a statement of the besetting problems of self-discovery in modern life – a theme to which the fact of total war is relevant, but which should not be obscured by its setting.

Streets of Night is a loose link in the canon, but since it was published after *Three Soldiers* and Dos Passos had revised it for publication, it may be taken as embodying the author's sensibility immediately before *Manhattan Transfer*. In fact, many passages have a clarity and strength equal or superior to much of the writing in the war novels. It is a spoilt but not altogether 'banal'[3] novel. Despite its youthful defects, *Streets of Night* is thematically serious. Wenny is a recognisable *confrère* of Howe and Andrews – trapped, hypersensitive, a frustrated rebel – and his choice of suicide has the merit of conclusiveness. He, too, is a victim of that fatal division between an inarticulate dream (creative, inspiring) and the call to action (dutiful, self-abnegatory). In his case, too, every interior tension is reinforced by pressure from without and every hesitant advance to freedom is vitiated by guilt and loneliness. He remains, of course, adolescent; but the central defect of the novel lies not in its use of an adolescent hero but in a failure of perspective. Wenny is too raw, too undigested artistically, Fanshaw and Nan are pale, over-schematised and lifeless. What Dos Passos' concern as a novelist demanded was a new synthesis uniting both psychological truth and representative significance to express the blend of social and personal forces that together establish the limits of freedom. *Manhattan Transfer* is a bold attempt to formulate such a method.

Here, in fact, is the first thorough prose demonstration of the techniques to be associated with John Dos Passos, which were treated by early reviewers for their novelty value rather than their suitability to the aims which the author had set himself. Continuous-narrative naturalism is abandoned. Replacing it comes a method both jarring and flexible, alternating the life histories of his characters with prose-poetic epigraphs, saturnine vignettes and interior monologues. *Manhattan Transfer* takes place in a crowded city on a crowded planet, though it is by no means an exercise in American 'unanimism'.[4] The individual protagonist is viewed in a context of modern urban institutions and representative types, but he is not extinct as a focus of sympathetic attention – indeed, he gains in significance from the author's supervision of the relative distances at which characters are seen. Moreover, Dos Passos is no longer writing the novel of pure stasis or congestion – energy contained or destructively turned inward. Motion is the key to *Manhattan Transfer*, and it is largely in order to convey the sense of motion – in space, in historical time, in consciousness – that the author has made his synthesis of technical innovations. But this movement never implies the possibility of hope. It is not dialectical, it heads towards no regenerating goal, it has no pattern except that of the rush and impact of separate self-interested forces at play in a giant twentieth-century metropolis. Made for man's convenience, the city reinforces the helplessness of the human will.

The movement of *Manhattan Transfer*, in fact, might be compared to 'Brownian Motion', the irregular jostling of small particles suspended in a gas or liquid, full of backtrackings and collisions, seemingly random but obeying the physical rules of matter. The characters of the novel, like the ball-bearings in the official model of Brownian Motion, have no sense of explanation for their conduct or their fates. Hence the fund of blindly providential accounts of human destiny – or 'the peculiar predominance of luck in human affairs', as Joe Harland phrases it. The personal will, a distinct but spasmodically effective quality in Dos Passos' previous fiction, dwindles to a gnawing itch for economic success or consumes itself in vain self-reproaches. Where before there had been a primary stress on the position of the rebel trying to found his struggle on personally acquired values, now the frame is largely filled by the many who can never shake off their conditioning. The characters are defined for the reader by their being placed in an arena of probabilities – whatever happens to them *is* them. The urban accidents with which the book is filled are often genuinely accidental in the sense that nobody bears direct responsibility for them. They are latent in the dynamism of New York. Is the reader to sympathise? *Can* he sympathise with the pygmy humans overawed and smashed by monstrous machinery full of undirected energy, impersonally presented like the Brownian model, supplied only with the information that this is how it happens to behave?

However, *Manhattan Transfer* is not a work simply based on the 'collective' formula. Most of the characters are drawn in a deliberately restricted fashion, but Jimmy Herf and Elaine Thatcher are not drawn to this scale – or rather, they are not shown in the same focus. On the face of it Herf is an unsettling influence, the unassimilated residue of Howe–Andrews–Wenny, a sensitive and self-pitying young man out of place in the city and the novel; and the proto-Herf who appears in one of Dos Passos' rare short stories undeniably is this.

This story – 'July' – appeared in the *Transatlantic Review*.[5] It takes place in Northern Virginia, and concentrates on the romantic sensations of the adolescent boy. 'In Egypt, Jimmy was thinking, there were no buggies; the rowers sang as they pulled on the long sweeps of the dahabieh.'[6] Such passages are familiar from the early writing of Dos Passos – the pagan nostalgia of Fanshaw McDougan, the pre-industrial itch that animated long sections of *Rosinante to the Road Again*. In 'July', though, these sickened fantasies, childish and literary, are framed by the running-off together of Ole Man Oatley, the neighbourhood stud, and the preacher's wife, who has poured out her suppressed longings to young Jimmy. This affair of the priapic Oatley with Mrs Chadwick (who, like Cassie in *Manhattan Transfer*, has all her life 'craved beautiful things . . . beautiful thoughts, beautiful friends')[7] seems likely to disillusion both parties. Jimmy, however, does not perceive this. He assists the lovers with a warning as they flee an angry posse. They have lived what he can only taste at the level of vicarious fantasy. Jimmy has to return to the household of Uncle Jeff and Aunt Emily, a temple of puritan respectability where 'romance' is harshly judged by the imperatives of Christian conformity and where 'the fried chicken and spinach and potatoes were ashes in his mouth'.[8] Dos Passos does not mean that Aunt Emily has burnt the dinner, but there is little doubt that Jimmy has suffered physically. At seventeen he inhabits a Freudian jungle of which the lushly exotic blooms, with their decadent shapes and odours, mimic the forbidden fruit of sexual passion. Disturbances ensue – 'a sick feeling in the throat',[9] 'the blood stung in his eyes',[10] 'a sharp pain in the forehead',[11] and 'he could hear nothing but the pumping of his blood'.[12] After a guilty sex-dream ('Her breasts were baked apples shrivelled to bursting . . . He was the god Ptah. It was red. It was Egypt')[13] he wakes up 'trembling and sick'.[14]

'July', a magazine story, gives no opportunity for Jimmy Herf to develop: it concludes with his 'epiphany'. But its hero is recognisably akin to the even younger Herf who, in Chapter III of *Manhattan Transfer* disembarks at New York with his 'Muddy' on Independence Day. Though this boy has a sentimenal impulse to kiss the ground of his native land, his background is cosmopolitan. The commercial mores of urban America, of which his Merivale cousins are the exemplars, are foreign and strange. He is shy, awkward and mother-eclipsed, and he is due to live in exile at the Ritz. From his first appearance, this anguished and lonely figure is portrayed with greater detail and urgency than the city's human detritus. The strangeness and excitement he senses arouse feelings comparable to the brain-nausea of 'July'. 'His legs ached as if they'd fall off, and when he closed his eyes he was speeding through flaming blackness on a red fire-engine that shot fire and sparks and coloured balls out of its tail.'[15] Fires and fire-engines are the central unifying metaphors of *Manhattan Transfer*. They symbolise the threat of apocalyptic destruction, and the panicky and unavailing human efforts to avert it. Even the harmless firecrackers of the Fourth of July celebrations are, to Jimmy, a feverish menace. 'Freedom' and 'independence' cannot be sustaining realities for him.

The Ritz proves to be the enclosed pinnacle of an endlessly stratified society, a kind of luxury prison. It is here that Jimmy becomes aware of the forces of base vitality, as he gazes from the window of his mother's suite. The reader, like Herf, can never strain his ears sufficiently to catch the talk of the common people. They are a mystery, not a class to be liberated but an aggregation of tangible spirits, both frightening and glamorous. And all round the block an identical miscellany of objects persists – 'A telegraph office, dry-goods stores, a dyers and cleaners, a Chinese laundry sending out a scorched mysterious smell.'[16] This is a list, rather than a significant selection, but a list made valuable in its alienating blankness. The objects are drawn within the whirlpool of Jimmy Herf's sensibility, in which the reader must also participate. New York can only appear whole if the synoptic perspective is matched by a view from within a distinct consciousness.

Thus Herf moderates the objective character of the passages from which he and Elaine are absent. There are no Jamesian depths to him, and he is largely incapable of development as a *person*, but as a character – depicted is a series of separate 'takes' – he illuminates the ubiquity of failure. On a diet of chocolate creams and suggestive encyclopaedia entries ('The Queen of the White Slaves')[17] he falls asleep, and wakes to find his mother dying of thrombosis. At this point he is released into isolation, and the surge of hopelessness that fills his mind is brilliantly rendered in a passage of exceptional intensity: the solitary boy in the great impersonal hotel squashes a fly on the window-pane; memories and fears of school invade his mind; he recalls his scarcely known father. Jimmy's rootlessness and his inadequacy to be a positive, masculine, self-sufficient person are underlined by the interposed contrasts with the domestic life of the Merivales, the smarter side of the family, cocooned (as in 'July') in a suffocating bourgeois domesticity. They had frowned on 'poor Aunt Lily's itinerant, unsettled existence. They are wealthy but have skeletons in their cupboard, such as the family outcast, Joe Harland, a black-sheep alcoholic, a former speculator fallen on evil times. Jimmy, too, disgraces himself with a *faux pas* and rushes off to the 'familiar crimson stairs of the Ritz'.[18] Jimmy's association with Harland is established implicitly through his social error committed while playing a financial parlour-game. The Merivales signify what he must reject if he is to realise his own nature – in the first instance because their pharasaical self-assurance is intimidating and later because he senses that there are worthier principles to be followed. But

Jimmy has to discover the limitations of merely avoiding uncongenial alternatives – and those limitations coincide with the innate restrictions on freedom.

Little more is learned of Herf's childhood. He next appears at the beginning of Chapter v, shortly before the death of Bud Korpenning. Bud had killed his tyrannical father, and by coming to New York had punished himself more terribly than could the law, which, despite his fears, never tracks him down. Jimmy has recently attended his mother's funeral: the mood is lyrical and vernal.

> Little worms of May were writhing in his blood . . . There is one glory of the sun and another glory of the moon and another glory of the stars: for one star differeth from another star in glory. So also is the resurrection of the dead . . . I'm so tired of violets / Take them all away . . . He walked faster. The blood flowed full and hot in his veins. The flaked clouds were melting into rose-coloured foam. He could hear his steps on the warm macadam.[19]

This is Jimmy's farewell to childhood. The sense of liberation by his mother's death bursts through in a realisation of the simple naturalness of life. It is a fragmented moment, relating Herf's carnal musings with the surrounding sense-data. Like much of *Manhattan Transfer*, it could be rendered cinematically. The sensuous immediacy of the situation calls for no psychological pursuit. Here is a young hero obliged to grow up fast and struggle for his independence under the shock of privation – and ready to make that effort.

The fade-out in medium shot pinpoints a special moment in the full context of Jimmy's experience. This passage marks the extinction of the Herf character taken over from the magazine story. The 'July' character, the sensitive filament, can no longer act as a satisfying centre of interest for a novel which surveys the hectic and complicated involvement of its characters with a variety of urgent difficulties. Herf's immediate problem is the problem of earning a living, and for a discussion of it he meets his uncle at the Metropolitan Club. Merivale plans for his nephew a career in the family tradition of work, prosperity and humbug. He offers his own definition of manhood, based on the philistine success-credo; Jimmy is unable to contradict him, yet as he leaves he foresees 'the revolving doors grinding out his years like sausage meat'.[20] At this instant Jimmy changes his mind, and almost in the words of Huck Finn announces: 'Uncle Jeff and his office can go plumb to hell'.[21]

Here is indeed a new Jimmy Herf, a sixteen-year-old capable of asserting himself against the formidable pressure of conformism and 'common sense'. One would not have expected from the younger Herf this kind of strength to make a fresh start on the basis of individual fulfilment, like

Stephen Daedalus. Herf had always been a person directed by others, whose own febrile yearnings clotted up inside him to cause circulatory trouble. And his stand is never as decisive as he imagines. Later he is forced to admit that 'Uncle Jeff keeps getting me jobs',[22] and he falls into circles of yellow journalism as bitterly futile and negative as the revolving doors of banking. Jimmy Herf's story in *Manhattan Transfer* signifies the end of Dos Passos' dream of the romantic hero who tries to assert his identity against forceful opposition and who, if he fails in the end to win, immolates himself in an existential tragedy that gives meaning to his rebellion. What was true of the earlier protagonists – that they guarded their integrity so vehemently that they would face death or imprisonment rather than surrender it – is no longer true of Jimmy Herf. The one-eyed man in the blind circle of determinism, he is seemingly no freer in practice to break out than Bud, Gus McNiel, Stanwood Emery or the other faces in the crowd. By showing at length the degeneration of a gifted and perceptive young man, the author spotlights with a dual focus the heartlessly random universality of Brownian Motion.

If the tendency of *Manhattan Transfer* is pessimistic, however, the method and style of Books ii and iii are notable for the energy and colour with which Dos Passos paints his portrait of misdirected movement. Herf reappears as an aimless young man with pink attitudes and a disorganised private life. The Sunderland theatrical boarding-house where he visits Ruth Prynne and the resident cast of unsuccessful actors are both treated with astringent satire. In Oglethorpe the sonorous ham, Cassandra Wilkins, lisping her virgin's prayers in a jungle of promiscuity, and Tony Hunter, the self-accusing faggot, appear the types of Dos Passos' theatrical and Greenwich Village years. The loosening of moral standards and the cynical levity of the talk prefigure the emerging shape of *1919*.

Into this half-world drifts Jimmy Herf, now a Columbia graduate who complains that big-city life is pointless and depressing yet inertly accepts it – an incurable city-dweller. Stanwood Emery, an aesthete–playboy, drawls in a succession of juvenile paradoxes his belief that the lure of material success is a will-o'-the-wisp. 'Why the hell does everyone want to succeed? I'd like to meet somebody who wanted to fail in life. That's the only sublime thing'.[23] The sentiments and the flip vocabulary are those of unproductive privilege, and Herf certainly finds little sublime about his own failure – a deeper failure than worldly failure. 'The trouble with me is that I can't decide what I want most, so my motion is circular, helpless and confoundedly discouraging'.[24] This self-reproach is only a symptom of the disease; Herf is more than an organised misfit. He is a sell-out, soured into premature bitterness. Between shame and brazen indifference, alertness and boredom, sardonic resignation and sudden revivals of the will, he is pushed about by mysterious and arbitrary forces.

Not to go to the war is to play the 'false Etruscan',[25] yet his excuse to Joe Harland – that he is 'poor at wangling things'[26] – rings hollow; he has been able to rely on Uncle Jeff to wangle jobs for him. Always he can fall back on the excuse of a 'hellish rotten job'[27] to justify the demoralising disgust and inertia which envelop him.

Thus, the radical opinions which he acquires from Martin Schiff are never developed beyond parlour-revolutionary 'opinionation' that matches so perfectly the seedy-romantic restaurant interiors redolent of *Streets of Night*. Schiff is a genuine radical, but Herf's major note is defeatism – 'Oh God, everything is so Hellish'[28] – and what most attracts him is not the urban American present but the rural European past. On his return from France to the post-war prohibition saturnalia, he wistfully recalls travelling in France – irresponsible, epicurean, behind the lines. 'Diddlede-dump, going south, sing the wheels over the rails down the valley of the Rhone. Leaning in the window, smoking a broken cigarette, holding a finger over the torn place. Glub-glub glub-glub from the bushes, from the silver-dripping poplars along the track'.[29] Here speaks Dos Passos the cultivated hobo who wriggles in the trousers of the novelist of social significance. Like the 'fine ram'[30] unearthed by Mr Perry on the building lot and the 'rickety . . . weatherboarded farmhouse'[31] still standing by the new apartment blocks, the memory denotes the irre-mediable deadness of the past and the secret yearning to recover it. No wonder Herf clings to this. Back in New York his problems are redoubled. The all-prevailing ethos of success, now on the crest of a Republican wave, baits and harasses him; he is oppressed by a clouded recognition that it is impossible to live as he does, straddling the two worlds of the conformist and the rebel. Unlike 'Long-legged Jack of the Isthmus', he will not be able to keep clear of the rising waters.

The climax of Herf's 'epic of disintegration'[32] springs from his rejection by Elaine, and extinguishes any residual hope for a life of integrity. His apathy, always profound, becomes total. He throws up, or is fired from, his job. In the 'Skyscraper' chapter images of the multi-faceted city, teeming with the sordid stories his work has brought him into contact with, flock around him. He identifies himself with the murderer Dick Snow – the ultimate outcast, who has 'met the demands of spring'[33] by composing in his death-cell a poem to be published by the 'Evening Graphic' – and with the alien radicals deported during the Red Scare.

James Herf, young news paper man of 190, West 12th Street, recently lost his twenties. Appearing before Judge Merivale they were remanded to Ellis Island for deportation as undesirable aliens. The younger four, Sasha, Michael, Nicholas and Vladimir had been held for some time on a technical charge of vagrancy. The later ones, Bill, Tony and Joe were held under various indictments, including wife-beating, arson, assault and prostitution. All were convicted on counts of misfeasance, malfeasance and nonfeasance.[34]

Here, and in the surrealistic fantasies of ribald celebrations that accompany the 'trial', Herf flickers to life as the wry intellectual, surveying with ironic understanding his internal conflicts and wasted opportunities, temporarily escaping the wringing self-torture of the 'hollow man'. By casting his uncle in the role of the officious A. Mitchell Palmer he exercises the ghost of family disapproval which has haunted one half of his mind.

But Herf is dogged by ambiguity to the very end. He remains the thinker who has realised the insubstantiality of mere words, echoing Hemingway: 'Don't talk . . . what you talk about you never do'.[35] Such disillusion is worth having; but it is a disillusion heavily tinged with regret for lost faith in the magical power of words to signify reality and to render it orderly and harmonious, which had been essential to Herf even while he abused it as a journalist. The recently exposed mass lying of the war-time propaganda agencies and the new discoveries in English style made by writers of his own generation ought to have persuaded Herf that language needed redemption, purification. Instead, he feels it to be itself a corrupt medium. Without such a faith, he seems to Ellen like 'a bastard mechanical toy'.[36] Herf takes to pieces the ruined mechanism of this toy to show his friends. Fascinated by the broken machinery of his own soul, he sinks further into acedia. While Martin Schiff walks off to take his life, Jimmy roams the streets, spellbound by a city that shines for him at every angle with the image of his loveliest sorrow. 'Ellie in a gold dress, Ellie made of thin gold foil absolutely lifelike'.[37] It is an exact picture – Ellie in gold foil is 'absolutely lifelike'. She is the vital illusion of the city itself – an illusion of expanding opportunities that hides the lethal trap.

Jimmy, in a terminal hysteria of despair, seizes on a contrary image. At a party given by the Hildebrands he hears the anecdote of the Philadelphian who 'wore his straw hat on the fourteenth of May'[38] and was killed for it by a town tough. Suddenly, this casually told story flaunts an ideal of idiosyncratic selfhood, the courage to step outside the bounds of propriety and risk the 'gesture of Castile'. Directly after the party, he leaves New York on the Hudson ferry which, at the start of the novel, had brought Bud Korpenning to look for 'the centre of things'. 'Then he walks on, taking pleasure in his breathing, in the beat of his blood, in the tread of his feet on the pavement, between rows of other-worldly frame houses. Gradually the fog thins, a pearliness is seeping in from somewhere.'[39] The pearliness of dawn into which he is walking scarcely suggests the 'symbolic suicide'[40] one critic has made of the final paragraphs. Yet it is lavish to call his departure 'the one progressive movement within the circle of futile and self-vitiating acts'.[41] Herf only knows that he is going 'pretty far'.[42] But he cannot be 'lightin' out for the territory'. There is no territory left. The past has been built over, and even upstate there flourishes the barbarous cruelty that made Bud Korpenning a parricide. Is not Jimmy Herf, like the pulp-heroes of a later fiction, 'running away from megalopolis; but in megalopolis's own product, the life-consuming machine. He'll be back; there is another town just ahead, just the same as the others. After that, another escape; and so on, till death puts an end to it'?[43]

What saves Herf from being a pure duplicate of previous Dos Passos heroes is his location in the context of a novel of which the form is carefully adapted to secure a reasonable aesthetic distance from the protagonist. The re-creation of a whole city through tropes of style – most successfully through the adaptation of cinema techniques – and the episodic treatment of an extended period both place Herf in a setting which reduces the author's licence to sanctify a self-image. Equally, other life histories contribute to a density and movement effective in marking the degree to which he is casualty. More fortunate than Bud Korpenning, less complacently successful than George Baldwin, he nevertheless suffers the blind misfortunes so casually inflicted by the metropolis. In his relatively closer focus he sharpens the readers' sense of confronting personal experience rather than a remote chronicle. If the 'poet and the world'[44] antithesis remains, it has been well integrated into a book which signifies a major advance in the author's art.

Still more impressive is a new Dos Passos creation. Ellen, though she moves at the pace and level of the swarm, illuminates them all, and by saturating the work with her infinite egoism gives to the fragments an essential unity. Herf exists as a strangely recurring fossil in the impacted layers of time and the city. Ellen colours them all with the refractions of her 'negative capability'. Around her spin the opportunistic shields and mirrors which dazzle her lovers or associates. Her upward progress, swifter and more sensational than Sister Carrie's, parallels the growth of the city: just as glamorous, just as lacking in social sanity. She commits emotional destruction on the scale of a runaway automobile, or the fires which continually ravage the city. 'She shall make mischief wherever she goes'[45] quotes Stan Emery, and only for him – because, as she half confesses, he dies too soon for her to tire of his driven vitality – does she experience something close to affection. George Baldwin, the man of iron ambition, is practically ready to kill under the influence of the passions she has awoken in him, and Ed Thatcher, after a life devoted to prudent acquisitiveness, lies spent in his retirement house at Passaic, scanning the gossip columns which report to him fresh scandals about the daughter for whom he has sacrificed so much.

Ellen Thatcher is the prototypical bitch, later to be more completely realised as Eveline Hutchins in *USA*. Unlike poor inhibited Nan she goes out to meet the world, turning her weaknesses into strengths. The falseness of Ellen, the sophistication she adopts for self-defence, is the falseness of city civilisation itself. Already as a young girl she is in love with the theatre, and whatever her gifts as an actress may be she adapts herself in a masterly fashion to the hegemony of the male. Her desire to change her sex, to be an aggressive and dominating influence, is realised through a clever exploitation of her female identity. Her recoil from the brute facts of sexuality in her honeymoon reveals her distaste for passivity, for undergoing penetration by another. And yet: 'She lay giggling on the far edge of the bed, giggling desperately as she used to do with girls at school'.[46] But one is not obliged to accept, on the partial testimony of Ruth Prynne and Cassandra Wilkins, that Ellen is just another hard bitch out for what she can get. She is not the most calculating of women, and her motives are never isolated and analysed: they merge, through the episodic text, with the vital metabolism of the city. Ellen is not simply *at* 'the centre of things',[47] she *is* the centre. Everyone recognises this, even George Baldwin, who is relegated to the position of one adoring male in a tableau of courtship. Like the Danderine lady she is part romantic ideal, part commercial fraud. Like New York, she sheds glamour and disaster arbitrarily.

Her behaviour towards Stanwood Emery reflects the real charm and tenderness of which she is capable. With Oglethorpe she strikes the attitudes of the aspiring actress; later she will become a poised woman of the world for her cocktail friends. Even the boy burglar whom she releases is overpowered by her magic. 'He grabbed the hand with the bill in it and kissed it; leaning over her hand kissing it wetly he caught a glimpse of her body under the arms in the drooping red silk sleeve . . . His eyes were full of tears'.[48] In the ironic sequel to this episode, Nick discovers that the cash he has taken from her apartment is worthless stage money. Ellen usually pays off in counterfeit currency. She is in tune with the metropolitan rhythm, and she shrugs off easily the disappointments that weigh down Jimmy Herf – 'Matrimony isn't much, is it?'[49]

Ellen is not inhumanly void of feeling but her quota of saving self-awareness is as ineffective as the fire engines that rush about the city to attend its ever-occurring conflagrations. Stanwood Emery's death and marriage do shock Ellen. She had so far lost herself with Stan as to risk her career, so that her dresser had reason to warn her 'Don't you ever let any fellow like that come to the theatre with ye. I've seen many a good trooper ruined by things like that'.[50] But Stan's own desperate irresponsibility had outrun Ellen's carelessness. His drunken runaway marriage to a chorus girl and his self-immolation by fire in their newly furnished apartment betray the unprotected completeness of his despair. Ellen suffers a pang for her dead lover – 'from the black · pinholes her pupils spread blurring till everything was black'[51] – but one which anticipates the ennui and aimlessness increasingly to beset her.

Unlike Jimmy Herf – such a nervous barometer of life's moods in the intensity of his chequered responses – Ellen has the benefit of a purely spontaneous self-deception. She never needs to contrive to mask her insecurity; but her need to be 'the centre of things' drives her on. Book II ends not with parturition but with abortionist's parlour and his 'dazzling sharp glass case of sharp instruments'.[52] The current of necessity in which Ellen lives sweeps aside personal emotion.

In the final section of the novel Ellen does appear with a child – Jimmy's child, Martin – yet the role of mother is one she finds it impossible to perform with conviction. Young Martin in his cot is prey to the fear and loneliness which both his parents had felt as children.

Ellen's rise progresses as she assumes the editorship of a society journal. In her recoil from the 'hobohemian', Greenwich Village scene she enters the plane of bourgeois success. She has 'arrived', and her arrival matches her with the politician on the make, George Baldwin, who regards Jimmy as 'a bolshevik pacifist and IWW agitator'.[53] Once again Ellen's seemingly heartfelt beliefs coincide with the new direction of her self-interest. Her awareness of the false face of the city mirrors the truth of her own situation: 'Under all the nickel plated, gold plated streets enamelled with May, uneasily she could feel the huddling smell, spreading in dark, slow, crouching masses, like corruption coming from the broken sewers, like a mob.'[54] Now a kind of urban Rusalka, she is a projection of the gaudily disguised pitfalls of New York. In particular her neurotic concern with appearances has all but extinguished the 'weakness' of natural human response. Only a bad shock can stimulate the vestiges of these responses, and the final transient indices of an alternative Ellen, capable of relating authentically to others, are seen after the fire at Madame Soubrine's, in which the seamstress Anna has been dreadfully burned. 'There are lives to be lived if only you didn't care. Care for what, for what; the opinion of mankind, money, success, hotel lobbies, health umbrellas, Uneeda biscuits . . .'[55] Yes: Ellen does care for those things enough to ignore the suspicion that her life is a fraud. She can no more undo the tendency to follow the metropolitan urge for smartness, sophistication and wealth than Brooklyn Flats can be cleared for snipe-shooting. But like the city she is an endlessly fascinating illusion. Dos Passos' portrait of Ellen is like his conception of New York as 'a great lonely man-killer, indifferent to the humanity she devours, at base romantic'.[56]

In *Manhattan Transfer*, however, the romanticism is latent, and is combined with a series of objectifying devices to create a much better novel than Dos Passos' earlier work. Brownian Motion is studied not with the disinterested curiosity of the scientist but through the prism of a growing sensibility. The famous romantic pessimism is more centred in a real understanding of the horrors of modern existence and conveyed with a much surer literary control. The first piece of narrative – fewer than eight lines – is an account of Ellen Thatcher's birth in a clinically repellent atmosphere of hospital smells. The process of birth is attended with no affirmations of emerging life. It is concentrated on the infant's appearance, borne by the nurse 'at arm's length'[57] as though it were a bedpan, squirming 'feebly, like a knot of earthworms'.[58] Such imagery links Ellen to Bud Korpenning, the upstate parricide who has sailed in on the ferry to search for 'the centre of things'.[59] Bud with his 'skinny turkey's throat'[60] and the aged violinist with his 'monkey's face'[61] are unloaded at the dock like coal or potatoes, no respect paid to their humanity. Just as Ellen falls involuntarily into the world, Bud is shoved off the boat, ignorant and afraid. He responds automatically to the big-city imperatives – 'EAT' – and the advice he is given by the owner of the lunch-wagon, when he explains his willingness to work, is 'It's looks that count in this city.'[62] Externals are everything – a principle recognised by the Jewish immigrant in the final sketch of Chapter I who shaves off his beard in dumb obedience to King C. Gillette's 'dollarbland smile'.[63] Mrs Thatcher wants to reject her child because 'it hasn't any label on it'[64] and therefore lacks an approved identity. At the smart restaurant in which Emile has found work appear a vulgarly plutocratic set – 'longtoothed', 'moon-faced', 'bottlenosed', 'weazlish'.[65] They drink to excess, talk loudly of sex and money, and finish their evening with a disgusting squabble. There is little doubt that mankind, in the opening chapters of *Manhattan Transfer*, 'is described in disagreeable or derogatory images'.[66] Moreover, men are not giant paragons of evil, they are mean and contemptible.

Yet:

There were Babylon and Nineveh; they were built of brick, Athens was gold marble columns. Rome was held up on broad arches of rubble. In Constantinople the minarets flame like great candles round the Golden Horn. . . . Steel, glass tiles, concrete will be the materials of the skyscrapers. Crammed on the narrow island the million-windowed buildings will jut glittering, pyramid on pyramid like the white clouded above a thunderstorm.[67]

Compared with its population of puny and ineffectual human beings, how glamorous New York is made to seem. It promises to rival the great cities of antiquity as a dominant civisilisation, though like them under sentence of doom. In this 'dust-reeking girder forest'[68] Bud Korpenning can easily lose himself 'like a needle in a haystack'.[69] The ironic translocation of the stock simile conveys his dreadful and inexorable loneliness. Cheated, pushed around or simply faced with indifference, Bud finds himself isolated beyond hope of recovery. This atomisation of the individual – the recognition that New York, apparently a single community of millions, separates and fragments the experience of the men and women who inhabit it – is a thematic keystone of *Manhattan Transfer*. But there is no suggestion that it can be cured by social reform. The insight is the insight of an artist – 'not so much the historian's verdict as the poet's lament'[70] – and it remains an accurate diagnosis not because the author is sociologically perceptive (though he is that) but thanks to the discovery of a form that will express for him a troubled and serious vision.

Manhattan Transfer is a vital advance on the books which preceded it because it has successfully synthesised what was previously strangulated, hysterical or unrealised. The form must be called a synthesis because its elements are not revolutionary or original – they derive from the efforts of true experimentalists (Stein, Joyce), from Carl Sandburg, from Dreiser, Hemingway and John Reed. But Dos Passos has not merely been alert and receptive, he has considered the relevance of the discoveries which he uses and adapts, and his skill in applying them to his own concerns is remarkable. Sinclair Lewis, writing from a more or less middlebrow point of view, seemed to half grasp this achievement when he wrote:

> *Manhattan Transfer* [is] more important in every way than anything by Gertrude Stein or Marcel Proust or even the great white boar, Mr. Joyce's *Ulysses*. For Mr. Dos Passos can use, and deftly does, all their experimental psychology and style, all their revolt against the molds of classic fiction. But the difference! Dos Passos is *interesting*! Their novels are treatises on harmony, very scholarly and confoundedly dull; *Manhattan Transfer* is the moving symphony itself.[71]

Despite the extravagance of the comparative literary judgements, there is a hidden truth in the assertion that Dos Passos is 'interesting'. For Dos Passos, with all his borrowings, is still a practitioner of American realism – an unacademic form, readable for its own sake by the unprofessional public and unrivalled in its facility to present the reader with a world he knows in his ordinary life. *Manhattan Transfer* is not 'difficult'. When it employs innovations, it uses them contextually and responsibly but in no sense esoterically. Mason Wade reinforced Lewis's description when he concluded that 'Dos Passos owes to Joyce the conception of a novel devoted to the life of a city . . . to Proust the use of significant detail and careful documentation, to Stein . . . people and the effectiveness of bald narration. But he added to his borrowings a great deal of his own.'[72]

What Dos Passos added was a concern to make literature *available*. He tended to write of his art as a craftsman solving technical production problems, and his amalgamation of modernist devices with a popular aesthetic makes *Manhattan Transfer* 'lively art',[73] accessible but not commercial. Thus the imagistic fragment, still part of his style three years after *A Pushcart at the Curb*, expresses the sweet–sour aftermath of a day in the speakeasies. 'Parlour-snakes and flappers joggle hugging downtown, uptown, hug joggling grey square after grey square, until they see the new moon giggling over Weehawken and feel the gusty wind of a dead Sunday blowing dust in their faces, dust of a tipsy twilight'.[74] The adequacy of the verbal effects – musical, atmospheric – is soundly judged. Too loose and casual to be satisfying on its own, the passage complements the narrative and psychological elements, and the impression of a teeming Manhattan arises from the flux and alternation of varying perspectives. The deployment of a changing focus is the essence of the process, and even where Dos Passos has frankly borrowed the borrowing is made to work for him. 'The man on the bench has a patch over his eye. A watching black patch. A black watching patch. The kidnappers of the Black Watch, among the rustling shrubs kidnappers keep their Black Watch. Ellen's toes don't kick in the air.'[75] The sudden inward plunge, the identification with Ellen's half-conscious fears of crude male sexuality, her shaky refinement, reach a level at which the reader is made aware of her significance. For Ellen, though increasingly made a symbol of the city, is a 'lead character'; she needs occasionally to live in her inwardness, to recall the impact on the individual organism of what is otherwise viewed broadly. Even so, the exploration of her fears is arrested at the level of pure sensation. To go further would be to risk explaining, to supply reasons for what is seen as basically random and mysterious.

Dos Passos' neglect of detailed psychology is largely mitigated by the choice of an episodic narrative; in each separate life the reader sees instances of the pattern, but never the pattern itself. Indeed, if the pattern exists it is arbitrary and not accessible to human control. Congo, for example, turns up at intervals throughout the book. We know that he tends a bar, loses a leg in the war, climbs probably more by luck than judgement to the status of a society boot-legger. 'The effect of the continual shift of scene and character is to fix them in a series of positions; we have to accept these positions as evidence of their fates, but we cannot follow in detail the steps by which they came to be'.[76] People rise and fall, propelled by forces associated with the opaque complexity of the modern city yet prevailing in life itself. Actually, Manhattan is life itself – there is no escape, no regenerating alternative. All the characters are at the mercy of a big, dirty, heartless town, but they 'won't go out of New York whatever happens'.[77] New York is both repellent and attractive, but even Jimmy Herf, who hates it most and has had an opportunity to contrast it with the European cities, cannot leave until he is virtually forced to do so by the collapse of his professional and conjugal relationships. The very discontinuity of the story isolates each life history into a series of engrammatic collisions with destiny. Drive, initiative and courage – even where they exist – have little correspondence with achievement. Achievement itself is nothing. Yet the book remains stimulating, in its panorama of failure and disillusion.

One major reason for this is Dos Passos' exploitation of cinema techniques, and those of the other visual arts, of which 'jump-cutting' is only one instance. The novel owes as much to his assimilation of movie grammar as to other fiction-writers. 'I suspect I got interested in Eisenstein's montage while I was working on *Manhattan Transfer*, though I can't remember exactly. Anyway montage was in the air. Notions of that sort spread like viruses, one hardly knows why'.[78] Dos Passos' sensitive nose for what was 'in the air' helps to explain his intelligent adaptation of cinematic methods. Though he had neither the peculiar fanaticism of Gertrude Stein nor Joyce's world-recreating imagination, he did possess, besides a naturally rich aptitude for words, a very keen visual awareness. The silent motion picture, then in the process of formulating its visual grammar, was an art uniquely suited to portray the qualities he wished to develop in fiction: movement, vividness, a sharp evocation of the concrete and a focal versatility allowing for rapid transitions between the particular and the general. Not only montage was available to him, but also the scenic division of the feature film and its capacity to alternate rapidly between the individual subject and his surroundings. Translated into literary terms, this facility gives a distinctly cinematic feel to passages in which a situation can be studied from several viewpoints as the location or angle of the controlling sensibility changes.

> Picking his teeth he walked through the grimy, dark entrance to Brooklyn Bridge. A man in a derby hat was smoking a cigar in the middle of the broad tunnel. Bud brushed past him, walking with a tough swagger. I don't care about him; let him follow me. The arching footway was empty except for a single policeman who stood, yawning, looking up at the sky. It was like walking among the stars. Below, in either direction, streets tapered into dotted lines of lights between square, black windowed buildings.[79]

The successive centres of attention – the tunnel, the man with the cigar, Bud's reaction, the policeman, the wider extensions of the city – are knitted into a complex entity that states with compulsive thoroughness Bud's problem and relates his fears to the implicit threat of strangers and policemen and the black, anonymous avenues of New York. Similarly, one senses 'in the air' of *Manhattan Transfer* the influence of metropolitan artists and caricaturists. Some of the tropes are quite specific: one of the most cutting episodes in the earlier chapters, for example, is the restaurant supper-party at which Emile, the outsider who wants to get on, witnesses the behaviour of a party of rich Americans. The table has been beautifully prepared – 'A goblet for Rhine wine hobnobbed with a champagne glass at each place along the glittering white oval table'[80] – but the company comprises the most hoggish kind of overfed business types and their brittle chattering girlfriends. Marco and the French boys wait on them, unnoticed as long as the service is satisfactory, mere 'animated dress suits'.[81] The venomous satire is familiar, an almost exact literary equivalent of the Berlin drawings of George Grosz, with whose work Dos Passos had become acquainted in Paris at the end of the war. It represents the same 'cirrhosis of nineteenth-century civilisation'[82] Dos Passos subsequently described Grosz as portraying. In later scenes – especially where the setting is Greenwich Village or the downtown speakeasy circuit – the prose acquires the Déco animation of the paintings of Joseph Webster Golinkin.

The ubiquity of failure in *Manhattan Transfer* is patent; but what often appears in doubt is the author's attitude towards the misery his characters undergo. There is little scope in the material for the comradely compassion of *Three Soldiers*. A 'mysterious occult force'[83] grips and represses humanity: this force is represented by the city, though it is more than the city. Occasionally, in a sketch aside from the main narrative, a pang of pity emerges.

> The old man in the checked cap sits on the brown stone stoop with his face in his hands. With the glare of Broadway in their backs there is a continual flickering of people past him towards the theatres down the street. The old man is sobbing through his fingers in a sour reek of gin. Once in a while he raises his head and shouts hoarsely 'I can't, don't you see, I can't?' The voice is inhuman like the splitting of a plank.[84]

In a painting by E. H. Suydam of Times Square in 1927 the huge skyscraper blocks with their signs and illuminations are shown dwarfing the crowds sketched in as a blurred mass at the bottom of the picture. To such a scene Dos Passos adds the pointed detail of the lost individual crying his helplessness. Yet the pity is not warm or involved – the man's cry is, after all, 'inhuman', and in illustrating the indifference of the crowd to this pathetic victim the author employs the 'indifferent sympathy' of the watchful artist. This has led to the accusation that *Manhattan Transfer* 'had the effect . . . of condemning the sufferers along with the disease';[85] yet in revealing the calamity of life Dos Passos does not despise the sufferers: he allows each detail to speak for itself.

Jimmy Herf, naturally, is a 'special judgement'.[86] Part Hamletian intellectual, part spoilt child, he acts as a reflecting consciousness to demonstrate the opposing tensions of the city as Dos Passos conceives it. New York is at one and the same time a megalopolis which with its aggregate of hostile 'things' cruelly chops off the exploring tendrils of human self-realisation and a glamorous whirlpool of experience. The machine – the Brownian model and its colliding streams of ball-bearings – is ugly and dangerous, but it is the only place to be. The past is dead, passing in a succession of nightmarish tableaux, and the future can never be what you want to make it. But *Manhattan Transfer* is not a tragedy of social determination and Jimmy Herf is no Clyde Griffiths. Dreiser's book *is* a tragedy because its pathetic hero undertakes the Herculean task of trying to become what his culture has falsely encouraged him to think he can become, and he ends by accepting a personal responsibility that will console those who survive him. An *American Tragedy* has genuinely radical implications: that the sacred dream of social mobility is an evil fraud, just as *The Great Gatsby* implies that the dream is more than a dream of material acquisition. The horrible powerlessness of Clyde and the matchless power of Gatsby to do everything but 'bring back the past' are weighty and heroic values. A rediscovery of America is suggested through a criticism of contemporary American practice. 'Tragedy' and 'greatness' are ruled out by Dos Passos. His book is named after a railway station, and its tone of flux and negation precludes heroism. One is most aware in *Manhattan Transfer* of the aimlessness of life: in its perpetual movement there is little discernible pattern, except for the repeated chance encounters with misery that wear down hope and energy. These moments – the 'engrams' of disillusion (commonplace and familiar yet perseptible even though the transient excitements of life) – provide the most definite and typical instances of the impossibility of happiness. They may be childishly personal – Jimmy getting only a small cup with his purchase of candy; or painful and absurd – Gus McNiel's accident on the trolley tracks; or vague and nagging – Stanwood Emery's failure to discover a mode of life that will put a stop to his compulsive hedonism. In every case, they suggest the disappearance of a grand strategy in life and its supersession by the global disease of ennui and anxiety. 'In headaches and in worry / Vaguely life leaks away / And Time will have his fancy / Tomorrow or today'.[87]

But *Manhattan Transfer* is a novel which defies its own pessimism. In denying the possibility of heroism, it aims for a truth close to the marrow of human experience. The overlying viewpoint of *Manhattan Transfer* – a neutrality breached by minimal doses to pity – is a recognition that civilisation, and specifically the city culture, is both necessary and harmful. Thus the accusation that 'the world he pictures is so completely dominated by a philosophy at variance with what he holds, that the ordinary reader is left with a dreary sense of human nature as a mean and shallow lot'[88] is a natural one. Yet it is made with an unfortunate illusion of hindsight, if it implies that *Manhattan Transfer* was the creation of an optimistic radical. Dos Passos' New York years (1922–5) saw the publication of two novels, a volume of verse, a travel book, the short story 'July' and finally *Manhattan Transfer*. His contributions to periodicals during these years consisted chiefly of travel pieces, and although his *sympathies* were broadly radical and humanitarian, his work showed few signs of a radical *philosophy* until *New Masses* started publication in 1926. Even during his association with *New Masses* and his involvement with the Sacco–Vanzetti case he was not a programmatic political thinker – at the time of *Manhattan Transfer* his professed aim was above all 'to put to the test existing institutions and to strip the veils from them'.[89]

This questioning and sceptical attitude may not reach definitive conclusions, but it is likely to seed a curiosity about the conditions of defeat. Specifically, these conditions lie in the manner in which people are obliged to live together yet cruelly isolated; perhaps an eternal fact of life, but brutally aggravated by the nature of the megalopolis. *Manhattan Transfer* is a milestone in Dos Passos's career, a work in which the maturing artist has begun to integrate his view of the world with a form that will most coherently express it. The shrinking explorations of the young aesthete have been transformed into an abrasive loneliness and alienation properly located in a social–historical framework, and the engrammatic pinpricks are painfully and realistically transmitted. *Manhattan Transfer* effectively contradicts the proposition that 'New York gives the directest proof yet of successful Democracy, and of the solution of that paradox, the eligibility of the free and fully developed individual with the paramount aggregate'.[90] In the idiom of a serious and mature, though unesoteric, novel it touches the pulse of the modern city fever.

4 America Can Break Your Heart: *USA*

1. 'A LOST REPUBLIC THAT NEVER EXISTED'

By 1930, when *The Forty Second Parallel* appeared in print, Dos Passos had associated himself with *New Masses*, the editor of which noted, towards the end of the decade, that 'the American artist is a split personality. His roots were partly in the machine age, which he damned, in the America which he fled; and partly in the culture of that Europe to which he now exiled himself'.[1] This had been true of Dos Passos, the immigrant's grandson seemingly unsure of his cultural identity, attracted by the 'gesture of Castile' which seemed to promise a greater relaxed spontaneity of life than America could offer. Now, while many of his contemporaries were surveying the world from Paris or the Riviera, he addressed himself to the task of treating the collective life of the nation in a major trilogy. He did not abandon the sensitive young man – indeed he presented him autobiographically in the 'Camera Eye' sections – but he aimed primarily for the amplitude of scope that enables the artist to be an imaginative historian.

In social and historical terms, America is two nations: although Dos Passos does not make this fact explicit until much later in *USA*, it supplies much of the energy that distinguishes the work. The political coloration here is central. But it is present in a specific manner, as an artistic *treatment* of the subject-matter, not as blunt didacticism. Michael Millgate has remarked that Dos Passos employs social–political categories to show the distribution of the author's sympathies.[2] But to call *USA* 'a Marxist epic' or to read its main intention as directly political is to miss the essence of Dos Passos' work. The author's sympathies, and his use of a political rhetoric to serve his literary concerns, do not amount to a principled revolutionary creed. A prophecy of this truth can be read from the epigraphical quotation to *The Forty Second Parallel*, a passage from Hodgins's *American Climatology*:

These general storms have been a subject of inexhaustible interest in all American meterological research and great labour has been expended on their various hypotheses in regard to their laws. Some of these laws, and particularly these relating to exterior features and general movements, may be regarded as very well determined; their general phenomena have been so conspicuous and so frequent of occurrence that some conclusion of this sort could not fail to result from the most imperfect observations . . .³

But these conclusions are purely external, since the paths, speed and direction of the storms are known, but little about their causes. Hodgins's cautious and weighty scientific language fails to conceal that these storms which rage along the forty-second parallel are ultimately mysterious forces. But to a Marxist, society is not mysterious: it has discoverable laws, by mastering which the observer can become agent, free to take part in assisting the movements of the dialectic. It is 'no accident' that Dos Passos has chosen to cite Hodgins. Brownian Motion has been superseded by a closer tracking and plotting of the characters in 'their exterior features and general movements', but Dos Passos remains agnostic in his refusal to draw any conclusions from these movements that will give meaning or hope to the aims of political radicalism. Hodgins may impress you with his meteorology from the lecture platform; but you will get rained on just the same. Dos Passos, wearing the licence of the artist, draws the reader's attention to his interesting examples of chaos. American chaos! Guaranteed more chaotic than all other forms.

This is not, of course, to say that his view of America is chauvinistic: the book's beginning is satirically ironic. 'CITY GREETS CENTURY'S DAWN' is the title of Section I, but the first big headline of Newsreel I is 'CAPITAL CITY'S CENTURY CLOSED', followed by a report of General Miles losing his seat and his dignity at a military review. The nationalistic oratory of Gilded Age windbags is set beside the memory of 'many a good man' who has died in the cause of McKinley's imperialist adventure. This is official America, the bully of the 'two nations', the spreader of popular dope and mystification. By contrast, Fenian McCreary's childhood is presented in terms of familiar, affectionate, innocent contacts with the world of youth. These perceptions and experiences are precisely what Mac has to lose. With the death of his father Mac is obliged to leave Connecticut for Chicago, where he will grow up under the influence of his radically minded uncle. Mac's own subsequent experience, including his sincere but fitful allegiance to Wobbly principles, is made to derive as much from his early home circumstances as from his practical understanding of the wage system: a matter of psychological reinforcement. Between this reinforcement and the exigencies of day-to-day living, Mac finds his grasp on his convictions tenuous and fluctuating.

Dos Passos, receptive as always to ideas that are 'in the air' uses the repressive character of capitalism alertly. Uncle Tim, an ineffectual rebel who talks more than he does, is bankrupted by Chicago business-men who buy up his outstanding debts. This is viewed as common justice by his wife, upon whom falls the burden of making ends meet and who makes no distinction between personal vices like excessive drinking and the holding of unorthodox opinions. The effect of the domestic conflict is to launch Mac, not into serious and disciplined work for the cause, but on a typical American adventure in the company of Doc Bingham. Bingham is the folk-figure of a huckster, almost a character from Mark Twain, for ever one jump ahead of the law or an angry cuckold, peddling uplift and pornography with the same dogged amorality and reciting Othello in the brass tones of a patent-medicine salesman.

Pure W. C. Fields, he is also Mac's third father; not the sick failure or the defeated radical but the worldly scoundrel who shows him the cynic's vision of 'things as they are': humanity is divided into gullible sheep and those who fleece them. Here is an outlook at variance with the Socialist analysis, of which it reflects in caricature only the ex-ploiter–victim syndrome. Even so, its partial truth is evident, and Mac never quite loses an air of rootless drifting. Moreover, another father-image lurks in the vicinity: Eugene Debs 'Lover of Mankind', the subject of the first Biography. Debs's brand of inspiratorial socialism – idealistic, quixotic, concerned with the setting of a personal example – is deeply in the American grain. He was a well-loved man, as Dos Passos' approv-ing cadences emphasise, but in his lack of revolutionary arrogance and cunning and in the naïve kindliness he showed even towards his jailors, he made of himself a victim rather than a true leader. In the 'gusty rhetoric' of the 'old kindly uncle' can be detected the attraction of Debs for Dos Passos and the general attraction of high-minded characters who find themselves beaten or lost. Doc Bingham's peripatetic dishonesty seems a better recipe for survival.

Following Mac's separation from Bingham, the fictional narrative is suspended for five consecutive Newsreel and Camera Eye episodes which bring into focus related public events of the time – about 1904–5 – and refract the author's own childish awareness of them. American news-papers report the Russo-Japanese war and the 1904 presidential cam-paign, while Dos Passos (at school in England) learns of them through the old British salt and an aggressive American boy. For him, they are subjects impossible to grasp except in a distorted, symbolic fashion through the reports of distant correspondents and the enclosed sensi-bility of a child. The Newsreel, working by reference to the public world, and the Camera Eyes, transmitting from within, supply fragments of a composite picture. Even so, causes and relations are irrecoverable. In the same way the characters of the main narrative strive but fail to interpret their experience – so real to them – into a satisfying pattern.

Mac's life becomes a sequence of temporary accommodations, though he is no fool, and in moments of hangover and spent resources he gropes for the clarity to formulate his aspirations: ' "I feel like hell . . . I wanta study an' work for things; you know what I mean, not to get to be a goddam slavedriver but to work for socialism and the revolution an' like that, not work an' go on a bat an' work an' go on a bat like those damn yaps on the railroad" '.[4] But 'PRAISE MONOPOLY AS BOON TO ALL',[5] shriek the headlines, and Mac succeeds in putting a stop to his repetitive drifting only by his marriage to the Lardnerian shopgirl Maisie, which in its enslaving futility and Maisie's passion for 'getting on' represents only the stability of stagnation. His escape to Nevada to support the local IWW in their struggle against the mine-owners is a transient effort to ward off Maisie, and he is forced to rat on his comrades when he learns she is pregnant. The picture of a Wobbly strike is well drawn, and Fred Hoff is of the utmost hardened revolutionary breed – perhaps more so, in the puritanical discipline of his allegiance, than were most Wobbly leaders, including Big Bill Haywood, the subject of the third Biography. The Wobblies' blend of pioneer stoicism and syndicalist agitation appealed to Dos Passos all the more because they were the great *failed* movement of native American radicalism. Though their membership was large, it was diffuse and shifting; their great successes were localised; their great days were ended by government persecution; they were notable for their martyrs. In this large-scale movement of losers appears the perfect Dos Passos image of the Byronic outcasts: there is an elegiac note to his celebration of their struggle.

Mac cannot hope to match the stature and dynamism of a mytho-logically great figure like Haywood. As the Newsreels build up a frenzied picture of capitalism dominating the labouring men who sweat and die to create its profits, Mac sinks further into the quicksand of compromise. Married life in California turns out to be a dispiriting affair, but Mac's realisation of the weak and dishonourable bargain he has struck is so much keener than his active resolution to do something about it that he moves on in a succession of blundering impulses. On arrival in Mexico he makes his grandiloquent vow not to be 'a goddam booster like the rest of them'[6] sound bold and definite. It is not. The movie-fade ending of Section I leaves him 'at the door of Encarnacion's little room that had a bed, a picture of the virgin and a new photograph of Madero stuck up by a pin. Encarnacion closed the door bolted it and sat down on the bed looking up at Mac.'[7] In his pitilessly objective description Dos Passos manages to suggest the material poverty of the Mexican girl bemused by a time of upheaval and the spiritual poverty which she and Mac share: intimate strangers, locked in the primitive Mexican shack with its bed and its cheap icons.

'Old Glory' begins with Newsreel 10, a patchwork of items from separate dates: the triumph of Madero (1911), Roosevelt's election victory

(1904), a denial of a report that General Grant (d. 1885) had undergone an operation for cancer, a popular son of 1911. The effect of mixing major and trivial news items is to suggest the inconsequentiality of the popular press and, more generally, the rush of miscellaneous data that the ordinary person has no opportunity to examine critically. The chaotic nature of modern society serves as sardonic commentary on the lives of the fictional characters. Janey Williams's story, now due to start, is prefaced by a Camera Eye which evokes through the frightening tales of a French maid about the 'Loup Garou' the nausea and fear Janey will feel about the carnal side of life and which she will seek, through the acquisition of 'refinement', to avoid.

Again, the basis for both Janey's and Joe's rejection of the family is laid in their early circumstances. Socially insecure, the Williamses inhabit a district also populated by negroes, to whom they must always try to adopt a desperate attitude of superiority. 'Popper', a clerk at the patent office and therefore a bureaucratic servant of real American know-how, craves peace and quiet in which to reflect on his secret disappointments. When disturbed by Joe, he beats the boy up with incredible viciousness. Joe's escape is into the streets; Janey's into the mass-produced fantasies of popular fiction.

> She liked to read and used to get books like The Inside of the Cup, The Battle of the Strong, The Winning of Barbara Worth out of the library. Her mother kept telling her that she'd spoil her eyes if she read so much. When she read she used to imagine that she was the heroine, that the weak brother who went to the bad but a gentleman at core and capable of every sacrifice like Sidney Carton in A Tale of Two Cities was Joe and that the hero was Alec.[8]

But Alec the dream lover does not see her as a desirable woman, and recedes as a frozen statue in her private pantheon. Even his death scarcely stirs her, though it does provide Joe with the impetus to leave home and join the merchant marines. It is Joe, in fact, who becomes what the young Dos Passos (Camera Eye 14) imagined himself to be – Philip Nolan, the man without a country. Joe shrinks, as the narrative adopts Janey's point of view, to a figure who sends 'a picture of the waterfront at Havana or the harbour at Marseille or Villefranche or a photograph of a girl in peasant costume inside a tinsel horseshoe . . . never a word about himself.'[9] Janey discovers that she can earn a reasonable living, thus freeing herself from dependence on her family, and she learns – within the scope of her pinched and narrow attitudes – to handle men; to be tolerable company and ward off their amorousness by acting the part of a the 'good pal'.

Camera Eye 15 takes up the family theme in the person of the writer's cantankerous Portuguese grandfather, who would throw his food out of the window in a fit of rage, while Newsreel 12 recounts dissensions in the national 'family'. Reports of political wrangling at the 1912 conventions are interleaved with press accounts of squalid, self-interested crimes. The immediately ensuing Biography of Willian Jennings Bryan sardonically relates the corruption of political power. 'Bryan grew grey in the hot air of Chautauqua tents, in the applause, the handshakes, the backpattings, the cigarsmoky air of committee rooms at Democratic conventions, a silver tongue in a big mouth'.[10] Then a further Camera Eye, once more centring on John Randolph Dos Passos, a man who grew so contemptuous of the hypocrisy of democratic politics that he 'couldn't get to be elected notary public in any country in the state not with all the money in the world'.[11] This convergence of the extra-narrative devices upon the machinery of politics is acutely relevant to this stage of Janey's story. She lives and works in Washington, where the presence of every facet and agency of federal power creates an atmosphere of wheeling, dealing, and sharpened knives. It also prefigures the subject of the next narrative strand, which concerns the childhood of J. Ward Morehouse, one of Dos Passos' most memorable creations. Morehouse's father is a drunken n'er-do-well; the son responds with an inordinate industry and ambition. His interests are entirely conventional:

> Outside of the Strenuous Life and a lovely girl to fall in love with him there was one thing Johnny Morehouse's mind dwelt on as he sat at his desk listing desirable five and sevenroom dwellinghouses, drawing room, dining room, kitchen and butler's pantry, three master's bedrooms and bath, maid's room, water, electricity, gas, healthy location on gravelly soil in restricted residential area: he wanted to be a songwriter.[12]

But even his first efforts in this field are 'boosting'. They hint at the J. Ward Morehouse to be, the pastmaster of mystification who handles words with such practical success and so thorough an absence of any personal conviction in what he utters. During the time he spends as a realtor's assistant in Ocean City (an episode enlivened by two of Dos Passos' cameos, the venerable frauds Strang and Wedgewood) the fast-maturing Morehouse psychology develops. Even emotional disillusion can supply the means for exploiting material advantages:

> For a while he thought he'd go down to the station and take the first train out and throw the whole business to ballyhack, but there was the booklet to get out, and there was a chance that if the boom did come he might get in on the ground floor, and this connection with money and the Strangs: opportunity knocks but once on a young man's door.[13]

His marriage to Annabelle – farcical as it is – reveals Morehouse as a stiff, solemn young man, quite impervious to any irony in his situation and possessed of an unquestioning attachment to self-help principles. He is naturally unresponsive to his wife's madcap hedonism (she, too, of course, is a fraud) but more than that he lacks any spontaneous warmth or enjoyment of it in others. 'Old Glory' concludes with a view of Morehouse stranded in Pittsburgh. But he is going places as a public relations pioneer in a society due to become increasingly dependent on the professional mystifier. His inborn priggishness guards him from self-criticism. In the letter breaking off relations with Annabelle he writes, 'I shall feel that when the divorce is satisfactorily arranged I shall be entitled to some compensation for the loss of time etc. and the injury to my career that has come through your fault'[14] – a reproach which, despite its lifeless commercial phrases, echoes a sincerer grievance than the reference to 'the great pain your faithlessness has caused me'.[15]

At this point in the novel – half-way through – the story has relied for its movement and significance on the variety and novelty of technique and the realistic low-key fluency of the narrative portions. Nevertheless, its interest has been the interest of kaleidoscopic display; more that of an extended 'Suite Americaine' than of a work founded on a stable organising principle. It is not hard to see why some contemporary reviewers made specious and marginal objections; they seemed to feel that, beneath the impressionistic outlines that divide up the story without ever quite reaching the tense reflexive allusiveness of poetry, there lay an essentially specious creation – something like the play that is brilliantly dramatic to watch but never seriously engages on a theme. But Dos Passos works gradually and by aggregation. The first two books of *The Forty Second Parallel* amount to a provisional placement of attitudes towards the corruption of the commonwealth, the individual in search of his fate, the child-artist's vision, the role of the hero; they await integration. In the last three sections these attitudes are amplified, developed and crowned.

'Twentieth Century: Eastbound' starts with a Camera Eye. The fourteen-year-old Dos Passos is struck by a sudden awareness of the universe beyond his own mind – 'Halley's Comet and the Universe'. The awesome infinity of these abstractions leads him to reject received religion and to sense the first pangs of mortality. 'You wondered if you'd be alive next time Halley's comet came around';[16] often his own infancy, relatively free and comfortable, contrasts with that of his characters. Eleanor Stoddard, the next one to be introduced, 'when she was small . . . hated everything'.[17] She has a father who puts her off. An office-worker in the Chicago stockyards, he enjoys telling repellent stories of the slaughterhouse to his family. Eleanor is driven into self-reassuring fantasies at an early age, somewhat after the fashion of Janey Williams. Her taste, though, is a cut above Janey's – no absorption in girls' romances. 'Art was something ivory white and very pure and noble and distant and sad'.[18] Eleanor meets her ideal self-image in Eveline Hutchins, and together they organise a provincial cult of art and self-improvement, with acquaintances like Maurice, the Berlitz teacher who paints, despite his extravagant claims of *Kultur-Bolschevismus*, 'the loveliest pictures in pale buffs and violets of longfaced boys with big luminous eyes and long lashes and longfaced girls that looked like boys and Russian wolfhounds with big luminous eyes, and always in the back there were a few girders or a white skyscraper and a big puff of white clouds'.[19] Here is an entertaining microcosm of early twentieth-century bourgeois culture, wittily aligned with the knockabout duo of Potter and Sportmann, Eleanor's superiors at Marshall Fields who struggle to outdo each other and to win the favour of their prize subordinate with the 'crisp little refined monied voice'.[20]

In truth, Eleanor is a sharp little piece, whose egoism, under a 're-fined' surface, enables her to cultivate Miss Perkins, more or less consciously for profit. The irony of the bequest she does receive is stinging – 'A handsome diamond brooch in the form of a locomotive',[21] the perfect example of Gilded Age taste. In the expensive trinket is summarised the monstrous greed and ruthlessness of the robber-baron financiers, whose epic bluff is remotely epitomised in Eveline's and Eleanor's interior-decorating business. Somehow, 'interior decorating' wipes the dirt off the money, and the enterprise is surrounded with arty pretentiousness. 'A photograph of Brancusi's Golden Bird over the desk . . . and copies of the *Little Review* and *Poetry* among the files of letters from clients and unpaid bills from the wholesalers.'[22]

When the two girls board the Twentieth Century Limited to work on a New York stage contract, they face the same portents that confronted J. Ward Morehouse on his arrival in Pittsburgh: 'the steelworks of Indiana Harbor, the big cement works belching puttycolored smoke, the flaring furnaces of Gary'[23] – all the ugly outward signs of industrial master-class hegemony, the processes that make money and consume life. The following Camera Eye (number 19: basically, the plot of 'July') speaks with the strangulated voice of the author recovering, from a whirlpool of memories, a real – though childishly innocent – sense of romance among brutal facts of success on the American plan.

What precedes the next instalment of J. Ward Morehouse's personal history is a Biography – that of Minor C. Keith. Keith is one of the least familiar biographical subjects and, as his name suggests, one of the few who are not overtly prodigious. He is a rat, a scavenger who, unlike so many entrepeneurs, dirtied his hands in close contact with the contaminated sources of his wealth. 'Limon was one of the worst pestholes in the Caribbean, even the Indians died there of malaria,

yellow jack, dysentery . . . Minor Keith didn't die'.[24] More important, he
founded the United Fruit Company, that pioneer of dollar-imperialist in-
tervention in the politics of South American states. The 'uneasy look'
in his eyes betrays the guilt and trepidation of his class as social an-
tagonisms intensify. Newsreel 14 had concentrated on labour unrest and
violence, and in Camera Eye 20 the death of a scab (a 'gentleman volun-
teer', perhaps mentioned in a conversation overheard by the writer at
Harvard) is recounted with an impassivity not far from gloating. The
time is now just pre-1914 and images of class warfare colour the mood of
the novel as the career of J. Ward Morehouse, only temporarily arrested, is
about to become a full-scale exercise in political deception.

Morehouse's job of reporter in Pittsburgh never satisfies his hunger
for success. The 'muckers' whose problems and difficulties surround
him arouse contempt in Morehouse, who lacks the humanity to sympathise with others – his intelligence serves ambition alone. When his
chance comes he seizes it to concentrate upon his chosen objectives
with an energy and single-mindedness graphically unlike the spasmodic,
faltering steps of Fenian McCreary. Morehouse, with the shrewd clarity
of the man who never halts to question himself, sees that his duties at
Bessemer Products can become more than routine apple-polishing. His
clever advocacy of a programme of 'educating the public', after the
bloody strike at Homestead, leads to his appointment as chief of an
'information bureau' for the entire Pittsburgh steel industry. And this
coup is supplemented by marriage to Gertrude Staple (and the Staple
fortune), followed by a second and more splendid European honeymoon.

But now the abyss is terrifyingly close. The 'war talk' which aborts
the Morehouses' year in Europe is prophetic; the nineteenth-century
afterglow is about to be dimmed. Camera Eye 21 has a wistful, elegiac
tone; it recalls Virginia farm-life in the dog-days of its entropy. 'The
land between the rivers was flat drained of all strength by tobacco in
the early Walter Raleigh John Smith Pocahontas days but what was it
before the war that drained out the men and women?'[25] For Dos Passos,
the rhetorical question marks his farewell to the innocence of the
Camera Eye device. With the advance of the 'blood-dimmed tide' it
ceases to be the deeply subjective, synaesthetic reflection of a child's
awareness. Increasingly, it will display the author as part of his public
world and not as a palpitating organism on whom the heavens may un-
availingly fall. Indeed, the next Newsreel (15) and Camera Eye 22
echo each other's phrases: 'WANT BIG WAR OR NONE . . . CZAR LOSES
PATIENCE WITH AUSTRIA . . . ASSASSIN SLAYS DEPUTY JAURES'[26], 'obliga-
tions according to the treaty of . . . handed the ambassador his pass-
ports . . . BRITISH FLEET DESTROYED GERMAN SQUADRON OFF CAPE RACE'.[27]
Sandwiched between them, under the title 'Prince of Peace', is a short,

coldly devastating attack on the Gospel of Wealth. In its laconic, literal statements, its reiteration of the words 'believed' and 'confidence', its telling use of simple poetic phrases and its final flat qualification it paints with great force and feeling the type of American successful man most despicable in the author's eyes – the non-productive financier and stock-market operator; the kind of man for whom John Dos Passos Sr juggled holding-company pyramids and negotiated tax concessions; the chapel-faced philistine who compounds his greed with the hypocritical and ego-gratifying vice of philanthropy, and who attempts to buy with his stolen millions the trappings of culture and lineage.[28]

Carnegie was the steel king of Pittsburgh, the interest which Morehouse has contracted to serve and which he continues to serve when after his return to the United States he founds his own agency. He has become a founder of the new industry of bamboozlement and legal lying – 'public relations'. He now draws towards him other representative figures who, beneath the deceitful labels – 'labour reformer', 'judge', 'press reporter' – are pledged to both self-interest and the interest of the class to which they are sold. Their fluency in the use of words, like Morehouse's own, is a treason to language. Words, no longer agreed symbols for certain objects and experiences, have been marshalled into an elaborate code of mystification.[29] Barrow and Judge Planet, caricatures though they are, are more significant minor characters than the cameo sketches of the novel's earlier chapters. Working in conjunction with Morehouse, they comprise a dangerous awkward squad of public misinformers, drawn like sharks to the smell of money. Morehouse, the smoothest of them all, wins his point with a drivelling and sentimental address to a Rotary luncheon on 'Labour troubles: a way out'. Beneath his oratorical soft-soaping, the attentive Babbits sense the usefulness of a spokesman against organised labour. Morehouse has found his market.

Newsreel 16 explodes softly in a starbust of trivial newspaper sensations, from the propaganda arm of commerce and industry to one of its satellite worlds – bourgeois art, show-business. There is an ironical disparity of effort between the two. J. Ward Morehouse conducts his affairs blandly and sedately; it comes naturally to him. Eleanor and Eveline, pitched on to Broadway, sweat and strain as set-designers for an ephemeral, stupid show which closes after two weeks. The satire on the New York theatre (of which Dos Passos had some disillusioning experience in the late twenties) is entertaining, but the chapter is important chiefly because it entails the first meeting-point of the separate narrative histories. Eleanor is a natural associate for Morehouse, who is almost dead emotionally and sexually, and she in turn finds her ideal man, who combines a generally gallant manner, an undemanding libido and the bromide of 'positive' American ideas.

. . . he explained about the work he was doing keeping the public informed about the state of relations between capital and labour and stemming the propaganda of sentimentalists and refomers upholding American ideas against crazy German socialistic ideas and the panaceas of discontented dirt-farmers in the Northwest. Eleanor thought his ideas were very interesting but she liked better to hear about the stockexchange and how the Steel Corporation was founded and the difficulties of the oil companies in Mexico and Hearst and great fortunes. She asked him about some small investment she was making and he looked up at her with twinkly blue eyes in a white square face whose prosperity was just beginning to curve over the squareness of the jowl and said, 'Miss Stoddard, may I have the honor of being your financial adviser?'[30]

This must be one of the nastiest moments in modern literature; what intensifies its repellent character is the fact that the two have instinctively recognised each other and relapsed into an unwonted frankness that is even less appealing than their customary starched poses. Morehouse does not usually speak like a Wall Street lout and Eleanor is much more dreadful when she is smitten with admiration for Morehouse than when she 'hated everything'. It is a meeting of the barren and self-serving. To be fanciful, one might view it as the instant of inspiration between the capitalist 'artist' and his muse.

Janey's story is resumed 'in the second year of the European war'. Reacting to the climate of hysteria, she leaves Dreyfus and Carroll, where German chauvinism prevails, and seems (like Eleanor) to be in danger of losing her economic independence when she too falls, by a combination of luck and despairing nerve, into the orbit of J. Ward Morehouse. All the different tracks of the narrative are now converging; their junction is Mexico where, a hundred and seventy pages earlier, Mac's story had been interrupted and where, in the aftermath of the overthrow of Huerta, Yankee activity is at fever pitch. The Mexican theme has been kept alive by repeated mentions in the newsreels. Now Mexico becomes a major centre of the action. Under the stress of a fluid and chaotic political situation normal attitudes are magnified, latent ones revealed. The printers and prospectors Mac meets in Mexico City, badly scared by the success of the revolution, have adopted proto-fascist opinions; the aged Pole, whose mental world of theoretical socialism has been ruined by the collapse of the Second International, takes refuge in eccentricity. 'He had a theory that civilisation and a mixed diet were causing the collapse of the human race'.[31] Amidst the collapse in Mexico, Mac's relative healthiness is apparent, though his political principles have more or less lapsed. He takes advantage of the local opportunities for sensual pleasure while his sympathies are still progressive enough to make him friendly to the revolution, though he is never part of it; his domestic and financial arrangements are congenially in order. By contrast G. H. Barrow, crossing the border on some shady mission, proves to be a disagreeable clown and has to be protected from the anger of the Mexicans, who have shed blood to affirm their belief that not everything can be bought for dollars. Barrow, though, is only his master's pilotfish; when he returns to the United States with a whole skin, Morehouse himself travels to Mexico with the aim, as he puts it,

> in a purely unofficial capacity you understand to make contacts, to find out what the situation was and just what there was behind Carranza's stubborn opposition to American investors and that the big business man he was in touch with in the States desired only fair play and that he felt if their point of view could be thoroughly understood through some information bureau or the friendly cooperation of Mexican newspapermen . . .[32]

In Morehouse's view, so conditioned by bluff and deceit, every contrary opinion must have something 'behind' it. Mac sums him up as a 'smooth bastard', but he is beginning to realise again that his own position is essentially false. The years of wandering, of choosing any way of life that seems temporarily appealing and never picking a definite outlook to be held at any cost, have caught up with him. He has become de-classed and de-naturalised. His personality has never matured. His flight to Vera Cruz and his initial panicky decision to return to the United States without Concha are due to a shaky individualism which has been at the core of his failure to grow and settle. Mac drinks a toast 'to the workers, to the tradeunions, to the partido laborista, to the social revolution and the agraristas'[33] – but he does so in the safety of Vera Cruz, open to the American fleet and far from the hinterland centres of Zapatista revolt. The drink has become more important than the toast, and nothing illustrates better Mac's fundamental lack of serious purpose than the motives which finally impel him to cancel his passage and remain an exile and observer. 'He was beginning to think it was silly to give up his bookstore like that. He went to the Ward Line Office and took his ticket back. The clerk refunded him the money and be got back to Concha's sister's house in time to have chocolate and pastry with them for breakfast.[34]

Mac has shrugged off all his major responsibilities in favour of lotus-eating. Partly, his story expresses a political truth, that in a system of individual interest the propertied classes can undividedly pursue their own and their class interests, while workers who take up radical politics are forced to make a debilitating choice between the two. But Mac's real affinities as a character are with the 'vag' tradition in Dos Passos' fiction. Dispossessed and in search of a secure identity, he drifts; the more he drifts, the more remote his chances of finding himself. Mac's freedom simply to *move* is a restricted and ultimately illusory freedom. His story terminates at the point where he has come to rest in a foreign country with a 'family' only loosely attached to him, neither true Mexican nor essentially American. Mac is a sympathetic character but no true proletarian and his defeat is the defeat of the isolated individual. Though he sees through the Morehouse philosophy, he lacks the will persistently to struggle against it, and his role is complete at a time when war-time contingencies are about to give Morehouse his big opportunities. Even so, he signifies, as engrammatic hero, the replacement of the sensitive young man by a new and tougher type. Mac is an interesting figure. He reveals the flaw in the American autodidact's odyssey and the limitations of a career so crammed with 'adventure'. Nevertheless, he is a member of the last generation to be able to lead such an existence; future prospects will be much grimmer.

As the Mexican imbroglio peters out in the months immediately before America's declaration of war, Morehouse's growing success is brought into focus through the admiring consciousness of Janey Williams. He has been gathering clients and is ready to swim with the tide of war sentiment. Various tensions have developed – particularly between Morehouse and Gertrude on the subject of Eleanor Stoddard – which threaten the supply of Staple capital on which he is still reliant. All this is refracted through the prism of Janey's idealisation of Morehouse: a device allowing ironical exposure of each party. Janey feels 'quite indignant'[35] about what she considers the malicious interference of Eleanor Stoddard. Every emotion she experiences is coloured by the false vitality of secondhand emotions. Janey is human life in clean gloves. By contrast, Gertrude Morehouse and Joe Williams are not afraid to express dissatisfaction in home truths. Gertrude understands the nature of her husband – 'Oh you're cold as a fish . . . You're just a fish. I'd like you better if it was true, if you were having an affair with her'[36] – but remains his prisoner. Joe, who has suffered the worst humiliations of the 'gob' merchant sailor in war-time, is greeted on his arrival in New York by a sister who has 'got on' and who judges him purely by the plebeian roughness of his manners and appearance. Joe has seen enough to realise 'the whole damn war's crooked from start to finish'[37] – essentially, a contrivance of the Morehouse operation by other means. The time is coming when Morehouse will depend on the war to save his hide.

'The Yanks Are Coming' opens with a confessive Camera Eye. The scene is a mass anti-war demonstration in New York at which Emma Goldman and Max Eastman rally the crowd with their speeches. The occasion is made to seem theatrical, histrionic; as the group moves from Madison Square Garden to the Bronx Casino and then to the Brevoort the great lion's roar of popular indignation dwindles to the parlour rhetoric of intellectuals who, 'eating frankfurters and sauerkraut . . . talked about red flags and barricades and suitable posts for machine-guns'.[38] Echoes of Vera Cruz – and in the final bathetic sentence, with its mimicry of Hemingway, scorn for the armchair revolutionaries: 'We . . . went home, and opened the door with a latchkey and put on pyjamas and went to bed and it was comfortable in bed.'[39] Set beside Newsreel 18, which cites Wilson's war oratory and reports Lenin's arrival at the Finland Station, it stresses the remoteness from proletarian experience of the radical intelligentsia, and the weakness of their convictions when they are put to the test.

Eleanor at this time 'thought that things were very exciting that winter'.[40] By now, she is the constant companion of J. Ward Morehouse and this relationship, 'pure as driven snow' in the sexual sense as Gertrude has suggested, is nevertheless a danger. It is largely responsible for the money difficulties plaguing Morehouse. The thought that he may have to abandon her to save his career gives her yet another pang of self-dramatising pity. 'She thought of her colored maid Augustine with her unfortunate loves that she told Eleanor about and wished she'd been like that. Maybe she'd been wrong from the start to want everything so justright and beautiful'.[41] However, just as she contemplates making a personal appeal to Gertrude which would almost certainly be a disastrous error, war is declared. The crisis ends in an orgy of sentimental humbug. Morehouse accepts a dollar-a-year post in Washington. Gertrude becomes magnanimously 'understanding', and Eleanor is once again able to place between herself and painful reality the familiar aspirational shields. 'How beautiful the room was, like a Whistler, like Sarah Bernhardt. Emotion misted her eyes.'[42]

With the United States about to launch into war, the historical movement of *The Forty Second Parallel* reaches a conclusion. Dos Passos, before he begins the story of Charley Anderson which is forty pages takes Charley through the time-scale of the whole book, appends one each of his experimental devices. Newsreel 19 is a brief compilation of press clippings, concentrated on the uplifting presentation of the nation's official war-aims and the colossal greed and dishonesty underlying them. Camera Eye 27 narrates, with a wry sense of emotions 'now' and 'then', Dos Passos' own voyage to France, drinking in with ardent zest the sights and sounds of his pre-combat experience, yet faced in the end with the Street of Lost Hopes and a suspicious French security agent. The final Biography aptly relates the career of Robert M. La Follette, Wisconsin's Progressive Republican governor and senator, one of the last great opponents of 'entangling alliances', who led the Congressional rearguard fight against Wilson's pro-Ally policies. The subject is treated with respect, but recognised as a loser, an anachronism: 'an orator haranguing from the capitol of a lost republic'.[43]

But the war itself is not to be the subject of this novel. The narrative resumes with the story of Charley Anderson – contemporary with Mac, but destined to be the new, Veblenian American. Charley is raised by a pietistic mother; up to the time he leaves home for Minneapolis, his childhood is serene and uncomplicated: little but the normal spasms of puberty disturb it. In Minneapolis he feels 'uneasy' at living under the discipline of Vogel's teutonic work-ethic, but his disinterested curiosity about mechanical things insulates him from the conflicts that worry his brother. Charley's early career is much like Edison's in outline and like Edison he is prone, through over-enthusiasm, to upset employers. Tinkering with machinery is for him an absorbing process which holds more attraction than any end to which it might lead. 'He didn't want to get married because that ud keep him from travelling round the country and getting ahead in studying engineering'.[44] His travels help him to mature and to broaden his sympathies, but at the same time he begins to feel the pull of self-improvement; this is no longer quite Edison's America of the freelance operator relying on luck and enterprise. Charley has what Mac lacked – a sense of purpose – and he is able to foresee the necessity of supplementing his personal gift with training and qualifications. 'Charley said he was going to New York because he thought there were good chances of schooling in a big city like that and how he was an automobile mechanic and wanted to get to be a C.E. or something like that because there was no future for a working stiff without schooling'.[45]

Under the influence of Doc Rogers, though, he chooses to enlist 'before the whole thing goes bellyup'. The final pages of *The Forty Second Parallel* recapitulate, from Charley's point of view, the general background of the final Morehouse–Stoddard episodes. For Charley, it is all confusion, 'too deep for me'.[46] Arguments against the war, as propounded by Benny Compton and the soapbox orator, mean even less to Charley than they do to Doc Rogers, who simply lowers his head and charges whenever he hears an 'unpatriotic' idea. Charley is also Mac's opposite in his complete ignorance of the theoretical aspects of politics. He is the practical man *par excellence*, and abstract discussion tends to give him a headache – in this respect he resembles Chrisfield, who can only act and needs John Andrews to think for him. Charley's 'manager' is Doc Rogers, upon whose suggestion Charley enlists – to leave for Europe on a French ship of which the crew will not even speak to him. The end of isolationism has not ended the isolation of the individual.

One critic has argued that 'Dos Passos does not call himself a Marxist, if he were more of one, he might have written a better novel.'[47] While this view is false – 'Art must make its own way and by its own way and by its own means. The Marxian methods are not the same as the artistic'[48] – it is central to critical misunderstandings of Dos Passos. The feeling persists that he *should* have been a Marxist. Marxism, after all, supplies a unique means of reconciling determinism and the exercise of free will – an antithesis which, under the specific terms of the dialectic, can be regarded as false. It states that there is a global tendency in history and that men can, by their own conscious efforts, help to realise it. Marxism insists that the behaviour of society can be understood and changed by using discoverable laws. To a writer like Dos Passos, instinctively drawn to the side of the governed and exploited, dealing with men in society, choosing as his protagonists men who lose hope and fail, Marxism ought, on the face of it, to be an attractive philosophy, both intellectually strenuous and optimistic. Yet the fiction of John Dos Passos persistently denies, in its atmosphere, situations and artistic logic, that human society can be rationally understood or that there is any reason to hope for radical improvements. The early heroes of Dos Passos had struggled to create a meaning for themselves in a hostile or indifferent universe, and all failed. Between the conditioning which limited their freedom and the illusory ideal of the self-realising individual, they lacked the will or energy to oppose the huge impersonal forces that defeated them – the army, New England morality, the pressures of metropolitan living. Ultimately, their failures are not *explained*: they are shown in some detail, and with increasing credibility as the author lays his hands on the tropes that enable him to render so vividly the constant engrammatic bombardment of social and personal defeats. *Manhattan Transfer* in particular stresses the adventitious nature of life: penalties and rewards are distributed by accident, but the direction of all events is towards loss and disappointment. On this evidence, life is a crooked gamble in which everyone is robbed. This is the outlook of romantic pessimism (the very opposite of Marxism) but it establishes its partial truth in *Manhattan Transfer* by the fast, vivid and dramatic pattern of its examples. The sea of circumstances in which Jimmy Herf drowns is portrayed in energetic detail, and in *The Forty Second Parallel* the method of *Manhattan Transfer* is extended to portray the society of a whole nation.

This method, the method of 'saturation', requires the sensitive exercise of a selective faculty. Accusations that this is just what Dos Passos lacks are balanced by contrary objections that he limits his scope to too narrow a segment of American society.[49] In fact, he has carefully selected characters of the lower-middle social strata, the ideal type of humbly-born American who is expected to 'get on' and for whom, in the sanctified tradition, America is the supreme land of opportunity. The significance of the narrative passages is to show that this is a profound illusion, that the actual freedom of the individual is limited, and that whether or not he suceeeds in 'making it' he is lonely and doomed. Those who decline to make it suffer materially; in any case, they compromise; their humanity is diminished by victimisation and by their personal inability to realise their principles. Those who succeed sacrifice so much in doing so. There is no contradiction in this attitude, any more than there is in the belief that personality is shaped by a combination of various circumstances – background, heredity, metabolism, conscious ideas. Dos Passos refrains from explaining: his eclecticism is entailed in the behaviour of his characters and in the accompanying data which he has chosen to include in the Newsreels, Biographies and Camera Eyes.

Hence the often-noted 'behaviourism' of his character-portrayal aims for a particular kind of truth: the truth as it is observed, the facts as they appear in immediate context. Dos Passos is not obliged to say whether he believes that men are alienated by the capitalist system of productive relations or by the nature of human life itself. Indeed, where capitalism rules, the two are effectively the same, and unless the novelist wants to play the social reformer he is not, as he works to produce a mirror of reality, required to distinguish between them. What he can do is to employ a rhetoric and imagery that expresses the shape of reality as he sees it, and for Dos Passos' purposes the imagery of class warfare could hardly be bettered. The force lines of class conflict within which his characters are drawn stand for the immediate everyday hardships of an unequal social system and for the permanent conditions of loneliness and misfortune under which mankind abides. Mac has three latent destinies corresponding to the three separate strands of his early life: ordinary sensual working guy, radical, wandering hedonist. He is incapable of making any final choice between them. Circumstances uproot him, and his fate, at the end of his personal history, is not evil or tragic but disappointing. The total weight of the novel's rhetoric contrives to suggest that he should have chosen a life of greater discipline and purpose – yet Mac is scarcely free to choose. He is free, however, to hope, no matter how inexorably his hopes are denied. The philosophy of proletarian revolution stands for his highest hopes, just as the American self-help philosophy stands for Morehouse's central aspirations, and the disparity betwen sustaining cultural myths and the manifold setbacks of life as it is actually lived is the major unifying tension of the book. Mac is a victim rather than an active traitor to his own ideology; his normative destiny is symbolic. Equally, J. Ward Morehouse, in one sense a Titan of self-discipline who prostitutes his talents in an unworthy cause, is in reality another victim. Whatever motivates him – and it is not a *conscious* desire to advance the class interests of the American bourgeoisie – leads him into the trap of the ruined individual. Such correspondences disqualify Dos Passos as a Marxist writer: a Marxist might agree that capitalism alienates both those who serve it and those who oppose it, but he could not describe their fates as individuals so even-handedly.

The importance of the individual to Dos Passos is underlined by his use of the Biographies, of which there are eight in *The Forty Second Parallel*. Only two are unequivocally hostile – those of Minor C. Keith and Andrew Carnegie, though if the last line were omitted from the piece on Carnegie it would be a bare collection of facts about a very rich man. Bryan is treated with a faintly compassionate satire – in 1930 he was only five years dead, but he stood, quaintly, for a much older America. Debs and La Follette took the risk of speaking out against the 'interests'. Burbank, Steinmetz and to some extent Edison are Veblenian heroes, the men of practical genius forced to mortgage their talents to the financial system. Each of these men is revealed to have some secret flaw or failure, but each – as T. K. Whipple has pointed out – seems to possess some superhuman quality, and they all overshadow the bleak and jaded lives of the fictional characters. Together with the imposing figure of John Randolph Dos Passos as he appears in the Camera Eyes,[50] they furnish a living reproach to the modern Americans who hobble blindly through the novel's narrative portions. The lesson may be partly historical – that the Gilded Age gave freer rein to the drives of the forceful individual – and partly political – that in a democracy only a few can expect to shine – but the principal effect is to suggest a contrast between those who dominated circumstances and those who are pushed about by chance or social currents. Even Morehouse, the shrewd, plausible opportunist is a flannel-suited puppet beside Bryan or Carnegie.

The author is not, however, proposing that historical progress depends on the activity of great men. Most of his biographical subjects were alive during the period covered by *The Forty Second Parallel*, but their achievements generally belong to the century before. The artistic value of the Biographies is to suggest the importance in himself of the individual and the variety of ways in which individuality can be expressed. There is little mention, for instance, of the advantages they drew from propitious circumstances or of how far each man represented a movement. La Follette is described as 'a wilful man expressing no opinion but his own' whereas Wilson had called him *one* of a 'group of wilful men', i.e. the Congressional rump of anti-war Insurgents. The contrast is deepened by this emphasis, and the society in which Mac, Morehouse and the others exist is given the appearance of a vast, disturbed ants' nest. Following his creations' movements, Dos Passos adopts the point of view of the dismayed ant who, observing the disaster at first hand but unable to determine its cause, runs helplessly about. The crowded yet atomised world which he depicts – a world superbly realised through the multi-faceted techniques of the novel – is not a world explicable as the product of strict historical laws. In refusing to be a social theorist, while at the same time using the observable facts from which social theorists would draw their conclusions, Dos Passos remains faithful to his vision. By throwing together the individual in all the patient and commonplace detail of his life-effort, the collective organism examined through its dominant beliefs and representative figures, and the subjective awareness of memory, he creates a nexus that refuses to explain or explicitly to judge, but which *displays* with energy and seriousness the developing life of a civilisation.

2. 'LIKE WRECKS IN A DISSOLVING DREAM'

In *One Man's Initiation* the reader finds studied notebook exercises in prose-poetic reporting – pictorial, imagistic. They are often formally redundant fragments in the narrative, they ignore grammatical and logical rules, and their tendency is self-consciously poetic. In *Three Soldiers* the imagery, though still intensely visual, is above all the imagery of natural sensation, of a reflective interchange between men and the environment in which they live and act. To John Andrews, Paris is not simply an impressionist canvas; it is rife with objects and people which he must learn to differentiate, judge, relate to. Soldiers bound for the front move, cough, and stamp their feet, while the corpse that Chrisfield stumbles across is a real corpse, undergoing decomposition, that modifies more intensely than propaganda his attitude towards the Germans.

Even so, a residual continuity of style is as noticeable as the development of a more assured and vital understanding of the craft of fiction. Certain distinct elements of composition – colour, form, a melancholy irony of elementary contrasts – remain constant. The real change in Dos Passos' handling of war occurs in *1919*, where the writing carries a brutal and sardonic edge, a reminder that hatred, disease and death are *routine*, a *dies irae* recited by a tired voice. It is the voice of hindsight: 'Tout est raconté comme par quelqu'un qui se souvient. . . . Chez Dos Passos, l'évènement reçoit d'abord son nom, les dés sont jetés, comme dans notre mémoire'.[51] But Dos Passos' 'temps de l'Histoire' has a deeper, more intimate quality than Sartre suggests. For in *1919* he recapitulates the setting and the specific character of his own war-time experiences in a much more complete fictional form than hitherto and with far greater control over his artistic means and purposes.

'Hell, I wanted to see the show'[52] was Dos Passos' account of his motives for not having taken, as he sometimes felt he should, the course of the principled pacifist. As the text of *One Man's Initiation* proves, a 'show' is basically the form in which the war is first represented: viewed, *pari passu* with the inward reflections of Martin Howe, as though it were à piece of assigned subject-matter on which the novice author could test his powers. John Andrews volunteered because he was 'so bored with himself'[53] and repelled by the unmanly privilege of the 'glittering other world'.[54] Each had a chiefly private motive, and in each of the war books the war itself, though necessary, tends to be a catalyst for foreground concerns and conflicts of a personal nature: the aesthetic explorations of Dos Passos–Howe and the adolescent value-struggles of John Andrews.

With Richard Ellsworth Savage it is otherwise. In the space of a few lines he is seen to abandon a priggish, lifeless pacifism for voluntary – though not ardent – service in the Ambulance Corps. Why? The reasons have to be inferentially drawn, but they help to place Savage.

> Everybody was drilling and going to lectures on military science . . . He managed to find time to polish up a group of sonnets called *Morituri Te Salutant*. . . . It won the prize but the editors wrote back that they would prefer a note of hope . . . Dick put in the note of hope . . . He discovered that if he went into war work he could get his degree that spring without taking any exams . . .[55]

This is not only a different *character* from the early protagonists, a man whose motivations are more complex and ambiguous; it is also a different *world*, a world to which the events of the post-war years have given, in Dos Passos' sensibility, a new meaning and, in his literary practice, a new style. In the terse and dismissive casualness of the prose and in the perspective that sets his characters within the collective world, instead of refracting that world through their personalities, appear the reconsidered judgements of the Dos Passos of the thirties. As Sartre writes, 'Dos Passos n'a inventé qu'une chose: un art de conter. Mais ça suffit pour créer un univers.'[56]

His 'created universe' is by no means one which he likes or wishes to accept, but it is an honest reflection of the world which he sees, more closely realised than the universe of 'organisation' that repelled Martin Howe or the Moloch-world of *Three Soldiers*. Dos Passos has not merely felt the prevalence of misery; he has lived through the doom of hope. The great pervading symbol in *1919* of the central fallacy of the modern organised world, the guarantee of failure and illusion, is American Progressive liberalism with its self-mystifying panaceas and its abstract faith in verbal formulas. Wilson is its arch-apostle. In 1968, confessing his 'hatred' of Wilson, Dos Passos wrote 'I still feel that Western civilisation would have been less imperilled if . . . Wilson . . . had used the threat of American entry to force a negotiated peace in the summer of 1917.'[57] He implies that he had always held this astonishingly unrealistic view; but actually *1919* uses Wilson in a subtler, more telling fashion. Like Morehouse, he is the man so practised in deception that he conceals his aims and motives even from himself – as Mencken put it, 'the self-bamboozled Presbyterian, the right-thinker, the great moral statesman, the perfect model of a Christian cad'.[58] In words stiff with contempt, Dos Passos paints 'Meester Veelson' (a title suggesting the false god of European public opinion) as a kind of disembodied larynx uttering its slogans in the soapy accents of moral certitude: 'Almighty God, Right, Truth, Justice, Freedom, Democracy, the Self-determination of Nations, No indemnities no annexations . . .[59] Cuban sugar and Caucasian manganese . . . machine gun fire and arson, starvation, lice, cholera, typhus; oil was trumps.'[60] Beneath the ectoplasm of high-minded abstractions lie the dirty facts of war, politics and commerce.

Wilson 'talking to save his faith in words'[61] echoes the despair of Jimmy Herf, who had lost his faith but could find no acceptable substitute – like the other early heroes he had attempted to construct a magical religion out of art or literature. Yet in *1919* things have changed: Richard Savage, though a descendant of Howe–Andrews–Herf, 'cannot be understood apart from the various devices of the novel – the camera eye episodes, the biographies, the newsreels, and other characterisations which overlap his own reality or help to define it'.[62] *1919* has the shape of a continuum, in which each technical mode and each individual 'destiny' converges to create a totality inaccessible through any one separate aspect. The perfection of the method ensures that *1919*, even more than *The Forty Second Parallel*, is a genuinely 'collective' novel – collective in its comprehensive relation of all its elements and approaches. Its theme is the betrayal of a civilisation – a betrayal not without its heroes and villains but at heart ascribable more to the remorseless dynamism of events than to any one man or group of men.

1919 takes pains to discipline its material. It is concerned not merely to be a 'dramatic documentary' or a 'large, loose baggy monster' vaguely and slackly surveying an entire culture. The formal problems already largely solved in *The Forty Second Parallel* are triumphantly overcome. The 'authorial voice', for example, which was responsible for many of the weaknesses in the early fiction in its inseparability from the hero's consciousness, needs careful consideration. Without it, no one can speak for the supervising creative intelligence, conveying his judgement or wonder, but the collective structure must not be violated by an intrusive subjectivism. The Camera Eye's function is to bridge this gap – though it has drawn unfavourable comment. '[it] is a survival from the aesthetic Dos Passos . . . why call it by such an objective, "documentary" name when it is such a subjective device?'[63] Yes, but Dos Passos *had* survived, was a sharer and participant, willy-nilly, in the turbulence that had helped to shape and modify his 'aesthetic' sympathies. And a camera is not an 'objective' article: it is used by a man who chooses the pictures he wishes to take. What a camera film does is to freeze time, to record a scene for ever as it appears at the moment of exposure. That is why there is justice in Sartre's idiosyncratic comments that

> Dos Passos s'arrête à temps. Grâce à quoi les faits passés gardent une saveur de présent. Ils demeurent encore, dans leur exil, ce qu'ils ont été un jour, un seul jour: d'inexplicables tumultes de couleurs, de bruits, de passions. Chaque événement est une chose rutilante et solitaire, qui ne découle d'aucune autre, surgit tout à coup et s'ajoute à d'autres choses: une irréductible.[64]

And in making a general statement about *1919*, Sartre accurately describes the effect of the Camera Eye in recording the endless engrammatic flow of sense-data on the consciousness of the artist. In fact, though the events are 'inexplicable', they are not the totally secret fragments of a personal sensibility. The Camera Eye is not an indulgent bow to the author's latent aestheticism but interrelates continuously with the other elements.

One index of the Camera Eye's success is to examine its manner of using familiar material, i.e. material which recurs in Dos Passos' writing. Such an image is that of the garden at Récicourt in which Dos Passos and his fellow 'gentlemen volunteers' took refuge shortly after their arrival in France. He first wrote of it in a letter to Arthur McComb dated August 1917:

> . . . a charming garden back of a little pink house of which hardly a shell remains. It smells of box and white roses and is full of tall phlox blooms – I can't imagine a more charming place, though even here lingers a faint odour of poison gas. Three lovely brown and white snails hang on a honeysuckle branch overhead. If it weren't for the guns that bellow out around us every few minutes and for the occasional Boche shells – and for the sausage balloon that hangs with ridiculous gravity in the very blue sky overhead – one would forget the war.[65]

In *The Best Times* this is worked up (probably from memory and from the original correspondence and notes) into a paragraph that dwells in more detail on the fate of the house and retains the plants, snails, honeysuckle and poison gas – though not the guns. It concludes with a nostalgic mention of the privy. 'It was a beautiful old backhouse, pale pink stucco with a tile roof overgrown with vines. Inside the earth closet with scrubbed deal seats was still clean. There were even a few squares of old newspaper neatly stowed in a box.'[66] The letter and the reminiscence reveal how strong an impression the villa garden made in its simple, eloquent contrasts: order, amenity, fragrance in the midst of war. But the same scene is used twice in *1919*. In Camera Eye 30:

. . . through the faint aftersick of mustardgas I smell the box and white roses and the white phlox with a crimson eye three brown-andwhitestriped snails hang with infinite delicacy from a honeysuckle-branch overhead up in the blue a sausageballoon grazes drowsily like a tethered cow there are drunken wasps clinging to the tooripe pears that fall and squash whenever the near guns spew their heavy shells that go off rumbling through the sky. . . . welltodo country people carefully built the walls and the little backhouse with the cleanscrubbed seat and the quartermoon in the door like the backhouse of an old farm at home carefully planted the garden and savored the fruit and flowers and carefully planned this war . . .[67]

The gardenscape is viewed in hallucinatory distortion through the 'aftersick of mustardgas'. The simple irony has been thickened and complicated by the association of the natural and mechanical worlds, and by the accusatory tenor of the last phrase. The whole taut, swollen, protesting narrative is alternated with curt lists of American patriotic clichés that run through the mind of the young initiate. It is personal — almost a parody of the early personal style — but it resonates not only through the following Biography (Randolph Bourne as the truth-teller versus 'Schoolmaster Wilson') but throughout the ensuing life-history sections on Eveline and Joe until, seventy pages later, Dick Savage discovers

a little garden at Récicourt . . . The garden had been attached to a pink villa, but the villa had been mashed to dust as if a great foot had stepped on it. The garden was untouched, only a little weedy from neglect, roses were in bloom there and butterflies and bees droned around the flowers on sunny afternoons. At first they took the bees for distant arrivés and went flat on their bellies when they heard them . . . What Dick liked best in the garden was the little backhouse, like the backhouse of a New England farm, with a clean scrubbed seat and a halfmoon in the door . . . He'd sit there with his belly aching listening to the low voices of his friends talking in the driedup fountain.[68]

The most idealised version is that from *The Best Times*: the tone of the letter is a relief rather than sentimental rhapsody. But the Camera Eye stresses nightmarish absurdity. Direct, unassimilated, like a neural snapshot, it arouses that instinctive sense of wrongness, hard to articulate but instantly recognisable, that strikes one in the presence of major contradiction in one's experience. The privy is like a farm privy at home — but of what use the catchwords of home? Such a collapse of familiar values threatens the sanity, and there flows into the author's mind a self-protective vision of human solidarity: '. . . après la guerre that our fingers our blood our lungs our flesh under the dirty khaki feldgrau bleu horizon might go on sweeten grow until we fall from the tree ripe like the tooripe pears . . .'[69] But there is no solidarity, only the common misery of victims. In Dick Savage's garden a satirical glow illuminates the pastoral atmosphere in which the dilettante ambulance-men bask. Their inexperience is underlined by their initial reaction to the sound of the bees' humming. Dick Savage is set apart by his aloof-ness and fondness for privacy. The scene about the ruined house is imbued with decadence. Dos Passos has found the means of distancing himself from the Harvard aestheticism of his youth, while making it a relevant part of his story. Dick, even though he feels 'happy and at home' in the backhouse (the implication is of mild contempt for the college-bred intellectual), almost flippantly strikes a chord of biological despair in his friend Steve. But the physical danger of war has been omitted.

In the sonorous echolalia of the Camera Eye lies the 'passé sans loi'[70] of which Sartre speaks. It is fixed and arrested, like the language which cunningly impersonates, without solemnly repeating, the narcissistic radiance of the apprentice work. Here is the 'récul esthétique'. But when the focus is altered to accommodate the entropy of universal disaster another picture emerges: Dick, Joe, Eveline are shown in social–historical context as men and women who have decisive relations with society at large. The totality of 1919 results from an overlapping of these images.

Dos Passos had begun his war service auspiciously, with the 'gentlemen volunteers' of the Norton-Harjes Ambulance Corps. The realities of the battlefield soon made the phrase seem laughable to him; he never for-got the sight of Dick Norton paying a pompous farewell to his men after the U.S. declaration of war had meant that they would be absorbed in the Medical Corps. To McComb he wrote, in the autumn of 1918:

Arthur . . . picture the scene . . . Richard Norton courtly in a monocle . . . in front of a large crowd of ambulance drivers – behind them a much shrapnel-holed barnlike structure, our cantonment – the section dog by name P2 wanders about uneasily. An occasional shell screeches overhead, makes the fatjowled gentlemen duck and blink . . . Mr. Norton has just finished his very modest speech ending with the won-derful phrase 'As gentlemen volunteers you enlisted and as gentlemen volunteers I bid you farewell.'[71]

In Camera Eye 32 this is expanded into a satirical sketch. Dick Norton constantly 'adjusting his monocle', lines up his section 'à quatorze heures précisément' because, it is implied, he wishes to flaunt his indifference to the shellfire which occurs regularly at that hour. Norton's performance is related with comic exaggeration. Preserving the moment with all the bold sharp outlines of its insane logic, the Camera Eye bears the imprint, both critical and impressionable, of the lingering memory. When the moment recurs in the narrative, proportions shrink as the focus is re-adjusted for a more distant, neutral, external view. 'Everybody got a copy of the section's citation; Dick Norton made them a speech under shellfire, never dropping his monocle out of his eye, dismissing them as gentlemen volunteers and that was the end of the section.'[72] The scene is built up laconically and dryly, from the personal detail of Dick's fondness for the European pastoral setting to the flat and conclusive 'end'. Decisions are taken; speeches are made; by some impersonal process of events people are shifted here and there. There is little time for analysis, little point in demanding reasons.

The Camera Eye does not invariably work merely by anticipating, in the idiom of the engrammatic moment of stress, what will later be observed as a part of the collective flow. But as a rule, it is used in this manner; and as a rule it succeeds. The Camera Eyes of *1919* actually cover the period from April 1916, when Dos Passos' mother died, to the spring of 1919, when, after a spell of scrap-iron shunting while the army hunted for his service record, he finally received his discharge. Except for two journeys stateside, Dos Passos was abroad for the whole of this time; had lost both his parents within the space of a year; had undergone a horrific rite of passage; had almost shared the fate of E. E. Cummings for his 'defeatist' attitudes; had travelled extensively in four European countries; and had chosen to become a writer. Some of these experiences were shared with other young men of his generation, but many were not. In any case, his artist's sensibility made him especially receptive to his participation in the drama of those years. In his first books, both sensibility and expression are still adolescent; the intensity of emotions has not been assimilated and brought under the distancing control of a mature artistic discipline. But while the vital emotions of adolescence there choke his urge to articulate them, Dos Passos worked to develop the the 'récul esthétique' that makes them recoverable and useable. The Camera Eyes successfully re-interpret the subject-matter of the first books and weave into the panoramic cultural biography a bright thread of personal history.

Outside of the Camera Eyes, Dos Passos takes pains to withhold from public events the highly charged current of his private imagination. The characters of *1919* exist through their relations with the 'loud world'; their adventures are generally beyond their control or understanding. But the 'determinism' has ceased to be the vague and lurking doom that used to fall on everyone like a sudden fog and is concretely associated with the self-defensive tyranny of institutions under threat. The holocaust of world war provides a dominant image universal and powerful enough to objectify the ubiquitous properties of suffering, betrayal and defeat. Dos Passos has risen to his subject with fresh reserves of clarity and control. Whereas in the Camera Eyes there resides the artist's shadowy inner triumph over the ghastliness of life – 'the mind's silent victory that integrity can acknowledge to itself'[73] – the narrative sections concentrate on the impotence and loneliness of the isolated individual under the conditions of total war: most notably in the story of Joe Williams.

Joe is a *lumpen* sailor, who is pushed and trampled on by the totalitarian machine. His fate is never to have a good time. For him, even the coarse fugitive pleasures of the 'submerged tenth' never quite live up to expectations. He copulates with stringy whores and aged negresses; 'sees the world' as a succession of foreign rat-holes; starts a voyage on his wedding night without having made love to his wife; and is nearly always broke. But Joe is not the victim of occult spiritual forces, demons or furies. After his desertion from the U.S. Navy he is a merchant seaman, and the merchant service is viewed not (as Conrad sees it) under the aspect of eternity but with extreme critical attention both to the physical hardships of shipboard life and to its war-time role as the logistic arm of American financial and industrial interests. The servant and scapegoat of institutional forces, Joe is badly treated: imprisoned in England on suspicion of being a German spy (a result of America's equivocal position at that time) and mocked by the specious lure of self-improvement courses. Nevertheless, though inarticulate, he is tough and far from stupid. He does manage to acquire a mate's certificate and he behaves as a rule with relative decency. Joe *struggles* – in his confused, instinctual way – but he can never shift the burden that presses him down. Just as in *The Forty Second Parallel* the sympathetic Mac and the repulsive J. Ward Morehouse are represented in a dynamism of contrasts – the 'vag' victim and the spiritually empty success – so Joe and Richard Savage move in a significant polarity throughout *1919*. Joe is the 'mucker' whose life is brutish and short, Savage the intellectual without integrity or conviction.

This typology is made live and credible not only by the author's keener sense of society in *1919* but by the narrative viewpoint he has chosen. Often it informs the 'hard and choppy'[74] style of the historical spectator: 'Joe Williams put on the secondhand suit and dropped his uniform, with the cobblestone wrapped up in it, off the edge of the dock into the muddy water of the basin. It was noon. There was nobody around.'[75] But Dos Passos also explores a vein of closer identification with his characters – with Joe in particular. The method is not profoundly inward – it does not attempt to explore the most secret recesses of consciousness – but it allows an exchange of dramatic tensions between the narrator's omniscience and the solipsism of the character.

'Next morning they were in court and it was funny as hell except that Joe was scared; it was solemn as a Quakermeetin' and the magistrate wore a little wig and they were everyone of them fined three and six costs.'[76] In mimicking the unlettered and colloquial tone of Joe's speech, the narrative gives that effect of a qualified sympathy which Sartre has noted. '. . . ce qu'il dit, le héros n'aurait pas tout à fait pu le dire, mais on sent entre eux une complicité discrète, le récitant raconte, du dehors, comme le héros êut aimé qu'on racontat . . . on dirait que c'est un choeur que se souvient, un choeur sentencieux et complice.'[77] Sartre, however, reviews *1919* as if it were all straightforward narrative (no distinction between the various modes) and as if all the life-histories were identical in their 'abondance triste' (no distinction between the characters) – in other words, he reads too much through the magnifying glass of his own assumptions. Actually, the 'chorus' is much more flexible than Sartre admits.

On the same page, for example, from which Sartre quotes the lines about Dick's teacher there is struck the note of petulant self-regard which so often characterises Dick, and the college-boy slang recurs at other moments when the Savage temperament – weak, narcissistic, undeveloped – is highlighted. 'Then he'd suddenly snap out of his argumentative mood and all the phrases about liberty and civilisation steaming up out of his head would seem damn silly too, and he'd light the gasoline burner and make a rum punch and cheer up chewing the rag with Steve about books or painting or architecture.'[78] 'Absurdity'[79] indeed – but the absurdity of Dick's own absence of settled beliefs as well as the absurdity of external circumstances. If (like Frederic Henry) he finds the value-loaded words meaningless and embarrassing, he cannot summon the effort to restore, by self-sacrificing actions, the meaning to any word. And thus his drift into the Morehouse limbo, where words simply have a pragmatic exchange-value like money, is plotted by these blind eruptions of self-pity, which display Dick's lack of moral resources, growing into cynicism, and the wider landscape of disintegration in which they occur. 'It was just like Ed said, you couldn't do anything without making people miserable. A hell of a rotten world'.[80] The method is that in which Joe's responses are conveyed. The world they inhabit is the same. But the implicit judgement varies: Dick's evasion of responsibility is contrasted with the social fraud that tries to palm off on Joe a false responsibility while denying his right to set its terms.

And this is true of other characters. Dos Passos' art is the art of the Stereopticon. Flat images are superimposed until they acquire the depth and roundness of relief. In words which echo the natural voices of individual characters, he lifts out from the conjunctive sentences and the accumulation of dense physical details their special traits or tendencies. Eveline Hutchins's neurotic, brittle worldliness is caught in passages such as this – when she comes home to find that Eleanor has invited her pet poilu to tea: 'She was glad to see him, because she was always complaining that she wasn't getting to know any French people, nothing but professional relievers and Red Cross women who were just too tiresome.'[81] The reckless, volatile temperament of Anne Elizabeth Trent is mimicked by terse, fast rhythmical sentences. 'It was crazy going up like this. She had to catch that boat. The plane had started. It was bouncing over the field, bouncing along the ground. They were still on the ground rumbling bouncing along. Maybe it wouldn't go up, she hoped it wouldn't go up.'[82] Benny Compton's inner life is a fiery blend of inspired dedication and the impersonal theorems of the totally committed revolutionary. His history is interlarded with phrases directly quoted from the *Communist Manifesto*, and it is not love or wealth that stimulates his hopes. It is certain words and phrases. 'Phrases like *protest, massaction, united workingclass of this country and the world, revolution*, would light up the eyes and faces under him like the glare of a bonfire'.[83] Throughout, the relief-effect of sudden switches of perspective gives to the characters a persuasively solid life. As Sartre perceptively observed, 'L'homme de Dos Passos est un être hybride, interne–externe. Nous sommes avec lui, en lui, nous vivons avec sa vacillante conscience individuelle et, tout à coup, elle flanche, elle faiblit, elle se dilue dans la conscience collective. Nous l'y suivons et nous voilà soudain dehors sans y avoir pris garde.'[84] Sartre's emphasis on suddenness is apt. But this intermittence of viewing angle, which does have the value of making lifelike and real figures whose minds are not deeply penetrated, is only one element of the entire composition. There must be added to the engrammatic punctuation of the Camera Eye and the refractions of the central narrative the more factually objective contributions of the Newsreels and the Biographies. *1919* is more than a clever illustration of literary versatility by a practised novelist: it is a case.

Three Soldiers had suffered as a book from Dos Passos' attempt to counterweigh the cruelties of the machine by an aesthetic credo in which he could not sustain belief. In comparison, the faith of *The Enormous Room* or *A Farewell to Arms* rings true: it is saved from appearing ridiculous in each case by the author's profound conviction and his urgent striving to embody it successfully in his art. Yet by the mid-1930s Hemingway could write a bad and silly novel with a collectivist moral – so untrue to the tenor of his life and work – which portrayed Dos Passos as a fake and a failure,[85] while Dos Passos had grown consistently as a fiction-writer. Their final political and personal quarrel did not reach a head until 1939, when they visited Spain together; but relations 'began to cool'[86] at about the time *1919* appeared. Politically, Dos Passos had made plain his radical sympathies, though he was never a 'joiner' and remained one of the non-party committed intelligentsia.

The 'faith' which energises *1919*, though, is not a confident belief in the socialist future. Yet despite its essentially negative character, it is more vital and authentic than his own earlier aestheticism, or Hemingway's later flirtation with the Stalinists. *1919 demonstrates*: it does not analyse. America is a hell of blighted lives; the sound-seeming precepts and institutions Dos Passos had grown up with 'during the quiet afterglow of the nineteenth century'[87] are in decay; 'faiths and empires gleam' – as Martin Howe slightly misquoted Shelley – 'Like wrecks in a dissolving dream'.[88] Dos Passos has nerved himself to accept the death of the old absolutes, but he registers a naked, passionate indignation against the pain and misery of modern society, especially as it is represented in the humbug of liberal capitalism. In his literary formulation of his rage and his incorporation of political and historical examples there is, as Sartre suggests, an implicit protest: the protest of moral despair, not an ameliorative programme.

1919 contains Biographies: the subjects include three radical publicists, two presidents, an investment banker, and two Wobblies. The final subject is 'The Body of an American'. The lives of John Reed, Paxton Hibben and Randolph Bourne have a special personal meaning for Dos Passos. They are the Sinbads, the men who got 'in bad'. All men of taste and intellect, they could have led secure, cultivated lives by obeying the trimmer's rule, 'don't monkey with the buzzsaw'. In the case of each, a conversion supervenes to amplify personal integrity into a pressing sense of social concern. Each declined to be satisfied with the easy comforts of privilege. They are not frozen public statues, the recipients of official testimonials. Dos Passos knew Hibben in Moscow shortly after the war, and Reed had influenced – through *Ten Days That Shook The World* – the very style of the Biographies. As well as serving the favourite 'Sinbad was in bad' motif, they symbolise, in their distinction and their fearless defiance of authority, an ideal of principled rebellion that implicitly rebukes those who are weak, timid and corrupt. The Biographies in *1919* are less purely formal than those of *The Forty Second Parallel*. They are generally longer, less poetic, more circumstantial and more heavily emotive. These three, plus those of Joe Hill and Wesley Everest, celebrate the major currents of opposition to the American establishment, both intellectual and activist. Fighters and martyrs, they are heroic: they commanded the rearguard fight against liberal shams as it was waged in the public life of the nation. They questioned the official slogans. They demystified conventional morality. Yet they are voices crying in the wilderness.

To underline the ethical discriminations of the Biographies, Dos Passos employs a naked, heavy irony in reciting biographical data. Occasionally, this takes the form of juxtaposing with the author's words data from *Who's Who*, or from the subjects' own speeches or writings. In this

manner, he is able to grasp some cliché of the ruling-class – say 'disinterested learning' – and crack open its shell with a scornful phrase:
'the rusty machinery creaked, the deans quivered under their mortar-
boards . . .'[89] 'he picked rosy glasses out of the turgid jumble of John
Dewey's teaching'.[90] The words of approval stand out in forceful clarity –
'husky greedy', 'unscared', 'cantankerous', 'truculent'. These connote the
antinomian virtues of the non-conforming individualist, and Dos Passos
plainly admires them as individuals. Yet like Debs they strove to assert
human brotherhood; to defy conventional opinion; to shed blinkers of
purely private happiness. They are the men who 'got in wrong'.[91]

Yet American history has not been dominated by such men, but by
the cautious, the deceitful and the self-interested. Roosevelt and Wilson
are examples of the latter type; despite the contrasts of their personalities they are treated with comparable antipathy. It is hard to quote
selectively from their Biographies – they are integral and conclusive in
the withering contempt of their rhythms and phraseology. They deploy a
brutally sarcastic inversion of the usual evaluative tone of American
idioms. 'Bully' and 'righteous' are repeated throughout 'The Happy
Warrior' to evoke the priggish pretensions of the man and the boyscout vulgarity of his public persona. Dos Passos lists with evidential
precision the significant facts of Roosevelt's career: the shop-window
reforms, the megalomania, the imperialist adventures. Nor is he blind
to slighter comic ironies – 'his life was saved only by the thick bundle
of manuscript of the speech he was going to deliver'[92] – or to a certain
scornful pity for the later, out-of-power Roosevelt. The most complete
denunciation is reserved for Woodrow Wilson. Even more than J. P.
Morgan (an out-and-out reactionary plutocrat for whom Dos Passos
feels an almost respectful horror) Wilson is the novel's major embodi-
ment of duplicity in power – the oratorial mystifying front for 'the elderly
swag bellied gentlemen who control all destinies'.[93] Dos Passos' Wilson is
basically the Wilson of Versailles, the Wilson of the Espionage Acts, the
sanctimonious, vindictive, dogmatic war president. 1919 is the novel of
the war and the Peace, but Dos Passos traces throughout Wilson's life
the strain of demagogic cant, the bigotry, the devious motives that made
Wilson into 'the greatest prophet [of] the current American theory that
political heresy should be put down by force, that a man who disputes
whatever is official has no rights in law or equity, that he is lucky if he
fears no worse than to lose his constitutional benefits of free speech,
free assemblage, and the use of the mails.'[94]

'The Wilsons lived in a universe of words linked into an incontrovertible firmament by two centuries of Calvinist divines, God was the Word
and the Word was God.'[95] In the biblical allusiveness of the language
Dos Passos parodies Wilsonian oratory. He parodies it to express his
dislike for its hypocrisy and he relates, as a means of enforcing the dis-

parity between its lofty, pious sentiments and the squalid realities of American political life, the crucial moment of Wilson's entry into politics.

> . . . *the sun meant to regenerate men, the sun meant to liberate them from their passion and despair and lift us to those uplands which are the promised land of every man who desires liberty and achievement.*

The smalltown bosses and the wardheelers looked at each other and scratched their heads; then they cheered; Wilson fooled the wisacres and doublecrossed the bosses, was elected by a huge plurality.[96]

The slogans and promises of Woodrow Wilson are printed, each with a short postcript to indicate its hollowness or dishonesty, rather in the manner of a partisan press campaign against the record in office of an unpopular minister. Dos Passos 'turns the moral values inside out to question the worth of a deed by looking not at its actual outcome but at its tone and style'.[97] *1919* is not exclusively concerned with private or public morality, but Wilson's tone and style are presented as being as objectionable as his policies; they are a metaphor for everything Wilson represents. For the creation of a rhetoric of despairing protest, they are brilliantly drawn on. Wilson's moralistic gestures and woolly, elevated speech-making are set among the 'rows of potted palms, silk hats, legions of honour, decorated busts of uniforms, frock-coats, boutonnières',[98] all the ostentation of privilege and power which divides the 'Old men shuffling the pack'[99] from the 'women in black, the cripples in their little carts, the pale anxious faces along the streets'.[100] In *1919* the Biographies are more than 'mythic poetry' of the national culture. Bitter and tendentious, they foreshadow the 'two nations' theme of *The Big Money*, and they integrate with the stories of the fictional characters by making familiar some of the leaders and apostles of the global forces which apocalyptically clash around the heads of Joe, Eveline, Richard Savage, 'Daughter', Ben Compton. In the later parts of the novel, the Biographies become threnodies for martyrs to repression and warhate.

Joe Hill's short Biography – it immediately precedes the first section of Ben Compton's life history – is recounted in simple, thumping rhythms that follow the pace and jauntiness of his songs. It is a piece of conscious mythologising, as is the sketch of Wesley Everest, whom Dos Passos associates with the legendary logger Paul Bunyan. These deaths, for which Wilson's Biography has prepared the reader, recall the death of another Joe – Joe Williams. Wesley Everest was lynched on Armistice Day 1919, exactly one year after the sudden, senseless death of Joe Williams in St Nazaire. Joe's death came in a sudden crash of oblivion,

like the apparently arbitrary accidents of *Manhattan Transfer*. Even so,
everything in his life was a preparation for it. Joe is a born loser: the soft
hotel beds, the chauffeur-driven automobiles, the smart clothes and expensive restaurants go to the Morehouses and their retinues. The particular manner and occasion of Joe's death are random, but such a
manner of dying is the natural outcome of such an existence. The unequal relation of the haves and haves-nots, which Dos Passos has kept
alive through the intermittent narrative chapters and the 'mood-music'[101]
of the Newsreel montages, is brought to an exceptionally powerful
climax with 'The Body of an American'. In these closing cadences the
author has concentrated the moral essence of his book. Simultaneously a
Biography, Newsreel, Camera Eye and life history, it amply justifies the
choice of Dos Passos' synthetic literary method, capturing not just the
eternal typicality of death, but the essential idioms and values of a varie-
gated culture.

   — busboy harveststiff hogcaller boyscout champeen cornshucker of
   Western Kansas bellhop at the United States Hotel at Saratoga Springs
   officeboy callboy fruiter telephonelineman longshoremen lumberjack
   plumber's helper . . .
   Thou shalt not the multiplication table long division, Now is the time
   for all good men Knocks but once at a man's door, It's a great life
   if Ish gebibbel, The first five years'll be Safety First, Suppose a Hun
   tried to rape your my country right or wrong, Catch 'em rough, Tell
   'em nothing . . .[102]

'John Doe' is the universal anonymous victim. In listing the clichéd
imperatives that have been fed to him in place of a free interpretation of his own life-experience, Dos Passos celebrates his poor body
with an ironic and dignified compassion. There is a more sincere
tribute in this final biography than in all the official pseudo-reverence —
the more so because the ghastly physical facts of death and decomposition are not shirked. 'The blood ran into the ground, the brains oozed
out of the cracked skull and were licked up by the trenchrats, the belly
swelled and raised a generation of bluebottle flies.'[103] And a coda adopts
the supremely bitter viewpoint of the hostile Biographies, with the 'unco'
guid' who had sat in safe billets and howled for blood queuing up as
at a select social function for the indecent pomp of the interment cere-
mony.

   There is hardly a line in *USA* that does not grow out of a considered
   concept of society, a concept, moreover, carrying with it certain
   implications as to where the root of evil lies . . . there is hardly one
   of his fictive or historical characters that does not in some way underscore the view of our society as one in which the profit system cor-

rupts or crushes, leaving those who climb to the top ruthless and unhappy, the intellectuals decadent, venal or escapist, and the lower classes wretched and abused.[104]

At each end of *1919* there is recorded an aspect of the war as experienced by those at the bottom of society's pyramid – Joe Williams slaving on board the vessels carrying *matériel* through the Atlantic submarine zone, Ben Compton caught up in the domestic war-scare and represssion. Most of the fictional sections between these two concentrate on the 'Cook's tour' war enjoyed by the middle-class characters in Paris and Italy. The bureaucratic wheeling and dealing of the Morehouse set and the raffish adventures of the 'grenadine guards' are the two related streams of narrative which flow together at the end of the war. Dos Passos is here handling material familiar to him at first-hand from his war and post-war experiences. Themes present in his subjective early fiction find sharper expression in the satirical portrait of Richard Savage, a Harvard intellectual who at each opportunity for a courageous assertion of responsibility weakens and surrenders, and in the life history of Eveline Hutchins – snobbish, second-rate, parasitic.

Unlike John Andrews, Richard Savage, as Stanley Cooperman writes, 'elminates both assertion and act and ultimately becomes what he most despises . . . If Andrews maintains his individuality through failure and futility, Richard gives up his identity to indifference and success.'[105] Savage does 'give up' the chance of saving his integrity, in a manner that makes each stage of his capitulation an authentic crisis which he declines to face. Unlike Mac – who otherwise shares much of his failure to connect words and deeds – Savage is not born to hardship. But in a world in which freedom has to be struggled for and positive choices are never easy, he invariably chooses the soft option. He represents the educated young men of his generation who, unlike Ben Compton, preferred silence and compromise to defiance. Though Dick has the impulse of defiance (he is constantly in peril of 'getting in bad') he sneaks out of every difficulty, performing his 'déclarations rituelles et . . . gestes sacrées'.[106] Through cravenly asking permission to 'explain his position' he ensures that the matter of his 'seditious' correspondence is dropped; and he murders Anne Elizabeth with lies.

It is Dick who revises his sonnets to include the 'note of hope' requested by the editors of *The Literary Digest*, and whose romantic self-image contrasts with his actual flexibility in accommodating himself to the world's ways. Already, he is in the Wilsonian sphere of self-mystification; but he has much further to fall before his nemesis as a public relations courtier. Dick remains half a man; in his alternations between self-pity and enjoyment of the febrile glamour of the 'glittering world' he resembles Jimmy Herf. But in the 'récul esthétique', through the technical variety of his medium and by the amplitude of his imaginative conception, Dos Passos extends the meaning of Dick's failure, revealing both the wantonness of the self-enclosed soul and the social infamy of his 'trahison des clercs'. 'We're the Romans of the Twentieth Century', Dick complains, 'and I always wanted to be a Greek'.[107] By such glib formulas does he shrug away the real choices, and his failure to choose with integrity and love.

Only in the characters of 'Daughter' and Eveline Hutchins does Dos Passos fail to make his novel as unified and consistent as a lesser book like *Manhattan Transfer*, where the figure of Ellen Thatcher serves as a cohesive presence. One woman critic, in identifying the discrepancy, has written that 'His women . . . often do come to life; in these cases they transcend the pattern; but by this very fact they show his real power of characterisation once it works free of an imposed design.'[108] But an 'imposed design', in the sense of an overall artistic plan, is essential to *1919*. In the terms of this plan, the two principal female characters are polarised: one belongs to the Morehouse world of selfishness, deceit, vanity; the other acts as a centre of spontaneous life brutally crushed out of existence – the corrupted survivor and the victim. Yet there is a little too much of Eveline's story, an 'over-determination' of the Paris circle of lies, and although Eveline differs from Eleanor (some of the internecine conflicts of the group arise from this fact, especially where the favour of Morehouse himself is concerned) it is not always simple for the reader, without carefully reconsulting the text, to bear this in mind. It is not until *The Big Money* that the separate relevance of Eveline's story fully emerges. Eleanor is virginal[109] and pietistic, Eveline worldly and shrewd, but in the last analysis the values they represent overlap so considerably that their identities merge. The picture of intrigue among the ancillary agencies of war would not be greatly altered if Eleanor, instead of Eveline, had been the reflecting consciousness through which it is viewed – or even if the life history of Morehouse himself had been continued. In one sense this is what does happen, especially during the general dissolution of the agencies into lobbying and partisan cliques at the end of war, since the people around Morehouse tend to become Morehouse-surrogates. In the brilliantly written sections on the post-armistice restoration of the 'good times', Eveline melts more and more into the 'conscience collective' until she cannot be reconstituted.

Daughter's case is precisely opposite. She does not fall irrecoverably into her context, she violates the context. She is the comic-strip heroine, the drum-majorette of a faintly crude and sentimental streak in *1919*. Dos Passos, despite his Latin ancestry, is not gifted at portraying images of natural human vitality – in particular he lacks the gift of evincing the intense energy of sexual passion.

Not to have fire is to be a skin that shrills;
The complete fire is death; from partial fires
The waste remains, the waste remains and kills.[110]

Dos Passos is a specialist in shrilling skins and partial fires. But Daughter's 'complete fire' never really catches, because the human–artistic equation is unbalanced. The character intended as a paragon of restless searching energy falls dead in its secret inner rhythms. Daughter ends her life dramatically, pressed on by her own 'crazy streak' and the treachery of Richard Savage; even so, it is the image of mechanical disaster which persists as the aeroplane is torn apart. 'A little wire waving loose and glistening against the blue began to whine . . . They were climbing again. Daughter saw the shine of a wing gliding by itself a little way from the plane. The spinning sun blinded her as they dropped.'[111]

These errors can be credited to the contentious problem for a male novelist of characterising women, endowing them with the proper kind of consistency and mystery. Though they faintly spoil the form of the novel, however, they do not diminish its meaning; they are minor blemishes. Dos Passos set out to write, in the trough of the depression, a novel not quite contemporaneous in its action that would be faithful to the recent data of American history and to the canons of his own judgement; to establish a continuity with *The Forty Second Parallel* – to show fluently and boldly the reflexive indices of a world-scale holocaust and a number of individual lives. Despite the superficial monotony of the procedure he chose, with its stress on the commonplace and relentless accumulation of contingent detail, he has more than realised a world that is tangible, concrete, recognisably real. He has succeeded in registering a vital concern about the conditions of life, for which twentieth-century America stands as a universal emblem – the horror of being manipulated by an impersonal and irresistible fate, the temptations of compromise, the awesome venality of moneyed power. Above all, he communicates a frozen pity for the lost, helpless, acted-upon individual. *1919* is not a tract. It offers no solutions. Only in the engrammatic summaries of *lacrimae rerum* is there latent a shocking, stimulating cry of protest. Sartre, for all his eccentric limitations, phrases this truth with eloquent understanding:

Nous reconnaissons tout de suite l'abondance triste de ces vies sans tragique; ce sont les nôtres, ces mille aventures ebauchées, manquées, aussitôt oubliées toujours recommencées, qui glissent sans marquer, sans jamais engager, jusqu'au jour ou l'une d'elles, toute pareille aux autres, tout à coup, comme par maladresse et en trichant, écoeure un homme pour toujours, négligemment détraque un mécanique. Or c'est en peignant comme nous pourrions les peindre, ces apparences trop connues, don't chacun s'accommode, que Dos Passos les rend insupportables. Il indigne ceux qui ne sont jamais indignés, il effraie ceux qui ne s'effraient re rien.[112]

But for all that, Dos Passos has substituted for any metaphysical version of human fate an accusing vision. The primary images of *1919* are Wilson 'talking to save his faith in words', the 'scraps of dried viscera and skin bundled in khaki' of the culminating Biography, and the omnipresent raging forces of destruction which connect the two: 'machine-gun fire and arson, starvation, lice, cholera, typhus'. Writing of an age in which 'mendacity, slander, bribery, venality, coercion, murder, grew to unprecedented dimensions',[113] Dos Passos drafts his petition of anguished protest with a Voltairean ferocity. In *1919* the novelist's reality can be appreciated entire: the spectacle of monstrous injustice, the impact of the component engrams, and the moral climate of the universe in which they interact.

3. 'WE COULD STAND THE WAR, BUT THE PEACE HAS DONE US IN'

Charley Anderson's war was omitted from *1919*, but Dos Passos opens *The Big Money* – as he had ended *The Forty Second Parallel* – with a view of Charley on board ship, hungover, edgy with carnal desire, and hoping (as Joe Askew phrases it) to 'get some of it away from 'em'[114] – the big-money boys, the established rich. Charley's experience, as the reader pieces it gradually together, has been less disillusioning than that of either the 'grenadine guards' who spotted the political chicanery or the dough-boys who bled in the trenches. He is intact; a decorated hero; able to return to the United States, thanks to his knowledge of aviation acquired during his service, with a plan for peace-time commercial success. It seems on the cards: Charley, a modest young man with the informal manners of the American west, has no painful history to darken his hopes – as Jimmy Herf had when he stepped off the boat with a new baby and hot-water bottles filled with smuggled liquor. Charley's life may not be *tabula rasa* – some family complications have already appeared in the first book of the trilogy – but it almost seems, as the warm sensations of his homeland synaesthetically recur, that there will be waiting, if he has the force and spirit to grasp it, a future as buoyantly complete as his imagination has forecast for him.

He sat there listening to the dancetunes, looking at the silkstockings, and the high heels and the furcoats and the pretty girls' faces pinched a little by the wind as they came in off the street. There was an expensive jingle and crinkle to everything. Gosh, it was great. The girls left little trails of perfume and a warm smell of furs as they passed him.[115]

So American, this equation of erotic and financial accomplishment. And yet: there lingers a cruel and tantalising air about these images of the good life. His senses rebound from the costly flesh-coverings that allure and conceal; in the trinket-words 'jingle' and 'crinkle' lurks the superficiality of these promised attractions, as of banknotes passed over a bar counter. Charley is left to intoxicate himself with the token invitations of odours that linger after the bodies have passed him by. It is 'great' to be there as a privileged spectator; 'great' to picture to oneself how, through luck and enterprise, one may share the glamour of it all. Charley cannot detect the fraud even when, as in the excitement of meeting Doris Humphries, he is treated not as a man with full human attributes but as a legendary hero, a walking medal. Her distant, perfunctory farewell makes more urgent and compelling his own fascination. 'It was just "Goodnight, Ollie dear, goodnight, Lieutenant Anderson", and the doorman slamming the taxi door. He hardly knew which of the hands he had shaken had been hers.'[116]

This scene, reinforced by the directly relevant and prophetic paragraphs of Newsreels 45, economically sketches the approaching lines of conflict which eventually ruin Anderson. For it is the recollection of this Aladdin's cave of delight that he carries with him back to Minnesota, where there lie in wait for him the irksomely dull entanglements of his past. Only one heartfelt commitment draws him there – his native concern for his ailing mother. Otherwise, Jim and Hedwig, now more affluent but indefatigably self-seeking, want him to settle down as a compliant drudge in their little grid of the system. Jim wants a bachelor mechanic who will give plenty and take little, but for Charley – a travelled man, who feels he has broadened his outlook – the drawbacks of this proposition are twofold. It is too consciously small-scale and niggling, and it lacks the thick gloss of charm that wipes money clean and surrounds the head of the successful entrepreneur with a halo of romantic enchantment. So Charley finds himself in a situation comparable to that of Krebs in *Soldier's Home*, who 'had acquired the nausea in regard to experience that is the result of untruth or exaggeration'[117] and who could not relate, after the war, to his family and friends in Kansas. Krebs's 'mal de vivre' springs from within, Charley's from outside himself, but each is sickened by the vividness of a disparity he always senses in his mind, and neither can respond to emotional demands by people who have not shared his experience and who assume that nothing has changed.

She felt limp in his arms. They danced awhile without saying anything. She had too much rouge on her cheeks and he didn't like the perfume she had on . . . Emiscah's voice had gotten screechy and she had a way he didn't like of putting her hand on his knee . . . As soon as he could Charley said he had a headache and had to go home.[118]

His re-encounter with Emiscah, who now means very little to him, is a more potent factor in Charley's determination to get away than his mother's death or the importunities of Jim and Hedwig. In his rejection of her – cold, cruel, yet not inspired by the chronic spiritual malaise that makes Krebs appear cold and cruel – are the incipient signs that Charley has begun to adopt the materialist doctrines of the twenties' boom climate. The vulgarity he repudiates in Emiscah is an outward vulgarity of manners only; her cheap perfume, her unmusical voice, her naïve view of courtship may be unattractive, but the girl is not reducible to these properties any more than Charley is reducible to his service record and medal ribbons. But for all practical purposes, men and women in *The Big Money* are reduced, by the ruling criteria of profit and success, to such bare indices:

It becomes indispensable to accumulate. to acquire property, in order to retain one's good name. When accumulated goods have in this way become the accepted badge of efficiency, the possession of wealth presently assumes the character of an independent and definitive basis of esteem. The possession of goods whether acquired aggressively by one's own exertion or passively through transmission by inheritance from others, becomes a conventional basis of reputability. The possession of wealth, which was at the outset valued simply as an evidence of efficiency, becomes, in popular apprehension, itself a meritorious act. Wealth is now itself intrinsically honourable and confers honour on its possessor.[119]

Wealth is the central value to which all subsidiary values of manner, taste and style accrue. It is no accident that *The Big Money* includes a Biography of Veblen, or that Charley's downfall is, in part, the destruction of a man who foraskes 'efficiency' for the prospect of sheer wealth.

It is Charley's misfortune to make his move eastwards too soon. As a result, he finds himself playing the part of Tantalus in New York longer than he bargained for. At every stage of his career, the future is recessive: each advance he makes breeds a fresh crop of frustration. Charley's spell as a beggar in the court of Mammon speeds up the dissolution of his serious, diligent, self-improving traits. At the same time, it increases the hunger for success which such qualities had been expected to help satisfy: in Veblenian phraseology, the aim of Charley's efforts switches from 'industry' to 'exploit'. He becomes alert for the quick speculative deal and the promising gamble rather than the Poor-Richard prospect of gradual, deserving, honest endeavour. He takes a manual job for the basic means of life, but most of his income is won at poker and he dissipates it in bars and brothels. Here he accepts the metropolitan way of life – fast, noisy, full of slick tricks and sudden surprises.

Charley is taken up, not for the military kudos with which he does have some personal connection, but in the identity of a stranger, by a girl who treats his innocent straightfaced remarks as the wit of a celebrity. At first he enjoys the 'great bright unexplored barn' of New York, but he will later be 'compelled to live in its disordered mind'. He hopes that his invention will provide him with the charismatic identity of the rich, successful man. As he awaits this apotheosis, Dos Passos finely builds up around him the loose and scattered impressions of an aspirant in the big town – its stretches of inanition, its sporadic high moments, and its routine of compromised pleasures. The extreme social and emotional discrepancies of his position start to wear Charley down. Mild persistent dissipation – a typical vice of the bored or lonely in large cities – overtakes him: 'It got so he didn't do anything all day but wait for Eveline and drink lousy gin he bought in an Italian restaurant'.[120] By the time Joe Askew is fit and ready to begin negotiations for the commercial manufacture of their aeroplane starter, the pattern is definite. Disappointment and tedium have sharpened Charley's crying need to get on; the *sauve-qui-peut* morality of urban living has erased midwestern ethical restraints. Charley's mind has become obsessed by the delusive rewards of large-scale material success.

At the end of the chapter this success is in view, and Charley has met the educated, smooth-talking men whose business is business. The narrative of his life story – a narrative carefully attuned to the 'intolerable neural itch'[121] of Charley's period of 'dangling' – has stressed the sordid and colourless round of work and vice interrupted only for tantalising glimpses of a magic kingdom he cannot enter. But another voice has served to counterpoint this story, the voice of the Camera Eyes. Camera Eye 43 opens with a lyrical impression of the author's return to the United States after his discharge, and the surge of memories and meanings that drift from his native shore as the ship docks. But the beginning is deceptive. The carefully chosen images of home and childhood – fresh, plangent – never become a panegyric. They give way to the sober testimony of the labour correspondent.

. . . the crunch of Whitecorn muffins and coffee with cream gulped in a hurry before traintime and apartment house mornings stifling with newspapers and the smooth powdery feel of new greenbacks and the whack of a cop's billy cracking a citizen's skull and the faces blurred with newsprint of men in jail the whine and shriek of the buzzsaw and the tipsy smell of raw lumber and straggling through slagheaps through fireweed through wasted woodlands the shantytowns the shanty-towns.[122]

And a few pages later the next Camera Eye sardonically stresses the surrealistic, out-of-place feeling Dos Passos had on his return from a tour to the Near East, where he had witnessed 'starvation, lice, cholera, typhus', when he found 'waiting again the forsomebodyelsetailored dress suit' in an America on the upswing of Harding–Coolidge prosperity. The Camera Eye's distinctive rhetoric, still counterpointing the narrative, has adult clarity and force. Childhood has been left behind, and the writer is both a man who has suffered personally and an observer–participant who relates with critical passion the contortions of a society drunkenly dancing on the edge of a chasm. The stringing together of related idioms or clichés, used in 'The Body of an American' to communicate an indignant pity, adapts itself to the task of seismographically recording the rift of America into 'two nations'. It is lyrical, satirical, and accusatory in turn: it points a finger at the well-fed businessmen who expect, from an artist-witness of the great catastrophe, the traditional received ideas and opinions of a young man on the make. The jolly uncle turns up as a prurient snooper in uniform. The America of lyrical memory has itself become, like Europe, a gigantic battleground – the land of violence and decadence. The Camera Eyes convey in a highly concentrated form the author's emotions of outrage, bemusement, and alienation; not rawly imposed on the fictive material, but relevantly accompanying or inter-penetrating the narrative. Their intensely personal attitudes suffuse the flat, dry, realistic fictional chapters. Despite the formal separation of the two, each is a necessary element in Dos Passos' 'double focus'.[123] Charley Anderson's pilgrimage in search of the big money synoptically includes a view of American society in which 'the pioneer virtues still survive in general parlance, but only as Musical Bank currency'.[124] On this huge canvas, a picture of universal corruption is painted, in which such early Biographies as those of Taylor and Ford furnish paradigmatic exemplars. The more stringent irony of the spontaneous engram, refracted through the hyperaesthetic optic nerve of the Camera Eyes, helps to stir the conscience of the reader who might otherwise fall into the moral sleepi-ness of the Colosseum spectator. And throughout the narrative sections there are other forces at work. The Big Money sets out to examine, with greater explicit attention than The Forty Second Parallel or 1919, the interaction of American social forces in the eight years following the Armistice and the particular roles of individual characters who con-sciously, instinctively or blindly choose the parts they will play in the struggle. The story of Mary French is the first of the life histories to de-pict a wholehearted and self-denying commitment to the cause of the working class, as opposed to the fluctuations of Fenian McCreary or the strangely guileless opportunism of the 'labour-faker' G. H. Barrow.

At its inception, it is a story familiar elsewhere in American fiction. Both Hemingway and John O'Hara took their own doctor-fathers as the models of the 'good doctor' in the Nick Adams tales and the Jim Malloy stories. The good doctor is the humane physician who gives his professional services to the poor, while the nagging doctor's wife[125] resents his unworldly dedication. But Dr French is more than a 'good doctor': he has a practice in the Wobbly mining country of Colorado, he votes the socialist ticket, and he implants in Mary – much to her mother's disgust – his own values. For the young Mary French these values have the radiance of religious beliefs, the tradition of Jane Adams and Hull House.

> She . . . lay in the Pullman berth that night too excited to sleep, listening to the rumble of the wheels over the rails, the clatter of crossings, the faraway spooky wails of the locomotive, remembering the overdressed women putting on airs in the ladies' dressing-room who'd elbowed her away from the mirror and the heavyfaced businessmen snoring in their berths, thinking of the work there was to be done to make the country what it ought to be . . .[126]

Her list of the social maladies to be cured is comprehensive and accurate; her training has seen to that, though her understanding of them is purely intellectual, lacking the final touch of experience. When that experience arrives it makes so real the deprivation she has vowed to fight (as real as the vulgar men and women on the train) that she finds Hull House principles inadequate to combat it. Her chief effort is the struggle to unite faith with the facts of experience, and this struggle – a protacted and painful effort – characterises the life of each of the figures whose stories are told in *The Big Money*. They strain to act, but their actions bring results that cast doubt on the premises from which they issued, and their life-goals fall apart into incompatible alternatives. Mary's affair with George Barrow – the least unsatisfactory sexual relationship in a trilogy distinguished by its roll-call of erotic failure – becomes for her a political betrayal once she recognises his hypocrisy. Yet Mary does press on, working her way to the centre of resistance, tolerating personal disappointments, just as Charley shoulders his way upward to become an overweight, hard-drinking, woman-hungry financial speculator. While still the Camera Eye records the inward symptoms of unease beneath the desperate energy:

> the personality must be kept carefully adjusted over
> the face

to facilitate recognition she pins on each of us a badge
today entails tomorrow
Thank you but why me? Inhibited? Indeed goodbye
The old brown hat flopped faithful on the chair beside
the door successfully snatched.[127]

Dos Passos writes of a Greenwich Village party. Such a retreat from the superficiality of 'hobohemia' is easily understood – but where does it lead? To a confused passivity in the face of the protean stream of life, ubiquitous but uncapturable, and still more attractive than the civilised babble of cocktail parties. In Camera Eye 46 the terms of this self-division are made more overt. The author has made a radical commitment of a kind, but he is oppressed by doubts. The ruling class is strong and ruthless, the masses are weak and divided; he senses the falsity of his own position as a liberal intellectual who, in his speechmaking, is expected to arouse his audience with dramatic slogans when he would prefer to urge on them his own attitude of sceptical enquiry.

'Peeling the speculative onion of doubt',[128] wearing 'the old raincoat of incertitude',[129] which he cannot agree to trade in for a doctrinaire creed, Dos Passos looks upon himself as 'an unidentified stranger hat pulled down over the has he any? face.'[130] The Camera Eyes of The Big Money are technically alert for the need to express the dimensions of crisis which overwhelmed Dos Passos when he got back from Europe. The former simple delight in basic sensory experience – as of a child, or a soldier plucking a flower in the midst of war – is denied to the adult civilian, and the poetic form tautens. Lyricism is sharpened by irony, blown up into crazy farce, or associated with the angry eloquence of social protest. Farce occurs in the pivotal Camera Eye 48: returning to the United States after his Spanish trip in 1923, Dos Passos overhears an obscure quarrel between some Cuban passengers on the boat. It signifies his farewell to the 'gesture of Castile' – natural, spontaneous private life, quixotically free from the shadow of institutions. Taking up life in America again means reassuming the problems he had previously attempted to face, and which had the effect of making him doubt his own sincerity. Predictions of crisis glow in a new cast of metaphor, as though Dos Passos had absorbed the works of English poets of the Auden school: 'the landscape corroded with literature' (Iberia); 'the multitudinous flickering dazzle of light' (from machinery); 'Venus's dangerous toe' (a venereal infection); cash difficulties 'as inevitable as visas'.[131] They suggest the galvanic shocks of a man poised between the actuality of his own consciousness and the hallucinatory whirl of the social reality he must focus on.

At this point – almost exactly half-way through the novel – each of the main fictional characters has reached a crisis point in his or her life.

Charley Anderson, on the rebound from Doris Humphries, has signed up with Tern Aviation of Detroit. Mary French has broken off her relationship with George Barrow and left for New York. Margo Dowling has eloped to Cuba. But each reacts differently to the patterns of engrammatic shock. Charley clings to an illusory success-credo with an increasing neurotic desperation that prevents him adjusting to reality. Instead, he resorts to anodynes that grow into addictive vices; when things go wrong he doubles his bets. He is trapped in a spiral of drinking, whoring, enervating late nights. Like a front-line pilot whose every mission may prove to be his last, Charley celebrates his triumphs with a juvenile recklessness and unwinds in repeated orgies of self-indulgence. In this behaviour-pattern lies the foundation of the charge that he has tried to cash in on his war record, has exhausted his credit. Ironically, this is true: the individualistic striver has become what others have made of him. For though Charley never counts coup or consciously exploits his wartime reputation, he retains the psychological habits of the active-serviceman and his associates see him as an ex-ace using his rank in civilian life. He is as trapped as a pendulum; whatever happens to him in Detroit and afterwards is additional proof that he has lost, and the dream recedes as fast as ever he stretches out to grasp it.

Mary French's story has an opposite significance: it is precisely by choosing to meet a bitter reality head-on that she forfeits her humanity. The humanitarian impulses she has learned from her father become narrowed and annealed, by inductive stages, into the iron militancy of the Communist convert. The steel strike in Pittsburgh is the first crucial encounter: Dos Passos paints – in the portrait of Ted Healey, the bigoted editor making a show of impartial news-reporting – a classic type of compromiser. Mary's political development is fully accounted for by such men and events: the concrete instances of cruelty or humbug which, in actual life-experience, may persuade one to change sides, or to adopt completely a previously hedged commitment. Mary's ironic fate is that she does finally align experience and belief – at a high cost. She had accepted long before, when she refused Joe Denny's stammered proposal, that she would have to renounce the consolations of personal happiness. But she discovers also that even such values as honesty, loyalty and comradeship are made victims of the exigencies of organised radicalism. With Benny Compton, and particularly with Don Stevens, there occasionally sputters the hope of a warmer personal relationship than that of fellow-workers in the cause – but the cause itself extinguishes such hopes. Mary voluntarily accepts misery and drudgery worse than that of the workers she is resolved to help – but at least she does so by intelligently facing the truth that one may be sentenced to choose between two incompatible objects of desire. Charley never realises this: as Arthur Mizener has pointed out, he shares the fallacy of Clyde Griffiths and Jay Gatsby.[132]

He equates material prosperity with spiritual self-fulfilment, and especially with erotic and romantic images of the good life. Completely unable to recognise the real nature of the fast, aggressive world into which he has plunged, he 'dies without ever understanding what has happened to him.'[133]

These two modes of choosing – risking all to win all, and losing, or subjecting the private self to a demoralising discipline of struggle – are mirrored in the anxious dialogue which the author conducts with himself in the Camera Eyes. But there is yet another way, at once hard-headed and fantastic, beset with vagaries, in which advantages are thrown away knowingly as a sentimental impulse, cruelties are compounded, good fortune stumbled across by bluff or coincidence and just as casually revoked. Several reviewers have written of Margo Dowling as though she were an amoral slut rising by pussy-power. Actually, she is 'a fundamentally decent human being ... shrewd and brave and tough enough to succeed in the savage world that has destroyed Charley'[134] – and her story keeps alive the otherwise curiously absent (except in the Newsreels) mythic quality of the twenties as it has survived in the popular imagination. Margo is unique; a real hybrid of the life- and death-instincts in her native civilisation, and Dos Passos' master-stroke of characterisation. She is the fantasy-woman counterpart to the nightmare-women in Dos Passos' work who are point-blank destructive. From the little girl feeling so 'proudhappy'[135] when her father is affectionately sober to the still young but obsolescent movie queen, she exhibits, along with native fascination, both a pardonable shrewdness of egoism and a responsiveness to the qualified, threatened warmth of human relations. While Charley Anderson and Mary French struggle through turbulent currents to disillusioning encounters with the unpleasant facts of the causes they had idealised, Margo floats on the wave-top like an errant, unsinkable cork. After a series of random adventures, she is washed up on the Barbary shore, where she, the tough and independent waif who does what comes naturally, is transformed by the Hollywood grotesque Margolies into a glamorous dream-idol of the nation. She, too, is fated to lose by her immersion into a huge, artificial fantasy; for only in its particulars does her personal history differ from those of the other characters. Each portrays one aspect of the twenties: the feverish industrial boom based on new technology developed during the war; the growing movement of political opposition that was to culminate in the violent polarities of the Sacco–Vanzetti case; and the new 'opium of the people' that reflected contemporary values in the distorted images of commercial entertainment.

The twenties began to be mythologised as soon as they were over,[136] but Dos Passos, though occasionally satirising their absurdities, is little interested in contributing to this process. Writing a trilogy that covers more than a quarter of a century of American history, he is more concerned in *The Big Money* to develop the themes foreshadowed in the first pages of *The Forty Second Parallel*, and his hand has grown surer as he has progressed. *The Big Money*, the longest of the three novels, is the most satisfying; the tensions chosen to dynamise its theme (which partly mirror the author's own divided outlook) are lucidly and coherently employed. The most fundamental tension is a political one, between the hope that the radicals are right, and will win, and the fear that their struggle contains the seeds of its own failure. From 1925 onwards, Dos Passos had begun to move – never unreservedly, but with deliberation – from the position of a sympathetic observer to a closer, more active association with proletarian politics. He had helped found the New Playwrights Theatre, where some of his own work was produced; had acted as 'contributing editor' for the *New Masses*; had, with Dreiser and others, investigated conditions among the striking miners in Kentucky, where he had been indicted under criminal syndicalism laws. But he never ceased to view himself as basically a writer and intellectual whose duty was principally to urge reform through the pressure of ideas. In 1930 he wrote:

> But there is a layer: engineers, scientists, independent manual craftsmen, writers, artists, actors, technicians of one sort or another who, insofar as they are good at their jobs, are a necessary part of any industrial society . . . If you could once convince them of the fact that their jobs don't depend on capitalism they'd find that they could afford to be humane. The time to reach these people is now, when the series of stock market crashes must have proved to the more intelligent that their much talked of participation in capital through stockholdings was just about the sort of participation a man playing roulette has in the funds of the gambling house whether he's winning or losing. As a writer I belong to that class whether I like it or not, and I think most men who graduate from working with their hands into desk jobs eventually belong to it, no matter what their ideas are. You can call 'em intellectuals or liberals or petty bourgeoisie or any other dirty name but it won't change 'em any. What you've got to do is convince the technicians and white collar workers that they have nothing to lose.[137]

Beneath the confused terminology and the horrible affectations of a 'popular' style appear two ideas. One is the Orwellian preoccupation with an appeal to the classes who may be tempted to turn fascist in the slump, the other a distinct *liking* for these classes as 'independent craftsmen' with a production ethic; it echoes Thorstein Veblen. Though Dos Passos tends to lump together technicians and the intelligentsia with an *omnium gatherum* of the skilled and professional classes, his fiction concentrates on the disintegration of intellectuals (Herf, Savage, Morehouse) who throw away their souls. Not until *The Big Money* is there a recognisable portrait of the Veblenian hero – and even there the hero shares the fate of the intellectuals. Charley Anderson features in a squalid anti-tragedy largely because he remains hypnotised by the quest for the big money. Charley reiterates, in phrases that grow hollower as they grow more and more remote from the reality of his practical work-life, 'I'm a mechanic. That's all.'[138] Yet apart from his early spells of aero-engineering at Askew-Merritt, Charley's connection with the avia-tion industry is as a frenzied financier of the most unproductive kind. He has joined the leisure class. And no wonder: the status of the money-man not only means big profits for the price of a phone call, but it is glori-fied by every current canon of social worthiness. Nothing illustrates this better than the echo of Charley's own words in Nat Benton's dismissive comment on the dead Bill Cermak. ' "After all" said Nat, "he was only a mechanic".'[139]

So Dos Passos never carries the cult of the self-sufficient technician to vulgar excess, because he demonstrates infallibly in his fiction all the dreaded situations which elsewhere he attempts to prescribe against. The technician lives in a global crisis which makes him choose, or suffer the consequences of failing to choose, his allegiances. Anderson is essen-tially an apolitical figure – completely so in the beginning, when he good-naturedly shrugs off Don Stevens's blunt question, 'Tell us what aviators think about. Are they for the exploiting class or the working-class?'[140] However, political events catch up with him. Thus when he faces a labour dispute at Tern Aviation his attitude is compounded of annoyance, self-justification and bewilderment; putting the manage-ment's case to Bill Cermak, he blurts out a kind of illiterate self-history – and the defences of a potential bully:

'But damn it, Bill, why can't you tell those guys to have a little patience . . . we're workin' out a profitsharin' scheme. I've worked on a lathe myself . . . I've worked as mechanic all over this goddam country . . . We've got a responsibility toward our investors . . . If every department don't click like a machine we're rooked. If the boys want a union we'll give 'em a union. You get up a meeting and tell 'em how we feel about it, but tell 'em we've got to have some patriotism . . .'[141]

This is the speech of a man who throws fistfuls of money about in nightclubs and fires servants in a moment's snap of temper: 'social existence determines consciousness', and Charley's consciousness has grown out of his role. Moreover, Dos Passos has set his story in a tri-angular frame of Biographies of eminent Americans who variously typify the aptitudes of Charley Anderson and the penalties or temptations to which they are subject. Frederick Winslow Taylor is chosen as the instance of the practical American engineer who, working at his craft with a selfless and impartial dedication, finds that his pioneer work is made to serve the interests of 'a lot of greedy smalleyed Dutchmen'.[142] Dos Passos stresses the actual neutrality of the *techniques* developed by Taylor (they are used by the young Soviet republic to train workers in its new industries) but his chief aim is to display how these techniques are perverted by a social system based on the profit motive, and this critique is echoed by the cadences in 'Tin Lizzie' that expose the meaning of Ford's mass-production efficiency and paternalism:

> The American Plan; automotive prosperity seeping down
> from above; it turned out there were strings to it.
> But that five dollars a day
> paid to good, clean American workmen
> who didn't drink or smoke cigarettes or read or think,
> and who didn't commit adultery
> and whose wives didn't take in boarders,
> made American once more the Yukon of the sweated
> workers of the world.[143]

Ford the 'passionate antiquarian' makes nonsense of the past by tearing its treasures out of their context and re-erecting them as a monument to his wealth, but it is hard to imagine the author sharing Taylor's sincere indifference to the European heritage. In the Biography of Thorstein Veblen, it is counted in his favour that he has not only read and translated the Norse sagas of his own cultural tradition but has acquainted himself with philosophy and the classics. Indeed, the Veblen piece is the most unreservedly favourable of all the Biographies in *The Big Money*. Veblen was not only an eccentric who 'got in wrong' by refusing to pay his ritual homage to Mammon, but a thinker who

> pointed out the alternatives; a warlike society strangled by the bureaucracies of the monopolies forced by the law of diminishing returns to grind down more and more the common man for profits, or a new matter-of-fact commensense society dominated by needs of the men and women who did the work and the incredibly vast opportunities for peace and plenty offered by the progress of technology.[144]

Here the author reveals all too plainly his defects as a polemicist. When he forsakes destructive irony to praise his subject, he only succeeds in diminishing him through the vague and windy formulations of straight political journalism. Yet the Biographies are not to be read in isolation, and Dos Passos' strength as a novelist lies in the manner in which he distributes stress and significance between the juxtaposed sections. The doubts and inconsistencies he is prepared to avow are re-fracted through his fiction in a dynamically proportioned conflict. Pat-terns established by the biographical sketches of real Americans – concise mixtures of fact and commentary – illuminate and deepen the stories of the fictitious characters, who are shown directly as they undergo their experience, fact and commentary inseparably fused. Charley may partake of Taylor's innocent pragmatism, Ford's egoistic ambition and Veblen's imprudent sensuality, but he is not a simple residue of these qualities; as a figure in the narrative he is entirely under the imaginative control of the author. The detailed concrete information about Charley that accumu-lates from moment to moment is specific and sequential: it gathers up his experience in a flow of sense-data which, in its full weight and worth, records what Charley is. The epic Americans of the Biographies are classic and monumental, each fact – Taylor's leather sleeping-harness, Ford's squirrels – picked to assume its place in a definitive summation. Charley's identity is thrown together piecemeal, compounded of innumerable stimuli, constantly built up like a coral reef until his death obliterates it. Often Dos Passos concentrates on the passive, impressionable side of Charley's nature:

> Charley was following Doris's slender back, the hollow between the shoulderblades where his hand would like to be, across the red carpet, between the white tables, the men's starched shirts, the women's shoulders, through the sizzly smell of champagne and welshrabbit and hot chafingdishes, across a corner of the dancefloor among the sway-ing couples to where the rest of them were already settled. The knives and forks shone among the stiff creases of the fresh tablecloth.[145]

At such moments, when Charley is pathetically intoxicated with the rare and pristine appeal of things – pitiful phantoms of his heart's desire – Charley Anderson the driven climber dissolves into the furniture. The pressure of social typology slackens; the Lardnerian situation of the dupe and his bauble melts in a pang. If Dos Passos were an author given to dramatic crises, it is at such moments that the crucial battles would be lost. All the motion and drama of the Biographies recedes, and in the syntactical progression is merely the ghost of an epiphany. The picture is rendered in detail, but the meaning emerges as a cluster of engrams: it stands for nothing else. Above all, such passages underscore the truth that 'his characters are primarily victims; they do not act as much as undergo things'.[146] In Charley's case, the one creative and purposeful achievement of his life – his invention of the new aeroplane starter – has occurred outside the action of the novel; everything thereafter arises by way of his reactions to the initiatives of others or through the effect of impersonal circumstances. A foggy but obsessive mythology clouds his brain. Whenever an example of one of his dream objectives wanders near (a rich, attractive woman – any rich, attractive woman) he reacts like a thermal fire-sprinkler automatically squirting water when a critical temperature is reached.

It cannot be said of Margo, however, that she *simply* 'undergoes things'. It is more that she manages to be in tune with things, infinitely adaptable and with the saving grace of resilience – though lacking the hollow hardness of Elaine Thatcher. In contrast with Charley's unthinking assumptions about the future (and his subsequent pained bafflement when that future fails to materialise) Margo is drawn as an active, planning creature: 'A career was something everybody had in New York and Margo decided she had one too'.[147] 'She'd get more for the ring at a hockshop if she didn't barge in on an empty stomach, was what she was thinking'. [148] Margo can even ask Charley for a cheque as he lies on his deathbed without appearing callous. And she relates naturally to the two 'show-business' Biographies in the first half of the novel. Both celebrate the charisma of individual American performers: Isadora Duncan, whose dedication to 'art' exceeded her gift for dancing, and Valentino the ghost-faced immigrant whose death caused a shock-wave of vicarious grief. They are the only biographical subjects in the trilogy to lay any claim to 'art', but actually many more serious candidates could have been chosen. What Dos Passos sees in their lives are the dithyrambic urges of the free spirit, identified with the frontier tradition of American democracy – 'She was an American like Walt Whitman; the murdering rulers of the world were not her people; artists were not on the side of the machineguns; she was an American in a Greek tunic; she was for the people'[149] – and the mass neuroses of the manipulated herd, who crave to fill the emptiness of their lives with images of the cinematic dream-lover – 'While he lay in state covered with a cloth of gold, tens of thousands of men, women, and children packed the streets outside . . . All the ambulances in that part of the city were busy carting off women who'd fainted, girls who'd been stepped on. Epileptics threw fits. Cops collected little groups of abandoned children'[150] – and Margo personifies both tendencies, inductively pursued through a bizarre and complicated private life until she surrenders to the Hollywood process which will institutionalise her for ever.

For Margo can never be a totally free agent. Fenian McCreary, leading an equally peripatetic life, found scope in the pre-1917 world for a series of rough and ready adventures. It was part of his failure that they led to no positive end. The chief characters of *The Big Money* are all eventually swallowed by one or other of the dominant collective organisms of their time. Margo is no exception. Under the tutelage of Margolies, she is destined to be 'the nation's newest sweetheart' – a commodity for public consumption until a newer sweetheart makes her appearance. In fact a fast-changing technology obviates her usefulness as the 'talkies' are developed. In *The Big Money* there is a protracted tension between the struggle of the human will and the social forces which parallels the central image of a conflict between the common people and the power of the 'interests'. This conflict is openly treated in the final sections of the book: the continuing history of Mary French and the later Camera Eyes and Biographies. 'Towards Margo Dowling . . . he maintains and communicates that attitude of wonder never quite dispelled'[151] – but what of Mary French? She is not unsympathetic, but her story is told with a detached pity, perhaps due to the author's conviction that 'I should stick to the position of observer, I did not think it was my business to picket or march'.[152] Mary French lives in the thick of the struggle; she does picket and march, sacrificing for her beliefs the affluence and comfort of the bourgeois existence that might so easily be hers. Yet in comparison with the impassioned denunciations of the last three Camera Eyes, Dos Passos' treatment of her situation is cool or satirical.

Mary acquires her political allegiance in the course of very particularised and first-hand experiences, but it becomes an all-consuming purpose: it allows her to ignore personal disappointments, makes personal matters in general less important. Yet for Dos Passos the prevalence of a disinterested passion that does not feed off familiar love-objects and people is suspect; and he is not naturally gifted at portraying its manifestations. While the descriptions of strikes and demonstrations are able and perceptive, the few lines of ideological discussion he gives to his creations are sketchy:

'I hadn't wanted to tell you, but they want me to lead a strike over in Bayonne . . . rayonworkers . . . you know the old munition-plants made over to make artificial silk . . . It's a tough town and the workers are so poor they can't pay their union dues . . . but they got a fine radical union over there. It's important to get a foothold in the new industries . . . that's where the old sellout organizations of the A.F. of L. are failing'.[153]

The ellipses are the author's, and one feels they would be unnecessary if Dos Passos' ear for dialogue had not failed him. Much more convincing are the cynical interpolations of Jerry Burnham. Wisely, the transliteration of radical debate is kept to a minimum. He shows respect for Mary, though in her final scene, after the execution of Sacco and Vanzetti, after her betrayal by Stevens, after the sickening party with Eveline Johnson and her crowd of parlour-pinks and bohemian plush-horses, she recommits herself to the battle. In the last sentence of the narrative, she is seen preparing herself for yet another protest campaign, ready to wear herself out or live life in the shadows for a cause she believes to be necessary and heroic.

But if Dos Passos is relatively aloof and cautious in his portrayal of organised dissent, he raises his voice in the Camera Eyes. Here he can identify the victims of oppression with the evidence of his own senses, and established his indignation on positivistic grounds of American history rather than on philosophical precepts. 'Walking from Plymouth to North Plymouth through the raw air of Massachussetts Bay at each step a small cold squudge through the sole of one shoe . . . this where the immigrants landed the roundheads the sackers of castles the king-killers haters of oppression . . .'[154] In the undeniable facts of personal experience and the almost equally vivid race-memories of what America has symbolised for the 'huddled masses yearning to breathe free' are the clues and images of his own protest. Dos Passos can be penguin-like with words. When he tries to argue polemically he waddles and flaps, but in the fresher water of poetic statement he achieves emotional power and lucidity:

. . . their hired men sit on the judge's bench they sit back with their feet on the tables under the dome of the State House they are ignorant of our beliefs they have the dollars the guns the armed forces the powerplants . . .

America our nation has been beaten by strangers who have bought the laws and fenced off their meadows and cut down the woods for pulp and turned our pleasant cities into slums and sweated the wealth out of our people and when they want to they hire the executioner to throw the switch.[155]

Such passages do have the air of a 'furious and sombre poem':[156] but they are not informed by any intellectual commitment to the left. Essentially patriotic, the deep, angry alienation which they convey is accompanied by an almost dismayingly reckless acknowledgment that the cause is lost. 'We stand defeated America'.[157] 'We have only words against / Power Superpower'.[158] *The Big Money* is not specifically Dos Passos' renunciation of his leftist sympathies but it is far from normatively radical in tendency. Dos Passos' sensibility is that of the artist, not of the conceptual political thinker; his attitudes are empirical, just as his primary tendency in literature is realistic. As a result, the imagery of political struggle in post-war America is harnessed to a view of life that stresses the immediate and specific – even if these are viewed along a lengthy historical time-scale. Despair predominates. It is undeniable that Dos Passos' writing is marked by a 'relative neglect of ideas and emotions';

in particular, a neglect of any discursive approach to political ideology. The supreme quality of the Camera Eyes is their seismographic closeness to areas of personal disturbance that are amplified in the main text. *The Big Money* is a novel of defeat. The deaths of Sacco and Vanzetti mark the end of a chapter, not a new beginning. The concluding Biographies deal with two 'rogue' millionaires who used the power of wealth to subvert the democratic process. Both Hearst and Insull were alive in 1936 (though Insull had been 'rumbled') and in the *ad hominem* reproaches Dos Passos addresses to each there is angry grief, as though they are the contemptible victors left on a battlefield of noble corpses. This, and the last famous picture of 'Vag' trudging along the highway while above him soars an aeroplane carrying 'big men with bank accounts, highly paid jobs, who are saluted by doormen',[159] round off the work with an image of universal hopelessness. 'Vag' is walking from nowhere to nowhere; the executive vomiting his lunch in mid-air is no happier or more purposeful. The striving for faith has been cancelled out by the persistence of doubt and pessimism.

The coexistence of political imagery and a fundamental scepticism in *USA* made it a needlessly complicated puzzle for critics: Lionel Trilling wrote:

> . . . to discover a political negativism in the despair of *U.S.A.* is to subscribe to a naïve conception of human emotion and human experience. It is to assert that the despair of a literary work must inevitably engender despair in the reader . . . the word 'despair' all by itself (or any other such general word or phrase) can never characterize the emotion the artist is dealing with. There are many kinds of despair and what is really important is what goes along with the general emotion denoted by the word. Despair with its wits about it is very different from the despair that is stupid; despair that is an abandonment of illusion is very different from despair which generates tender new cynicisms.[160]

Yet any number of liberal categories of despair will not erase the fact that the typical feeling of *USA* is entropic despair. True enough, the man who felt despair-in-the-bone might never write at all, but the quality of the author's energising impulse is precisely the artist's commitment to record experience in a manner that honestly registers its significance. And Dos Passos' conception of this duty is highly traditional – the selfsame conception that has underlain his work since the story of Martin Howe: '. . . pencil scrawls in my notebook the scraps of recollection the broken halfphrases the effort to intersect word with word to dovetail clause with clause to rebuild out of mangled memories unshakably (Oh Pontius Pilate) the truth.'[161]

Yes, what is truth? Dos Passos' art springs from the patent, empirical (and partial) observation of truth. This is not, though, simply the 'inner truth' of the introspective writer seeking spiritual verities: it is cinematically alert for all the detritus of experience – personal, material, historical. America of the post-depression years, with its time-honoured myths exploded, offered to artists like Dos Passos the perfect landscape of devastation. As his fellow-author on the Harlan County investigations observed:

> Faster cars, more efficient machinery, more and more towering sky-scrapers erected in record time, subway trains screeching the extreme necessity of speed, more and larger cities, more business, more cares and duties – as though we, of all people, were ordered not only to mechanize but to populate the world! But just why? For any known event or spiritual reason? Rather, it seems to me that in this atmos-phere, the mental and physical condition of millions of people have already 'blown up' or are about to. They live and die without tasting anything really worth while. The average individual today is really tortured; he is so numerous, so meaningless, so wholly confused and defeated.[162]

But to pass from the certainty of observation to the exhausting and contentious path of active opposition is no easy matter. The strength of *USA* lies in its honest, unflagging exegesis of the particular in a form that presents life with the brilliant yet limited accuracy of the novel; Dos Passos had dug into his native culture for the words and symbols to realise it in all its variety – and in its essential entropy. *USA* is not informed by the global philosophy of Marxism but by a view of human existence as ultimately planless. Dos Passos' treatment by critics on the left, at first effuse and later hypocritically savage and abusive, illustrates both the relevance of his chosen subject-matter and the neces-sary risks of being misunderstood that are run by an author who at-tempts to adapt the novel to the kind of reality so powerfully conveyed by the cinema – a graphically mimetic persuasiveness, a versatility of scope and angle, an ability to blend poetic and realistic modes. Whatever Dos Passos' extra-literary associations with the platforms of the left may have meant to him personally, they cannot be adduced as evidence in judging his trilogy, which is *sui generis*. The resonance of its protest, expressed in a chosen and practised medium, is not reducible to a four-square political argument, and Dos Passos cannot say with Ruskin that 'I feel the force of mechanism and the fury of avaricious commerce to be at present so irresistible, that I have seceded from the study not only of architecture, but nearly of all art; and have given myself as I would in a besieged city, to seek the best modes of getting bread and water for its multitudes.'[163]

Even so, it is not possible to dismiss the question of politics. The rhetoric of radical dissent is an inseparable part of the content of *USA*. It is relevantly there as a facet of the total reality surveyed, but additionally as a major element of structure and meaning. The most prominent of the fictional characters – Mac, Morehouse, Eveline, Richard Savage, Joe Williams, Charley Anderson, Mary French – lead lives that are heavily touched by defeat. They are not all losers of the same kind: some, in their own terms, succeed, but only at the cost of denying every worthwhile human impulse. Others – Joe, particularly – experience nothing but misery and injustice. Losing is so universal that it overlays the 'two nations' theme. Yet one of the means of dramatising that boundless gulf between the legendary promise of what life in America ought to be and the hideous facts is to show the two in suspenseful interaction. As the trilogy progresses through its three stages the reader is enabled to contrast engrammatic defeat and disappointment with the national dream of individual opportunity; the liberal dream of inspirational war-aims; and the supernational dream of the libertarian future. In this fashion, the lesson that life can never live up to the expectations men place in it, that men themselves cannot live up to their own aspirations and that the world cannot be meaningfully interpreted for our comfort emerges powerfully from the aesthetic data of the trilogy. In the rhetoric of *USA*, radical dissent contributes – especially in *The Big Money* – a provision for judging and placing the efforts of the various characters in their blind and futile struggles to redeem the absurdity of the world they inhabit. It also helps to substitute for the bleak neutrality of *Manhattan Transfer* the writer's protest against the entropy he must accept – a protest self-contained in the pages of the trilogy itself. For this reason, among others, *USA* must stand as a major work of defiant pessimism.

5 'Rejoining the United States': *District of Columbia* and the Later Fiction

'It was somewhere during the years of the early New Deal that I rejoined the United States'.[1] Dos Passos' private secession at the time of the Sacco–Vanzetti executions had not led him to join any organised movement of dissent: he retreated, as he wrote, into this 'private conscience'. But he was still politically alert, and his activities led him naturally into contact with Communists. His experiences were disillusioning. Among the Harlan County miners and in Spain, Dos Passos was shocked by the ruthlessness and cynicism of those who professed to be fighting for the just society. Even in *USA*, one had sensed the repercussions of this in the harsh discipline of the party tacticians, the treatment of Mary French by Don Stevens, the air of conspiracy and deceit. Yet there it had formed, in the total context of the work, a mid-point of reflecting ironies between the terrible tragedy of the Sacco–Vanzetti affair and the entropic lives of the characters enmeshed in a sordid struggle for wealth and power. There was no direct assault upon the Communist faith.

However, Dos Passos' next book – and the first of a succeeding trilogy – begins to show a new line of development. The individual hero of the novel is Glenn Spotswood, son of a Columbia professor and the heir to a family tradition of moral idealism. This idealism is predominantly Christian. Glenn's grandfather, Old Soul, speaks of Andrew Jackson as a 'great heart and a Christian Gentleman'[2] to Mrs Spotswood, his daughter-in-law. Herbert Spotswood, the father, loses his academic post through his opposition to American involvement in the First World War. The unpopularity of his stand is mirrored in the family quarrel at Thanksgiving dinner, in which Uncle Mat provokes Herbert by his outspoken denunciation of 'conscientious objectors and disloyal elements'.[3] Herbert's religious tendency is not purely contemplative, but entails the application of Christian precepts to social and secular matters. For this reason, he 'gets in bad' and the family is divided (rather along Herf–

Merivale lines) between the Spotswoods and their conforming cousins. Tyler, however – Glenn's elder brother – accepts the draft.

Herbert Spotswood's ethical rigour limits his practicality and his ability to understand those who do compromise or adapt. Though Glen resents his father's preaching, it is he who is destined to follow the path of idealism. But it is not a route he at first chooses for himself. 'The parental bent' is a source of irritation to him, and as he listens to his father's complacent reminiscences over the tea-table he feels 'his mouth hardening with dislike' at the basic egotism of Herbert's conversation. Glenn, like Jimmy Herf, has been closer to 'Muddy' – and her death has both emotional and practical consequences for him. It means that her annuity ceases, and he is obliged to 'go out and scratch', as he puts it.

Adventures of a Young Man is therefore Glenn Spotswood's personal odyssey, and to relate the story Dos Passos has jettisoned the multifocal techniques that he employed in the creation of *USA*. 'The result is a book that reads more like other people's novels than anything Dos Passos has written'.[4] Glenn Spotswood, though, is not drawn to the life of art, as the heroes of the early work were, but to the cause of political radicalism, and it is the successive stages of this process which supply the core of the book.

Glenn's first job is as camp counsellor at Camp Winnesquam under the tutelage of Dr Talcott. Glenn is sixteen and his adolescent self-consciousness is pictured in the familiarly flat, concise sentences: 'He fell into a kind of daze looking at half his face in the narrow strip of mirror that edged the dial of the scales. He hated how he looked. His nose had a knobbly pasty look. His reddish hair had a silly-looking wave in it. One gray eye looked back at him dolefully.'[5] Glenn is never quite to lose this uncertainty and self-doubt. Unlike his father, who never questions the rightness of his own imperatives, Glenn has a fatally divided nature. One side of him responds to Paul Graves, the Southerner only 'a couple of years older than Glenn'[6] who has immense self-possession without taking refuge in dogmatism or blind inflexibility. 'Paul has the pragmatic experimental, and inductive qualities of mind that mark the scientist and the democratic American'.[7] Instinctively, Glenn follows Paul's leadership – follows it into hot water when Paul is fired from the camp for having invented a game for the boys based on the civil war raging in Russia. Glenn 'gets in bad' with the hideous Talcotts for supporting his friend. As a result, he is more or less disowned by Herbert Spotswood, whose pompous letter of reproach echoes the accents of Wenny's clergyman father.

The developments of the first section have therefore concentrated on placing Glenn in a familiar position – that of a virtual orphan who must seek his own way in the world. Glenn's manner of facing the 'temptations and brutalities'[8] that lie ahead of him is classically predictable. He becomes a 'vag'. At the end of his first year in a 'cow college', Glenn takes off West, in the company first of a fellow student who accepts the doctrines of Henry George, then of a Wobbly 'working stiff', Ben Doe. Ben preaches working-class direct action, but his taste for liquor, gambling and whores proves him to be as inadequate a guide to practical living as the pious single-taxer. Glenn's vacation adventures, though, have introduced him to 'real life'. He has been prepared to accept the influence of his next mentors, Mike and Marice Gulick. In the company of this bohemian–academic pair, he moves to New York.

The Gulicks are essentially shallow people who flirt with ideas: Dos Passos brings to his satirical portrayal of them much of the contempt he has shown previously for hobohemia. But through their milieu swim types who are less foolishly inconsequential and whose portraits are drawn with a thoroughly vindictive animus. Boris Spingarn and Gladys Funaroff practically compete with each other in their dry and abstract fanaticism. There is much talk of 'bourgeois liberalism' and 'social fascists', and the thickening atmosphere of political intrigue is accompanied by a depiction of the radical intellectuals' private lives which suggests low standards of personal morality. Glenn himself is rather the poor relation of the scene, but his growing commitment to the revolutionary cause is serious. Hard on the heels of his sexual disillusion with Gladys comes a vision – reported in a style familiar from *Manhattan Transfer* – of a future in which his life will acquire meaning from its service to a greater, impersonal end:

> Inside his head he was standing on a platform in a great crowded hall hung with red bunting, haking himself a speech: Wasn't it about time Glenn Spotswood stopped working himself up about his own private life, his own messy little five-and-ten-cent store pulpmagazine libido . . . The new Glenn Spotswood . . . was going on, without any private life, renouncing the capitalist world and its pomps, the new Glenn Spotswood had come there tonight to offer himself . . . to the revolutionary working class.[9]

The tone of solemn mockery is patent: it is almost Jimmy Herf to the life. Yet Glenn is not to remain a half-baked, hypersensitive young man picking at the scabs on his soul. His faith will grow more intense – despite the villainous factional disputes he observes at first hand, and despite the author's clumsy and mystifying handling of the story. For the very next chapter opens with an episode repeated almost entire from *Manhattan Transfer*, even to the 'lamb chops and baked potatoes'. Herbert Spotswood proposes to his son that he should accept a position in Uncle Matthew's bank. Herbert, though still avowing his pacifism, claims that he has come to recognise that 'there's a certain selfindulgence in extremism'.[10] Glenn answers in a series of stereotypical Marxist slogans. But the conflict is curiously dissipated. Glenn agrees to try the job – for what reason is never made clear – and the scene ends with Glenn leaving for a visit to Paul Graves, who has found his vocation as a plant geneticist. Glenn's enthusiasm for the radical cause is not to Paul's taste. His cultivation of the dispassionate methods of the scientist have begun to supersede his former political sympathies, and his attitude to the Soviet republic is modified by caution. 'The only thing, Paul said, yawning and shaking the sand off his feet on the porch, was not to make up your mind before you began the experiment. If you really wanted to find out facts you had to take your preconceived notions and put them in a tin box and lock them up in the safe.'[11]

The empiricist warning against Utopian doctrinaire schemes could not be much clearer. It will be Paul Graves's function throughout the novel to act as a kind of 'control', illuminating by contrast the errors and misconceptions of Glenn Spotswood, and he is revived in the final volume of the Spotswood trilogy in much the same role. Glenn, meanwhile, is headed for Horton, where the East Coast National Bank is awaiting its college-educated recruit. But even here, under the aegis of his Uncle Mat and Aunt Harriet, Glenn feels the pull of politics. He finds the opportunity to meet workers actively involved in class struggle – the striking Mexican pecan-shellers – and he encounters another life-guide in the person of Jed Farrington. Jed has 'got in wrong' by his blend of dissipation and unpopular opinions; he is sympathetically portrayed, as are the Mexicans. They are genuinely exploited, and their efforts to improve their lot through the only method they have are admirable; but the central theme of conflict between the concrete, familiar and practical and the formulations of political dogmatists is repeated with the arrival of a party agitator from New York.

> As soon as Jed opened the door of the back office he could hear a loud Brooklyn voice saying, 'We must turn every courtroom into a school for the workers'. A thin young man with closecropped hair and goldrimmed tortoiseshell spectacles was walking up and down with his necktie flying. 'It doesn't matter if we lose one case or a hundred cases as long as the workers are made to realize the significance of revolutionary Marxism'.[12]

This is Irving Silverstone, the party gramophone quite impervious to the ordinary human needs of the workers. Silverstone is calm and rationalistic, seemingly in contradistinction to Mr Punjabi, the bogus mystic handling Aunt Harriet's financial affairs. But in the last half of the novel it becomes plain that characters like Silverstone, Jane Sparling and ultimately Jed Farrington are frauds and parasites. Glenn's next step is to take the part of organiser with the Kentucky miners: this section occupies two long chapters, and represents a severe weakening of the author's powers. When one recalls the 'Mac' chapters of *The Forty Second Parallel*, in which Dos Passos' imagination produced and rendered his character's adventures with clarity, tension and versatile sympathy, the Slade County episodes seem almost inexplicably dull and awkwardly handled.

The failure is not inexplicable, though: for Dos Passos has begun to write fiction in which the hero's defeat is not *shown*, engrammatically, but *ascribed* to one principal cause or defect. The displacement of the agnostic desire to exhibit the nature of defeat by a reductive urge to account for it strikes at the living core of Dos Passos' art. Situations previously dramatised with a resourceful skill are now manipulated to serve a hypothesis or a prejudice. In *Adventures of a Young Man* this condition has not become absolute. Much of the confusion which disfigures the latter part arises from this uneasy mixture of two incompatible attitudes. The old Dos Passos – the writer who could evoke with cinematic completeness all the immediate sense-data of a situation, is not dead; but he coexists with a sour, cantankerous and crudely didactic journalist. Within a few pages of each other, for example, one can find passages like this:

> He couldn't sleep. He lay on his back staring at the flicker of the firelight among the cobwebs that hung looped from the rafters overhead. Cold spurts of wind came in through the chinks in the boards under his back. Excitement made his heart thump and made the skin round his eyes feel tight; his face had a scalded feeling from the long drive through the winddriven rain.[13]

And this:

> 'Here we have a chance to organize a group of absolutely untouched militant American workers. It's the start of a series of real revolutionary industrial unions. These miners drink the class struggle with their mother's milk.'[14]

No one would deny that Marxist bureaucrats tend to speak in clichés: but Silverstone and his ilk are *reduced* to clichés. They do not even share the reality of their liberal dupes like the Gulicks. The fact that Dos Passos is working a familiar vein of realist prose at the same time as he produces monsters of one-dimensional characterisation weighs against Arthur Mizener's argument that Dos Passos is a satirist *tout court* writing in the tradition of Johnson and Swift. Mizener argues that

Each subordinate character fits his part in the whole by being what Jonson would have called a 'humor'. You cannot easily forget Marice Gulick or Comrade Irving Silverstone or Chuck Crawford or Herbert Spotswood, you remember them not because they seem 'real' to you but because, like Sir Epicure Mammon, they are classic representatives of their types, warmed to the kind of life all great satirists can create by the anger and grief of their author at finding them what they are.[15]

Yet this is to ignore the imbalance imposed by the disjunction of sympathies over the whole novel: and in praising Dos Passos' contingent gift for satirical portraiture it ignores the direction in which the novel's rhetoric of disapproval is applied.

For *Adventures of a Young Man* is a philistine work, in the last analysis. The writer's targets are all people with intellectual pretensions, thinkers, reformers. The Slade County chapters have some success in depicting ordinary people, but the ordinary people seem to be admired not only for their courage and honesty but for their lack of education. And the entire drama is spoilt by a narrative obscurity and the introduction of supernumerary characters who never spring to life as they do in the cameo sketches of *USA*. The background to the episode is the Comintern's change of line in the mid-thirties: but it is poorly dramatised in the book. The impression is left that the big-city schemers have cheated the miners, deceived Glenn and reversed their former positions all for the satisfaction of their own cleverness. With the conviction of the accused miners, and their subsequent deaths 'while attempting to escape', Glenn suffers yet another major blow of disillusion. He, who has attempted to share the life-experience of the workers – and has adopted the name 'Crockett' to do so – finds himself classed with the turncoat 'leaders' and theoreticians.

Glenn's disillusion, however, does not lead him to cynicism – only into a desperate, lonely existence as a fringe radical. His isolation from the mass movement is complete. Only Paul Graves, returned from the Soviet Union where he had been a visiting American expert, remains loyal. Paul's experience has convinced him of the wrongheadedness of applying Marxist political imperatives to the practical, scientific business of social engineering, and he has rediscovered patriotism:

'They gave me everything in the world, but as soon as I'd got a station started the goddam party line would cave in and they'd shoot my best guys or put 'em on forced labour and send me off somewhere else . . . I could have stayed on but I got sick of it and came home . . . damn good thing too . . . the New Deal's got the fiveyear plan knocked for a row of red squares as a social experiment . . . I began to hear the eagle screaming'.[16]

But Paul and Glenn are unable to communicate. Despite their common mistrust of the party, each has sought a path of his own – Paul reconciled to American capitalist civilisation, Glenn conducting a hopeless fight in an ultra-left splinter group. Glenn's urgent desire to serve the working class by personal effort is undermined by his intellectual self, i.e. by his criticism of party strategy. As Less Minot tells him, 'you got too much eddication for an organizer'.[17] The final repudiation persuades Glenn to enlist in the International Brigade: an act of despair and self-sacrifice, since it effectively places him in the hands of his Communist enemies. Glenn is arrested almost immediately on his arrival in Spain, and released only to perform a suicide mission. He dies a soldier of the republic, but the circumstances of his death make it useless and unheroic.

While Glenn has misspent his legacy of political idealism, his brother Tyler, in *Adventures of a Young Man*, has appeared as a 'normal', safe, materialistic figure. It is he who, during Glenn's involvement with the pecan-shellers' strike, issues the judgement of conformity. Yet in the succeeding volume, *Number One*, Tyler himself is politically committed. He has become the secretary of a Long-type Southern congressman. Chuck Crawford talks constantly of 'the people' (rather, like Charles Foster Kane, as if he owned them) but despite the folksy oratory with which he decorates his public speeches, the people to him are an abstraction, only real in so far as their votes will lift him to power. Five 'poetic' forechapters deal in turn with a subsistence farmer; a radically minded garage mechanic; a young store-clerk and radio 'ham'; a miner; a businessman. An epilogue pronounces that 'the people are you'. The narrative consists of five discontinuous episodes concerning the ruthless rise of Chuck Crawford and the disillusion, disgrace and ruin of Tyler Spotswood.

The story of Chuck and Tyler is related for much of the time with credibility and concision: Dos Passos' facility for rendering the tangible impedimenta of experience – the hotel bedroom, the campaign office, the political rally, the nightclub – has not deserted him. Yet the homiletic end which this talent is made to serve are now even more obtrusive than in the previous novel. Tyler Spotswood's motivations for assisting Crawford's rise are insisted upon. One is his love for Sue Ann Crawford, but this is a minor element, and leads only to a scene of doggish self-abasement. Principally, Tyler has caught the Spotswood disease – a dedication to political abstractions that is essentially un-American, Utopian and dangerous. Tyler's idealism and his ability to shut out unpleasant facts when they disagree with his image of Crawford's mission is apparent from the start. Accepting Number One more or less at his own evaluation, Tyler rebukes Ed James for his inopportune references to the base facts of political advantage. 'Ed the trouble with you is you've been in the East too long . . . You've gotten cynical . . . You've forgotten how the folks feel back home'.[18]

Tyler is prone to drink and venery, and in this respect resembles the traditional Dos Passos failure-hero; but these vices are either immaterial set beside his prime intellectual fallacy or contingently related to it. Crawford himself is an energetically drawn character-type, who does 'everythin' in the first person'. He is actually not the kind of man one would expect to take in the Tyler Spotswood of *Adventure of a Young Man*, and Tyler does, in his moments of self-disgust, find himself thinking of Number One as a 'bigmouthed bastard . . . that son if a bitch . . .'[19] Tyler is – as the author over-explicitly phrases it – 'a man reconciled by a few drinks to the deceptions and disappointments of life',[20] yet his loyalty to Crawford, or the Crawford ideology, is prodigious. Crawford is plainly a crooked opportunist; Tyler, however, tends to resent only personal mistreatment, and his faith in Crawford's political sincerity is unshaken by his close association. 'A man's got to have a crazy streak to appeal to the American people'[21] is his rationalisation. Chuck's 'crazy streak', his personal charisma, is matched by his calculating wiliness. While he is clever enough to mimic the received rhetoric of what Dos Passos called 'the illogical law-abiding, law-twisting procedures of our peculiar type of political evolution'[22] though subverting its essential being, Tyler lives politically in an unreality as complete as his hopeless love for Sue Ann. He cannot recognise this consciously, but it is baldly stated by Ed James, himself no innocent.

> Ed went right on: 'Toby, I meant what I said. In my line of duty I run into plenty people who think the world of you and they wonder why the hell you run with this Every Man a . . . shoot, I can't even say it . . . Chuck'll go pop like the weasel one of these days.'
> 'You put in some time on him yourself, don't forget that, Ed.'
> 'You win . . . But I'd like to see you on your own . . . Honestly, Toby, you're as bad as your kid brother, only he wore himself out to save the world for the reds . . . What ever happened to him?'
> Tyler reddened. 'Let's get a move on,' he said sharply.[23]

And he denies with a signal lack of conviction to Sue Ann that he is 'one of those starryeyed idealists like my kid brother'.[24]

Tyler in following his star becomes, like Glenn, an exemplar of the *trahison des clercs*. But hand in hand with his naïve faith in Chuck's mission goes the personal morality preached by his father, which he has never quite shaken off. It is the puritan American morality of justification by works, which he has briefly articulated to his confidante Sue Ann.

' ". . . if you do things too often that makes you feel like a skunk, then after a while you get to be a skunk, ever thought of that?" '[25] At the crucial moment of his career, when he is about to be called to testify at the inquiry with the State Park Bottoms oil leases, Tyler finds this ethic reinforced for him in his brother's posthumously delivered letter. 'After all it's what you do that counts, not what you say. One thing I've learned in my life is that everything every one of us does counts.'[26] Though Tyler has been swallowing martinis, this letter has the effect of filling his mind with 'bright clear sorrowful light'. The letter has stressed the primacy of honest experience over 'the "ism" talk', and it concludes with an injunction to believe in America and 'make more and more of the promises come true'. So Glenn Spotswood, whom one had seen inscribing a 'mock-heroic' testament on his cell wall, bequeathing his hope of a better world to the international working class, becomes the persuasive ghost who beckons Tyler back to decent behaviour and the Stars and Stripes. The effect is meant to be dramatically serious, and Glenn's injunction is plainly freighted by the author's approval, but it gives to *Number One* an ending of contrived sentimentality. Tyler Spotswood 'takes the rap', and while Chuck Connors harangues a radio audience with the verses of Henley, he editorialises on the lesson he has learned. ' ". . . We can't sell out on the people, but the trouble is that me, I'm just as much the people as you are or any other son of a bitch. If we want to straighten the people out we've got to start with number one, not that big wind . . . You know what I mean. I got to straighten myself out first, see . . ." '[27]

One reads with horror and disappointment the platitudes that Dos Passos evidently means to be accepted as the moral conclusion of his book. To present Tyler as an idealist who repudiates his commitment to a sullied cause in order to identify himself with General Custer and Old Glory mocks the purpose of fiction-writing and grotesquely falsifies human psychology and the nature of political belief. The coda of the novel, a passage otherwise comparable to the prologue of *USA*, climaxes in what is, frankly, flag-waving guff:

> weak as the weakest, strong as the strongest,
> the people are the republic,
> the people are you.[28]

The fault of *Number One* is not that it embraces conservatism but that it attempts to deal directly with political ideas at all. The relative weakness of Dos Passos' handling of ideas is dismayingly exposed in *Number One*, and his efforts to make a *roman à thèse* out of contemporary events spoil the modest but real success of his portraiture. The comparison is easily made with *All the King's Men*: Robert Penn Warren's much more sophisticated treatment of a like subject fully explores the thematic potential of the Long story. But Dos Passos, himself preaching against deceptive abstractions, is insufficiently practised at handling ideas to convey them with any depth. The result is that his situations never dramatise the novel's underlying concepts. Dos Passos views political arguments with the awful, childish clarity of the convert and he makes prescriptions through Manichean melodrama.

The paradox of his method, therefore, and the root of his artistic failure lies precisely in the vagueness of his political formulations, which constantly undermines his efforts to locate 'the people' as presences made concrete. Writing of the opening forechapter, Louis D. Rubin acutely notes that

> The passage is filled with details, and yet paradoxically it is a completely abstract piece of writing. It is not a particular place or individual being described, but merely a farmer – any farmer: 'the people'. Something of the same effect might have been achieved had Mr Dos Passos chosen to include a painting as a prelude, instead of the prose passage.[29]

The effect of this contradiction is to diminish Dos Passos' 'mystical Transcendental faith in the people'[30] as the countervailing value he intends it to be. The literary habits he has formed are unsuitable to his aims:

> Dos Passos' effects have always depended on a violence of pace, on the quick flickerings of the reel, the sudden climaxes where every fresh word drives the wedge in. No scene can be held too long; no voice may be heard too clearly. Everything must come at us from a distance and bear its short ironic wail; the machine must get going again; nothing can wait.[31]

Number One is crudely resolved in Tyler's regenerate impulse to take moral responsibility for what he might legally evade, and the crudity arises from Dos Passos' insistence on pressing him a political moral.

For Tyler's failure – the general failure to understand the corruption he has associated himself with and the conventional failure of his disgrace – is explained in terms which rob it of the truth one has recognised in the failure of *Manhattan Transfer* and *USA*. The novelist who had solidly refused to explain his characters' lost souls has descended to accounting for his ruined protagonist in terms of intellectual apostasy to a native political tradition. Moreover, he allows his hero to verbalise this explanation in a novelettish fashion: the people is us, we must put ourselves straight. 'Don't say it – prove it' is the rule that criticism has established, and in violating it Dos Passos has lost his way. That this wrong turning is not accidental and temporary is demonstrated by the final volume of the trilogy, the subject of which is a full-scale scrutiny of politics at the national level.

The Grand Design is punctuated by snatches of a Mother Goose rhyme beginning 'A man of words and not of deeds / Is like a garden full of weeds'. The aim of the book is to show the weed-ridden garden of federal politics and to anchor the blame for it in Rooseveltian policies. There is no *a priori* reason why a novel conceived in such terms should not work: most omnivorous and flexible of literary forms, it can properly claim as its subject-territory the whole of human experience, and its purposes may be unashamedly didactic or partisan. Yet in Dos Passos' case, a special fictive sensibility is applied to ends which can only frustrate it. The result is a vulgar, embarrassing, hypostatised product, which expresses its author's discontent in inartistic contrivance instead of as a settled and integrated reality.

The method of evocative forechapters has been retained, though as the story progresses they are increasingly invaded by authorial comment. The narrative starts with the departure for Washington of Millard Carroll, and identifies Carroll's idealism with the frontier tradition. In the territory between Texarcola and Washington are the historic survivals of a bygone America – the zig-zag fences, the smoky cabins, the old woman in a poke bonnet of whom Lucile Carroll remarks that 'It was like talking to Dan'l Boone's mommer'.[32] The sense of an America of potential plenty is established as a contrast to the atmosphere of Washington's political salons, which are populated by undesirables. The Carrolls meet Mike and Marice Gulick – last seen as fellow-travelling stooges in *Adventures of a Young Man* – and with them George Dilling – 'a tall too youthful-looking sallow man with a certain pomp in his manner'[33] – and Mack McConnell, who speaks with 'a flutelike note of selfsatisfaction in his voice'.[34] These two, however, are minor characters, and like most of *The Grand Design*'s proliferating minor characters, they appear only at intervals and only to utter their two cents' worth of moribund dialogue. Dos Passos' growing incapacity to colour his minor characters is only one sign of his devitalisation.

The central villain – and 'villain' is by now not an inappropriate term for a Dos Passos character – is Walker Watson, head of the New Deal agency for which Millard Carroll is to work, who exemplifies all the crimes and fallacies of the Roosevelt administration: a character of such multifarious vices that he scarcely exists at all. He is naïve and calculating, superstitious, pathetically loyal, egoistic – in short, not 'only unreal but grotesque',[35] and rendered implausible by being made to talk in an idiom hopelessly removed from ordinary speech. Walker's vulnerability to the hypnotic charm of the President is suggested thus:

'He told me things I'd never dreamed of, quoted whole passages from Senator Benton. He especially admires Jackson for not trying to serve a third term. He doesn't believe in breaking with the two-term tradition. He's got good reasons for everything he's doing and not doing. He explained the whole situation and asked my advice and I agreed with him he was doing the right thing . . . You ought to have been there to hear him talk about Farm Economy . . .'[36]

Likewise,

'Hitler's attack on the Soviet Union is the best thing that ever happened to the movement in this country. For the first time we are marching shoulder to shoulder with the great masses of the American people. In the common war against the Nazi aggressor we have direct access to congress and the Administration.'[37]

Judge Oppenheim, who has abandoned judicial impartiality for a bigoted support of the Democratic administration, speaks with the same robotlike portentousness: ' "Perhaps . . . if we had more of their devotion to the public interest and were less blinded by the self-seeking incidental to the profit system by which we were all conditioned from the cradle we should be able better to understand their problems" '.[38]

If this were merely satire, it would be artless and over-stated. But even the 'good' characters – those whose attitudes are tacitly underwritten by the weight of the novel's rhetoric – 'don't *talk*, in the usual sense of the word; they recite fragments of editorials'.[39] Paul Graves, for example, the 'hero' of *The Grand Design*, is portrayed as a thoroughly American figure, whose native good sense rejects the alien doctrines that are using the New Deal to further un-American interests. Paul's wisdom and clarity of vision derives from his field trips, which enable him to contact and speak to 'the people', yet he too pronounces his views in the stale, mechanical phraseology of a popular newspaper column: ' "Your relationship with people changes when you try to organize them into doing things. You have to kind of lower their consequence. First thing you know it's your career instead of the work gets to be the important thing. I suppose that's how politicians are made. Oh God, don't let me turn into a politician . . ." '[40] Like Millard Carroll the successful businessman who has proved himself in action, Paul Graves the empirical scientist becomes disillusioned with a government that is full 'of words and not of deeds'; additionally, he is made the spokesman for the author's anti-communist persuasion:

'We've been having leaks in the office. The investigators have pretty well caught up with the Nazis but they are babes in arms when it comes to Reds. The leaks can in my opinion only come from the communistic brethren . . . I know a good deal about the Russkis but I don't know much about the brethren in this country at least not since way back when one of my best friends went that way. But from what I do know about the Russkis I know they can no more get out of the conspiratorial habit than fly to the moon'.[41]

Paul's conversion, and the minatory nature of this analysis, are meant to be taken seriously, and his suspicions are heavily reinforced by the portrayal of the communists themselves. Joe Weekes is a repeat-performance of Don Stevens. Jed Farrington reappears, now a sinister cartoon-Red far removed from the Southern rake of *Adventures of a Young Man*, who had seemed like a prototype for civil-rights lawyer in *Easy Rider*. Jane Sparling and Winthrop Strang are sexual deviants, personally repellent in a way latently associated with the creed they profess – and they are shown (the last resort of the embittered polemicist) to be hypocritical in their enjoyment of private luxuries. What is lacking is a governing sense of reality – not simply about politics, but about the need for art to speak to its audience with a voice that acknowledges everyday actuality yet concentrates it through an imaginative effort that springs from a real willingness to face what is complex, discomforting, or obscure. In his novels of the twenties and thirties – and especially in *USA* – Dos Passos had appeared to possess such a voice. The engrammatic vision and method had provided him – a synthetic writer – with an instrument for recording the fragmented structure of human experience with irony, sympathy and graphically realistic conviction. The strength of this instrument lay in the writer's refusal to seek generalised explanations or draw reductive conclusions. He had unremittingly sacrificed for this special purpose the deep and subtle exploration of motives and states of consciousness. In *District of Columbia* he sacrifices the gains his former attitude had allowed him, with no corresponding advantages.

This is especially clear in the case of Herbert Spotswood, who completes the family history through his role in *The Grand Design*. Herbert returns from Switzerland (where he had been employed by that supreme agency of futile idealism, the League of Nations) to propagandise for collective security. The symbol of Herbert's function is the recording machine which he carries with him and which he uses to rehearse his radio speeches: a vain, concupiscent old man whose religious zealotry, which once made him a pacifist, has now turned him into a proponent of an anti-fascist war: ' "If there is a murderer at large on the streets . . . you have to call the police and have him apprehended before he shoots someone else, apprehended or shot . . . There can be no compromise between civilisation and barbarism" '.[42] Herbert's moral fanaticism is seen as especially dangerous since he is a radio orator with an audience of millions. And Herbert finally is used. Persuaded to address a 'memorial meeting' for Americans who had fallen in the Spanish war, he finds himself speaking to a 'party rally' in the opproved slogans of pro-Soviet agitprop. 'The Red Army has done what the broken remnants of the forces of the decadent capitalist democracies of Western Europe were not able to do. It has stopped the Wehrmacht dead in its tracks'.[43] The fantastic naïveté of Herbert Spotswood is matched by the diabolism of the communists: helped by the easily penetrable, cranky and dogmatic federal administration they are summoning American energy and faith in support of an anti-American cause.

And 'rejoining the United States' seems exactly to mean this to Dos Passos – producing a trilogy from which the multifaceted vitality of *USA* is dismally absent, a kind of fictional equivalent of John T. Flynn's *The Roosevelt Myth*. Even as satire it fails, though there was a subject here. H. L. Mencken had urged Sinclair Lewis to ridicule 'the vermin . . . of the Roosevelt and past-Roosevelt years . . . the rich radical, the bogus expert, the numbskull newspaper proprietor (or editor), the career-job-holder, the lady publicist, the crooked (or, more usually, idiotic) labor leader, the press-agent and so on'.[44] *District of Columbia* has nothing like the kinetic unity of *USA*, and the family who provide the common character element are conceived as failures in terms very different from the figures in earlier novels. It is true that 'all three members of the family arrive at exactly the same frustrated and empty philosophical position',[45] but that failure should entail the adoption of a 'philosophical position' at all indicates the distance which the author has strayed from his familiar material and attitudes. The ideological errors of all three stem from a political idealism that places 'the grand design' of a misconceived programme of betterment above the particularities of actual situations and individual people. Glenn is led to a pointless death on a remote battlefield; Tyler undergoes legal ruin; Herbert is made a puppet of the 'reds'. The exemplary and tractarian use of these characters to underwrite a political argument – an argument itself as monstrously simple and one-eyed as the error it professes to counter – distorts and reduces their effective reality. The attributes each has as a separate identity are insufficiently related to the basic courses and purposes of their lives. They are tacked on, almost automatically, as the traditional vices of the Dos Passos victim, but pale and dilute beside the unwieldy construction of a patriotic 'case' to which the Spotswoods as persons are subsidiary. One critic has written: 'Perhaps what is wrong with Dos Passos' later fiction is simply that the tension finally disappears: the individual sensibility is subsumed at last within an asserted collective historical experience – however different in its nature from that postulated by the earlier fiction.'[46] And while failure is expressed as the result of political misconceptions, the antidote is summarised in action – most particularly in the action of Paul Graves, who concludes the trilogy by enlisting in the U.S. Navy, as Tyler Spotswood had earlier done. Graves signals the appearance of the new Dos Passos hero, who repents his mistakes and prepares to rectify them. The failure to find a dynamism for their lives in real American roots is shared by all members of the Spotswood family, the Washingtonian 'cliff-dwellers' who have little contact with the ordinary life of the nation. But the tautness and controlled relevance of the contextual stylistic devices in *USA* have slackened to a weary rhythm that aims more at hectoring the reader with received ideas than realising a particularity that he may observe and judge for himself: 'a man in his twenties, maybe, scrawny neck red and creased from the weather sticking out of the ravelled sweater, brows bent under the bluevisored cap, riding the jangle of castiron and steel over the caked clods (it's clayey land an' a rainy spell came on before he got shet of his winder plowing).'[47] Efforts to picture the reality of individual people who comprise Chuck Crawford's audience are made in just this fashion; like cheap pottery figures they have neither individuality nor a true representative quality, and the tricks of style are exposed by the feeble pressure of significance. Dos Passos' personal mannerisms become positive annoyances, like the increasing negligence of the comma in his narrative sections. And as the sharpness of studied detail ebbs from his writing a barren and neurotic stridency appears: ' "After the war one of the preconditions of a lasting peace will be the greatest possible freedom of trade," said our President. It was a time of Caesars: the Heads of State declared a few new freedoms to order the tortured world; the battlefield was the whole blue globe'.[48]

The flag-waving oraculism is repellent. Coarseness – sheer intellectual coarseness, artistic coarseness, and an unfeeling and bigoted treatment of the human qualities he caricatures in the sympathetic and unsympathetic characters alike – has invaded the work of Dos Passos. When one compares the ending of *Adventures of a Young Man* with the final pages of *For Whom the Bell Tolls* one realises that Robert Jordan's terminal dialogue with Maria and with himself, though it occurs at the end of a very peculiar novel, is of a piece with the ambiguous motivations and beliefs that have propelled him all along. Glenn Spotswood's death, though equally sacrificial, is a kind of Awful Warning against choosing to believe in a wicked political philosophy. In one case the last image is of palpitating life, in the other of blank extinction; and the reader, though he feels pity for Robert Jordan, has no way of involving himself in Glenn's death, since Glenn has never existed with engrammatic positiveness: he is a victim of ideological mischance, a mistake to be rubbed out.

At the time of completing his second trilogy, Dos Passos had come to believe that 'it's political methods and not political aims that count.[49] This dangerously simple creed has found its way into the novels as an onslaught on preconceived plans, systematic control, centralised direction which signifies the end of Dos Passos' career as a sceptical enquirer – a role directly suitable to the writer of fiction. The consequences are lethal: books suffer not only in terms of drama and fictive tension but from a deficiency of basic craftsmanship. His usual disdain of plot gives way to a reliance on coincidence; the narrative is clogged with redundant passages; episodes are too casually juxtaposed or related; dialogue based on a sound ear for the rhythms and idioms of ordinary speech vanishes, and a monstrous, barbaric alien language issues from every mouth. Where the novelist's art floats free from his political obsessions, an occasional episode comes alive – Chuck Crawford protean and histrionic to bend others to his will, the silly private life of the Gulicks, the astrologer's part in *The Grand Design* – but these serve to illuminate the impoverishment of so much else. *District of Columbia* resumes the theme of failure, but its *parti pris* attitude prevents it from demonstrating failure as a fully conceived actuality; instead, it is reduced to the level of an imputed historical fallacy, and the talent which had concentrated on virulent nodes of despair dissipates itself in ill-natured rhetorical squabbling. Moreover, the new positives which the author has acquired have led him to need a visible prototype of success; if the values are right, they must promote tangible instances of fulfilment. Paul Graves in uniform foreshadows the arrival of the Dos Passos self-realising hero – an ominous image, which would not disgrace the *Women's Home Companion*.[50]

The fact has to be faced that in his later fiction John Dos Passos is a failing novelist rather than a novelist of failure: a failing novelist largely because he has ceased to be an effective novelist of failure. It is scarcely possible to believe that the author of *USA* is producing books of which none is a vitalising pleasure to understand and evaluate, but it is true. Worse still, he is a writer whose deficiencies are no longer enlightening objects of critical attention, but one whose art is radically weak even in its most elementary aspects. The novels degenerate not simply in their incapacity to develop fresh thematic energies, but in the restless juggling of technical approaches, in the repetition of over-used and faded material, and in the slackening of the craftsman's hand that used to deal so readily with such fundamentals as the establishment of time, place and mood.

Chosen Country, as the title implies, is a tribute to U.S. civilisation and an announcement that the author has aligned himself with the most authentic tradition of American cultural identity. This is meant to be the Jeffersonian tradition; unfortunately it savours more of the elderly, comfort-loving, *Time*-reading, Republican-voting, stockmarket belt – the thinnest crust of any tradition. The author of *Facing the Chair* creates a hero of Italian descent who, after an early life of waywardness, 'comes home' to the United States. The story is written with a complete disregard for the nature of conviction and personal development and culminates in a section entitled, with supreme vulgarity and despite the fact that much of it is set in Canada, 'O My America My New Found Land'. Jay Pignatelli's rediscovery of his native land is accompanied (needless to say) by his marriage to a girl from an 'old family'. There seems little doubt that the writer considers this arrangement to have *put everything right*, and this belief alone measures the distance he has travelled.

Immediately before the start of the concluding section of *Chosen Country* there occurs a crucial passage. After his involvement in the Sabatini case, Jay's thinking of his messed-up life and Communist perfidy:

> Sitting stooped in the chair in the dead air of Mulvaney's empty office he could hear Dandy's voice dim out of the past: 'Failure is a word I don't admit in my vocabulary'.
>
> 'But if you do fail . . .' he said aloud and jumped to his feet and grabbed his hat and slammed the door on that stale remnant.
>
> 'Then admit failure', he shouted into the empty hall, and waiting for the elevator began to think that henceforward . . .[51]

For the first time, Dos Passos offers himself as a novelist of the happy ending, and by doing so relegates his art to the level of the sentimental film or the Norman Rockwell illustration. Moreover, the two quoted passages are not exceptionally disgraceful examples of the style and content of *Chosen Country*, which begins the story of Jay Pignatelli's father, the son of a Garibaldino who, unlike his brother Joe, adopts the United States as his fatherland. James Polk Knox Pignatelli is patently John Randolph Dos Passos[52] in a thin disguise, and he is introduced in the first of the sections titled 'Prolegomena', 'biography'-like interludes in the narrative that tell the story of Jay's parents and Lulie's father. These life histories will eventually merge in the long-postponed relationship of the hero and his wife. Other similar portraits deal with Eliot Story Bradford (a fictional counterpart of Richard Norton), Anne Comfort Welsh, one of Dos Passos' destructive women, and a lawyer named Elisha Croft who is evidently modelled on Clarence Darrow. The practice of basing characters overtly on actual people is repeated in the figure of George Elbert Warner, an egoistic and accident-prone young man based on Ernest Hemingway.

Chosen Country is a novel of almost five hundred pages, and because of its length it painfully demonstrates how thin Dos Passos has stretched his material. The absence of dramatic pressure and positively relevant incident, often amounting to even plain tedium, is highlighted by the reduction of the narrative style, for the most part, to a bare sequential recitation. In his effort to restore a measure of vitality to his fiction, Dos Passos makes use of his family history in a manner that has contingent interest but is never fruitfully integrated. The whole of his artistic logic has been inverted to create a fairy tale of error, reform and conversion.

Accompanying the ebbing of fictive tension there is, fairly naturally, a proneness to absurd and distorted self-parody. Chapter 1 introduces Jay Pignatelli as a passenger on a train (he is a habitual and dedicated train-traveller) dreaming, or recalling, Herf-like detailed memories of his childhood. Suddenly he has an involuntary orgasm: 'He woke up all wet, saying to himself disgustedly; damn and double damn there ought to be something a man could do to help it . . . In the narrow toilet that stank of puke and was full of gut and filthy papers underfoot, he scrubbed himself off with scrunchedup paper.[53] Sexuality, though never precisely a sin, has always been a value associated with the ethical lassitude of Dos Passos' heroes, but here it is inexpressively used. The wet dream, the humiliation, the stinking lavatory are staples; but they echo only the special note of Dos Passos' most popular effect, they do not significantly contribute.

Inadequate, too, are the parallel chapters on Lulie Harrington and her set. The contrast with Jay's background is striking – the Harrington clan are secure, confident, outdoor people with a touch of *noblesse oblige* – but the characters die on the page. Dos Passos is never as ponderous as Dreiser, but he falls into the same trap of catalogue realism. Joe Newcomer, Zeke, George Elbert Warner, Jasper Milliron are like remote strangers in the pages of a compulsive diarist. Paragraphs run on randomly, carelessly garnering names and objects and piling them into an aggregate of undifferentiated abstractions. Lulie herself is reverentially treated, and therefore deprived even of the colour and life that Dos Passos' malicious caricature bestows on Anne Comfort Welsh. Even George Elbert Warner is pale and indistinct; here are the very weakest chapters Dos Passos has ever written.

Jay Pignatelli's history is offered as a success-story, and his marriage to an old-stock American implies that the Union has fulfilled its paper promises and discovered a unique strength through blending native and immigrant traditions. Whatever the ultimate merits of this point of view, it is not dramatically validated in *Chosen Country*. Jay's choice is a puppet's twitch. The articulated skeleton of the novelist's former self maintains Jay as the residual legatee of other, more memorable incarnations; it is incapable of realising him as a man making deliberately, out of experience and self-correction, a significant decision.

Failure continues to be treated as enslavement to foreign political doctrines in the next novel. *Most Likely to Succeed*. The setting this time is varied – the New York Theatre and Hollywood, both of which

Dos Passos had experienced professionally – but the protagonist is Jay Pignatelli's evil twin and his function is to discredit Communism as an exempler of its power to ruin decent human values. The purpose itself is naïvely didactic, and its putative objectifications are little more than slovenly rags in which the crusading spirit is thinly dressed. Once again sex and travel are the immediate correlatives of the opening situation. The seduction on the liner, which entails the rusty symbolism of Jed Morris's transfer from steerage to first class accommodation, raises the demon of 'bad sex' again, and the entire first section, 'Morocco', (it does not precisely take place in Morocco) exhibits a central character who is tirelessly unpleasant. From his very first remark – 'Ain't is perfectly good grammar. Shakespeare said ain't'[54] – to his parting from Jane Marlow ('Just a rich bitch, he said almost aloud')[55] Jed Morris is a monster heel. His crime is worse than the common Dos Passos vice of almost voicing intimate or tactless ideas in public: he is a believer in dialectical materialism. Besides, he is an artist – in the sense that he is a professional dramatist – and the reader is prompted to wonder if he is confronted with the *volte-face* of Dos Passos' appearing as the spokesman of ultra-conservative philistinism. But while Jed is not intended to be a good artist, he is certainly meant to be a failure – and not just because he becomes a rich and successful screenwriter. In fact, he does not develop into a failure, he is simply designated one, and most of the novel consists of supplementary proofs that Jed Morris is irredeemably vicious.

Purely conventional – even old-fashioned – in form, *Most Likely to Succeed* aims for the most obvious of the ironies suggested by the title. Not only does it miss electrifying the platitude that a man may be a success by all worldly canons yet fail humanly – compare J. Ward Morehouse – but it sets a positive puzzle for the reader by its inattention to prime requisites of the novel. The failing novelist, himself execrated by the critics and with the fear of professional perdition haunting him, has lost the 'récul esthetique'. He is no longer an intelligible writer in the basic idioms of his craft. For instance the action of 'Morocco' takes place in 1926, as the hero explicitly announces on the first page; prolific allusions to Paris, the Ballet Russe and Dada certainly date it in the twenties. But there is a bewildering lack of temporal actuality. In erasing the landmarks of his own past – here Dos Passos aims at wiping out the New Playwrights' Theatre, as he had earlier wiped out Harvard, Roosevelt, Sacco and Vanzetti – the author has left obscure necessary delineations of circumstance.

'Morocco' establishes Jed as emotionally dishonest and self-deceiving and introduces the image of the Soviet freighter 'with her tiny speck of red in the stern'[56] that will become a sinister recurrent signal of the American machinations of the Comintern. 'Theatre' concentrates on the metropolitan milieu of committed, experimental theatre and reveals Jed as a despicable mirror-image of Jay Pignatelli. Like Jay, he has a father whose philosophy has dominated his life, though J. E. is an elderly Jewish semi-paranoid who has spent his life conducting a futile struggle against J. P. Morgan and the 'interests'. Felicia Hardestie, like Lulie in *Chosen Country*, is a member of an eccentric upstate family. Her father is an opinionated veteran goat whose conversation turns to pronouncements like 'Without the intense purification of the sensual . . . a man cannot free himself from his own libido'. His attitude to radical politics is distinctly in line with the development of Dos Passos' own views: 'The trouble with the revolutionary movement is that it's as materialistic as capitalism. He would have us all be paid full wages for marching in columns of four . . . *Onward, Christian Soldiers*, and nobody must walk on the grass.'[57]

Thus Scho denounces the idealist. Jed *is* the idealist, or at least the victim of idealistic illusions. In practice, this means he is saturated with the maximum of personal corruption. 'Throughout his climb to success and fame' runs the publisher's endpaper blurb, 'he clung to a destructive philosophy of life that cut humanity out of his soul'. This, alas, is a reasonable summary of the content. The Craftsman's Theatre is a squalid arena of competing egos and interpretations of the party line. It aims to bring theatre to the people, but actually mounts productions chosen more or less for their political orthodoxy and achieves neither popular success nor mass political influence. It reflects the self-contradictory instincts of Jed's nature, which he desperately articulates to Felicia: ' "We've got to put it over. It's our one big chance . . . The Human Race is a sure thing, feller. It's revolutionary. That'll bring in Lew's theatre parties, see? On top of that it's box office, see?" '[58] But the tension is only stated; never does Jed fully exist as an individual whose essential inner conflicts, tellingly dramatised, impede the mature development of his character. He is a rat on all counts: for espousing the Communist faith, for simultaneously desiring conventional rewards, for his animalistic sex life, for attempting to incorporate Marxist doctrines in his plays and for failing to capture a popular audience for them. The objectification of primary reality has vanished. Jed is a target buoy, washed around by pages of fictive special pleading, vague and complicated intrigues, lifeless dialogue. Sam Faust, George Pastor, Eli Soltair, V. F. Calvert and others surrounding the theatre project, are dim, pasteboard figures.

They also found in the later sections, observing or abetting the apotheosis of Jed Morris as a highly-paid servant of the motion-picture industry. Jed's facility with words (of which the reader otherwise has no evidence) makes him useful to producers of prolefeed; but there is the sinister suggestion that his slavish loyalty to Comintern policy ensures that his success is fast and ample. There is little organisation of dynamic incident in the latter half of the book. Jed's personal life disintegrates *pari passu* with his professional advancement. Like almost everyone else involved in party work – and few of Dos Passos' Hollywood people are not – he eventually comes under suspicion. Fear of party retribution compels him to betray a woman with whom he has evidently found true love. The Moroccan nightmare has come true, and the final page shows Jed in the throes of a heart attack after interrogation by Sam Faust and V. F. Calvert, empowered by the 'Control Commission' to investigate him. The sheer melodramatic vulgarity of so many situations recoils against the author's passion to expose the red menace. Political talk is reduced to dead parrotting – 'Anybody with any knowledge of dialectical materialism can figure these things out ahead'[59] – and Jed's flickering awareness of the pit of horrors into which he has stepped is rendered by such banal formulae as 'We believe in different Americas . . . but love makes us one'[60] or 'Who am I, Mark? Sooner or later every man has to ask himself that question'.[61]

The novel presents a hero-failure who never convinces in any dimension. It suffocates under a cold-war blanket of hatred. Dos Passos has proved nothing about failure and he has falsified a critical period of history; any consciousness of the giant threat of fascism is absent from *Most Likely to Succeed*. So is the sense of life among ordinary people. Like other anti-Communist revivalists of the fifties, Dos Passos equates Communism with wealthy, parasitic 'elements', and by aiming at this barn-door irony he extinguishes deeper, subtler ironies – and truth. Jed Morris is a total failure. The author says so. But it is not a failure which can touch or persuade the reader, it is contrived. It rings with the infallible false note of the counterfeit.

The remaining two novels published during Dos Passos' lifetime illustrate a further weakening of artistic control, and in each of them a man of about the author's age and with the author's own experience is shown at the end of his tether. Roland Lancaster, in *The Great Days*, comes alive only when he thinks of the past; his affair at the age of fifty-nine, with a much younger girl, is a series of humiliations and cross-purposes. To underscore the contrast, the narrative is divided into two alternating sections. In one, Lancaster gives a first-person account of the key episodes in his life. The other, impersonally narrated in the dramatic present, concentrates on the Cuban trip with Elsa. Lancaster has grown world-weary through the exhaustion of experience: 'Hasn't he always entertained the dream of boxing up his old wornout life and sending it to dead storage?'[62] Elsa embodies his last hope of self-revitalisation, and Cuba the opportunity to mend his professional fortunes as a journalist.

The Great Days partially returns to the use of engrammatic perceptions – Lancaster is used up as a result of a cumulative barrage of assaults on his energy and integrity – but it takes pains also to accommodate Dos Passos' ideological grudges. Potentially the most interesting theme of the later works – reassessment and *apologia pro sua vita* by the aging novelist – is dissipated. Dos Passos has worked in much of the material from which his later journalism derives, and the positive values are cemented in with egregious reliance on cliché. 'Heroism: I had never understood the meaning of the word not even in France in the old war until I went to England. Those stodgy stubbly Britishers. Civil defense; their dogged selfeffacement as they went about their grim chores.'[63] In scraping around for subject matter, he has leaned heavily on his friendship with Hemingway (George Elbert Warner of *Chosen Country*, now grown up and very much 'Papa') and his 'tour of duty' as a war correspondent. The First World War–Greenwich Village–radical upsurge settings are abandoned, but what replaces them is tedious and flatulent, especially the long account of warfare in the Pacific. The first-person narratives survey Lancaster's life from 1929 until the immediate post-war period, and include a wealth of unassimilated and unrelated matter: his friendship with Warner, with Roger Thurloe – who later enters government and resigns because his preaching of anti-Communist vigilance and preparedness is ignored – his marriage and the death of his wife, his professional assignments. The tenor of these episodes is Lancaster's failure to make himself into an influential prophet of the benefits of American democracy, in line with Roger Thurloe's exhortation:

'We've got to know what we want to do . . . It's up to fellows like you to spell.it out for us . . . Not in detail, but in outline. There ought to be an American democratic theory like there is a Marxist theory.' I told him I had been beating my brains out on the project all winter. I wasn't the only one. Hundreds of other men were trying to put it into words.[64]

But *Blueprint for the Future* – Lancaster's attempt to 'put it into words' – drops dead in the face of public indifference. His image of the débâcle is that of sailing a boat against an ebbing tide.

In addition to his inability to arouse national opinion, Roland Lancaster learns that his relationship with Elsa is ultimately destructive and must be renounced. The discovery is a painful one, but bears the consolation that 'the worst is over. Life just by itself has meaning'.[65] Ro and Elsa are a curiously parallel couple to Colonel Cantwell and 'Daughter' in *Across the River and Into the Trees*; however, though the portrait of their relations is not so disablingly invaded by fantasy it has nevertheless far less depth and substance. Elsa is young (or youngish) but timeworn. She has made a disastrous marriage, drinks too much, and is frankly interested in a man who can afford to give her a good time; Ro has almost emptied his bank account to pay for the Cuban spree.

Elsa's personal history is familiar: working at a dancehall in her teens, runaway marriage to a bandleader, pregnancy, escape. Once the two are isolated in Havana, their relationship reveals its latent tension. At one moment Lancaster senses harmony: 'The river is the color of washing blue with a sheen of gold on it. The boats are golden white in the slanting sun. Terns fly overhead. They are looking at the same things, feeling the same things'[66] The next, a discussion of H. G. Wells reveals the gulf between their conditioned attitudes. Lancaster, out to impress, makes an absurd spectacle of himself while Elsa seeks her own gratifications. Street-canny but uneducated, she insists 'I believe in art. I don't believe in current events'.[67] Her tainted innocence and his corrupted idealism lead them down a blind alley.

The reader is left to draw the conclusion that Roland Lancaster's personal and professional impasses have left him on the edge of nothing, where he can acquire the impetus for a fresh assault on life, repudiating the vanities that have plagued his career. Yet his failure is loosely and rather opaquely described; it is never thoroughly established as a life-like consequence of impelling circumstances. The depletion of a talent is apparent in nearly every line – not just in the extensive use of unintegrated reportage and the heavy-handed editorialising but in the limpness of characterisation, dialogue and atmosphere. One catches echoes of the erstwhile Dos Passos: 'The beauty of the dim crowded streets where you walked with all your senses sharpened by the knowledge that a ton of bricks might drop on your head any moment. The tiny blue crosses of the traffic lights. The way faces bloomed out at the striking of a match.'[68] But the words occur as by the automatic reflex of an organism that has specialised in one function which it can no longer perform with spontaneous life yet cannot adapt to fresh purposes. The war-time London streets, Lancaster's feeling of isolation, the facile conclusion of his story – all substitute acquired tricks of technique for living art. The great days are irrevocably past: Ro's hollow moralising reveals the exhaustion of the author's creative vitality.

In *Midcentury* creative exhaustion is terminal: not even a reversion to the manner of *USA* can disguise it. If *The Great Days* is Dos Passos' last attempt to get outside himself, *Midcentury* is his final effort to penetrate society. The penetration is not deep, though: the theme of the book is the extinction of the self-willed individual by the power of large group interests and monopolies but it is expressed in querulous and bigoted accents. Organised labour is the villain: though labour 'racketeering' is the ostensible target, coercion and corruption are seen as the dominant weapons of the movement.

In the opening section, 'Your Place in the World', two principal characters appear: Terry Bryant, a returned soldier of the Pacific war, and Blackie Bowman, ex-Wobbly and now the aged and broken resident of a

Veterans' Hospital. While Terry is shown attempting to find himself and his destiny as an American in the post-war society now so changed and forbidding, Blackie delivers an autobiographical monologue. The content of this monologue is classically time-honoured – hobo life, the IWW, Greenwich Village, promiscuity and dipsomania. One accepts that it is the novelist's farewell to his halcyon days, but the first-person narrative is wearisome and thinly related to Terry's story. Punctuating these fictional chapters are three other types of statement: 'Documentaries', biographical profiles, and 'Investigator's Notes'. The Documentaries stress the reification of life by the process of scientific discovery, the profiles eulogise General MacArthur and castigate Freudian psychoanalysis and John L. Lewis, while 'Investigator's Notes' is based upon the reports of intimidated workers to the McClellan Committee. A Prologue in the author's prose-poetic style sets the infinitude of space beside the neural sensations of the individual being. This pattern is repeated for the second section, 'A Creature That Builds', at the end of which Blackie Bowman dies. The final part, 'Systems of Enterprise', weaves together the story of Terry Bryant with that of Jasper Milliron, one of Lulie's suitors in *Chosen Country* who has become a major executive of a cereal products corporation.

Midcentury is loose, barren, and repetitious. Blackie Bowman is potentially the most interesting character, but his experiences are little more than yet another version of the essential John Dos Passos tale, and they lack scope and density. General MacArthur and Dean are praised for their patriotism, a value now unambivalently good. The Documentaries miss the variety and ironic juxtaposition of the Newsreels in *USA*. The seven abstracts of Investigator's Notes are seven separate pieces of evidence against labour corruption – one would have served, especially as five of the profiles (Bridges, Harry Lewis, Reuther, Tobin/Beck/Hoffa, Senator McClellan) treat the same subject. The lyrical intention of the three prefaces and the epilogue – to warn that 'institutional man' must 'sacrifice individual diversity'[69] – is rendered as a blunderbuss assault on Big Unionism (to a minor extent, on Big Business and Finance); the interplay of tension between social and individual forces is neglected. *Midcentury* is not so much pessimistic as grievance-ridden.

The outcome of the Duquesne taxicab war, in which Terry Bryant is martyred, illustrates the compromises imposed on personal initiative (Jasper Milliron's son-in-law, Will Jenks) by the strength of the big combinations. The taxicab war is the most exciting portion of the narrative; but it does not end the book. For there follows an extraordinary attack upon youth, and by implication on the coming future. Dos Passos has already denounced the moral deficiency of the young American conscript soldiers who, taken prisoner in Korea, had collaborated with their captors:

Idealism without ethics is no compass.

'One of the most difficult problems for a prisoner is maintaining his judgement,' General Dean told Worden.

For judgement read sense of right and wrong.

No one had told those kids that right and wrong was the inner compass that points true north.[70]

Now he proceeds to express his contempt for the adolescents of the 1950s.

Documentary 24 includes one item on a discothèque riot, another on the motorcycle invasion of a town in California. The ensuing profile of James Dean, 'The Sinister Adolescents', with its gloating and scornful phrases, is aimed not only at the morbid cult of Dean (a fine actor, who won immense professional respect from many of his colleagues in the motion-picture industry) but at an entire post-war generation. The general accusation is that teenagers have been betrayed by affluence and security, miss the 'glory of life' and attempt to restore it by hero-worship, violence and rebellion. The treatment of Dean and his followers is in repellent contrast to the author's apple-polishing attitude towards another of his profile-subjects, Sam Goldwyn. The closing chapter 'Tomorrow the Moon', consists of the interior monologue of Milliron's nephew, Stan Goodspeed, who has run off with Jasper's credit cards. He is an old man's nightmare of a typical adolescent, as the premature cynicism and poorly hit-off jive talk show.

'Stan Goodspeed's throwing a ball. Yeah man' are the novel's final words: in 'Sendoff' the conscience of the author speaks up for another voice — 'the still small private voice that is God's spark in man'.[71] It is a spark which has ceased to illumine his fiction. *Midcentury*, professing to defend the individual against the enveloping institutions that threaten to crush him, only reflects a jaundiced disappointment. Maladroit in its construction, rife with traces of the magazine origins of much of its material, it embodies a sorrowful deterioration.

Dos Passos ends as the fulminating enemy of youth, having begun as its spokesman. Romantic failure is turned into cheap, patriotic self-regeneration and scepticism hardens into dogmatic fetishes of belief and repudiation. Nevertheless, it is an injustice that he should now be widely out of print (at least in Britain), forgotten and despised. The wonder is not that he should have ceased to be a widely respected literary figure, but that he should have left an œuvre which, despite the relatively small proportion of first-grade work, contains so much that is admirable.

In *Manhattan Transfer* and especially in *USA* Dos Passos had faced up to a universe which bore no objective meaning and in which the existential struggle to create meaning in volitional life-activity itself seemed hopeless. The 'impassioned objectivity'[72] of his manner and his technical resourcefulness helped to make him an author of genuine distinction. Dos Passos at his most accomplished communicates that most frightening sense of a world in which the impedimenta of a human-created civilisation refuse to yield any human meaning for the individual who reaches out to their lethal or recessive profiles. Fitzgerald wrote, wisely, that he spoke 'with the authority of failure';[73] that he could use the phrase suggests how failure is a kind of qualification for making authentic judgements on life – and the significance of the remark is sharpened for Americans. When Dos Passos shows the sickly futility of a life – shows it in the accumulated detail of daily defeat, shows it transformed (to use Sartre's term) into a 'destiny' – he overcomes the ignoble facts by the truth and courage of his portrayal. This task it is the duty and justification of art to perform. That he omits other truths – the transcendence of pervading misery by the intensity of man's perceptions and will to understand; the supremacy of love, however transient its realisation; the deep satisfactions that come out of struggle – no more invalidates his attitude than the existence of happy marriages disproves Hemingway's view of male–female relations. The reader who has shared in the life of our century turns the pages of Dos Passos with the shock of self-recognition.

When the fiction of John Dos Passos ceases to draw energy from a nexus of alienation and doubt it loses artistic cohesion. The persona he chose, or grew into, was increasingly inimical not simply to his earlier purposes as a writer, but to the essential character of his literary ability. When Dos Passos 'came home', when he published crude magazine polemics and volumes of sentimental popular history, he surrendered the insight which underlay his major trilogy and which is so finely expressed by James T. Farrell: 'Time slowly transfigures me just as it transfigures all of us. There is no security in an insecure world. There is no final home on a planet where we are homeless children.'[74] Farrell has also paid tribute to the vitality of the naturalist tradition, including *USA*: 'They have been written in the spirit of truth. If they are part of a tradition, that tradition has had more force and more impact, and has been able to nourish and give more energy to successive generations than any other tradition. This is especially so in America.'[75]

For it remains the case that Dos Passos is an American writer; he had no need to resort to anti-Communist bluster, Barry Coldwater and the *National Review* to assure himself of this. The great American theme of success, from its enshrinement in popular self-help mythology to the beautifully controlled resonances of *The Great Gatsby*, entails its own corollaries of failure, despair and disillusion. Fitzgerald recorded such emotions in typically personal terms: '. . . an over-extension of the flank, a burning of the candle at both ends; a call upon physical resources that I did not command, like a man over-drawing at his bank . . . a feeling that I was standing at twilight on a deserted range, with an empty rifle in my hands and the targets down'.[76] Yet not for nothing is Fitzgerald associated with the *zeitgeist* of inter-war America. What distinguishes his self-analysis is its freedom from rancour or blame; his artist's objectivity served him well. Similarly, the best work of Dos Passos – even where it draws on personal and political sympathies – never identifies a single source of error, a single evil. 'Impassioned objectivity' – more objective in *Manhattan Transfer*, more passionate in *USA* – allows him an exceptional freedom and versatility; antithetical properties (success/failure; radicalism/conservatism; mass institutions/ the private consciousness) are deployed with extreme skill and tension. When this tension is dispersed by crude polemicism, the vital framework collapses. A primitive world-view is matched by severe technical regression. Dos Passos' disservice to himself arises not from craft-experiment, but by the sincere yet damaging change in his viewpoint that persuaded him to re-interpret failure, success, morality and history.

It is especially deplorable that Dos Passos concluded his career as a novelist with a malevolent portrait of American youth. If there is any heroism in our time, any self-denying actions comparable to the heroism of the Spanish workers who fell on the barricades of their murdered republic, much of it has been contributed by a generation of young Americans who denied the limitless power of their government to coerce the individual and who showed their opposition by active resistance. But the great wave of contemporary organised outrage in the West is spent; despite the growth of an international youth counter-culture, one is more aware of fragmentation than of unity or harmony. Here are two themes perfectly in key with the interests of the novelist whose life ended in Baltimore on 28 September 1970. Such a novelist might be the chronicler of a world grown even more complex, uncertain and bewildering in the fifty years since *Manhattan Transfer*: not to point at causes and solutions, but by mirroring our dilemma and frustrations through the medium of art to amplify our awareness of our own situation, to provide us with an alternating focus on ourselves as social and individual beings. The time is due for Dos Passos to be re-read, as he wrote, with both sympathy and impartiality – and above all, with a seriousness equal to the most worthy of his aims and achievements.

Notes

INTRODUCTION

(All passages quoted are from the author's working copies as identified in the notes. Original editions of the works are given in the bibliographical listing.)

1. Edmund Wilson, *I Thought of Daisy* (Penguin edition, 1963) p. 45.
2. Carlos Baker, *Ernest Hemingway* (London: Collins, 1969) p. 649. Baker's identification of Dos Passos as the 'pilot-fish' is consonant with the text of *A Moveable Feast* (see note 8).
3. Malcolm Cowley, *Exile's Return*, rev. ed. (London: The Bodley Head, 1961) p. 9.
4. Randolph Bourne, 'Twilight of Idols', in *War and the Intellectuals*, ed. Carl Resek (New York: Harper Torchbooks, 1964) p. 63. The original essay appeared in *The Seven Arts* II (Oct 1917).
5. John Dos Passos, *The Fourteenth Chronicle*, ed. Townsend Ludington (London: Deutsch, 1974) p. 99.
6. John Dos Passos, *The Best Times* (London: Deutsch, 1968) p. 141.
7. Ibid., p. 144.
8. Ernest Hemingway, *A Moveable Feast* (New York: Scribner's, 1964) pp. 207–8.
9. Baker, p. 585.
10. Alfred Kazin, *On Native Grounds* (London: Cape, 1943) p. 315.
11. Ibid., pp. 326–7.
12. Leslie Fiedler, *Waiting for the End* (Pelican edition, 1967) p. 15.
13. Ernest Hemingway, *The Old Man and the Sea* (London: Cape, 1952) p. 103.
14. John Dos Passos, 'The Business of a Novelist', *New Republic* (4 Apr 1934) p. 220.
15. Ernest Hemingway, *A Farewell to Arms* (London: Cape, 1929) pp. 284–5.
16. John Dos Passos, *Three Soldiers* (New York: Modern Library, 1932) p. 205.
17. Ernest Hemingway, *To Have and Have Not* (Zephyr edition, 1947) p. 172.
18. Arthur Mizener. 'The "Lost Generation" ', in *A Time of Harvest*, ed. Robert E. Spiller (New York: Hill and Wang, 1962) p. 79.
19. Henry James, 'Guy de Maupassant', in *The House of Fiction* (London: Mercury Books, 1962) pp. 144–5.
20. John Dos Passos, 'Books', *New Masses* (Dec 1929) 16.
21. Ernest Hemingway, Preface to *The First Forty-Nine Stories* (London: Cape, 1939) pp. 7–8.
22. John Dos Passos, 'A Note on Fitzgerald', in *The Crack-up*, ed. Edmund Wilson (New York: New Directions, 1945) p. 343.

23. *The Best Times*, p. 130.
24. Henry Dan Piper, 'Fitzgerald's Cult of Disillusion', *American Quarterly* (spring 1951) 72.
25. John William Ward, 'Lindbergh, Dos Passos and History', *Carleton Miscellany* VI (summer 1965) 22.
26. Arthur Mizener, *F. Scott Fitzgerald* (formerly *The Far Side of Paradise*) (London: Eyre and Spottiswoode, 1958) p. xiii.
27. F. Scott Fitzgerald, *The Crack-up*. p. 77.
28. F. Scott Fitzgerald, *The Great Gatsby* (Penguin edition, 1963) p. 8.
29. Ward, p. 21.
30. John Dos Passos, *Manhattan Transfer* (London: Constable, 1927) p. 273.
31. *Gatsby*, p. 126.
32. Tony Tanner, *The Reign of Wonder* (Cambridge University Press, 1965) p. 360.
33. Ward, p. 25.
34. F. Scott Fitzgerald, *Tender Is the Night* (London: The Bodley Head, 1969) p. 75.
35. Arthur Mizener, p. 244.
36. William Troy, 'Scott Fitzgerald—The Authority of Failure', in *Modern American Fiction*, ed. A. Walton Litz (Galaxy Books, 1963) p. 135.
37. *The Big Money* in *USA* (New York: Modern Library, 1939) p. 517.
38. *Tender Is the Night*, p. 259.

1   THE ETHER CONE: HARVARD AND STREETS OF NIGHT

1. Charles W. Bernardin, 'John Dos Passos' Harvard Years', *New England Quarterly* XXVII (Mar 1954) 3.
2. Ibid., p. 9.
3. *The Harvard Monthly* LVI (July 1913) 173.
4. Ibid., p. 174.
5. Ibid., p. 176.
6. Ibid., p. 178.
7. Ibid., p. 179.
8. Ibid., p. 179.
9. Ibid., p. 179.
10. *The Harvard Monthly* LVII (Feb 1914) 158.
11. Ibid., p. 162.
12. Ibid., p. 163.
13. *The Harvard Monthly* LIX (Dec 1914) 77.
14. Ibid., p. 77.
15. Ibid., p. 79.
16. Ibid., p. 80.
17. John H. Wrenn, *John Dos Passos* (New York: Twayne, 1961) p. 35.
18. 'Dos Passos was uncertain when he began *Streets of Night*': David Sanders, ' "Lies" and the system', *South Atlantic Quarterly* LXV (spring 1966) 226. According to Wrenn (p. 121) it was completed in Spain.
19. John Dos Passos, *One Man's Initiation: 1917* (Ithaca: Cornell, 1969) p. 12.

20. John Dos Passos, *Streets of Night* (London: Martin Secker, 1923) 27.
21. Ibid., p. 30.
22. Ibid., p. 35.
23. Ibid., p. 36.
24. Ibid., p. 37.
25. Ibid., p. 34.
26. Ibid., p. 37.
27. Ibid., p. 47.
28. Ibid., p. 57.
29. Ibid., p. 63.
30. Maxwell Geismar's phrase, from *Writers in Crisis* (Boston: Houghton Mifflin, 1942).
31. *Streets of Night*, p. 65.
32. Ibid., p. 232.
33. Ibid., p. 170.
34. Ibid., p. 171.
35. Ibid., p. 135.
36. Ibid., p. 23.
37. Ibid., p. 74.
38. Ibid., p. 39.
39. Ibid., pp. 65–6.
40. Hayden Carruth in *The Reader's Encyclopaedia of American Literature*, ed. M. J. Herzberg (London: Methuen, 1963) p. 304.
41. *Streets of Night*, p. 48.
42. Ibid., p. 61.
43. Ibid., p. 54.
44. Ibid., p. 188.
45. Blanche H. Gelfant, 'The Search For Identity in the Novels of John Dos Passos', *PMLA* LXXVI (Mar 1961) 138.
46. *Streets of Night*, p. 187.
47. Ibid., pp. 190–1.
48. Ibid., p. 197.
49. Ibid., pp. 215–16.

2 'GETTING IN BAD': ONE MAN'S INITIATION: 1917 AND THREE SOLDIERS

1. H. L. Mencken, *Selected Prejudices*, 2nd series (London: Cape, 1927) p. 38.
2. Ibid., p. 41.
3. *One Man's Initiation*, p. 5.
4. Ibid., p. 51.
5. Ibid., p. 54.
6. Ibid., p. 64.
7. I should make it clear that I am going to use the word 'engram' – 'the durable mark caused by a stimulus on a protoplasm' – and its variants to indicate what seems to me central in Dos Passos, i.e. the unheroic wearing-away of the human spirit by an accumulation of petty sufferings and defeats.

8. *One Man's Initiation*, p. 61.
9. Ibid., p. 47.
10. Ibid., p. 60.
11. Ibid., pp. 71–2.
12. Ibid., p. 148.
13. Ibid., p. 159.
14. Ibid., pp. 160–1.
15. Ibid., p. 162.
16. Ibid., p. 165.
17. Ibid., p. 170.
18. Ibid., p. 180.
19. Ibid., p. 5.
20. Stanley Cooperman, *World War I and the American Novel* (Baltimore: Johns Hopkins, 1967) p. 175.
21. John Dos Passos, *Three Soldiers*, p. 22.
22. Ibid., p. 3.
23. Cooperman, p. 177.
24. *Three Soldiers*, p. 17.
25. Ibid., p. 17.
26. David Sanders, ' "Lies" and the System: Enduring Themes from Dos Passos' Early Novels', *South Atlantic Quarterly* LXV (spring 1966) 222.
27. *Three Soldiers*, pp. 225–6.
28. Ibid., p. 373.
29. Ibid., p. 378.
30. Ibid., p. 427.
31. Ibid., p. 452.
32. Ibid., p. 469.
33. Cooperman, p. 177.
34. Ibid., p. 179.
35. *Three Soldiers*, p. 145.
36. Ibid., p. 145.
37. Ibid., p. 146.
38. Ibid., p. 147.
39. Ibid., p. 17.
40. Ibid., p. 32.
41. Ibid., p. 209.
42. Ibid., pp. 466–7.
43. Ibid., p. 458.
44. Sanders, 224.
45. James Steel Smith, 'The Novelist of Discomfort: A Reconsideration of John Dos Passos', *College English* XIX (May 1958) 335.
46. *Three Soldiers*, p. 178.
47. Ibid., p. 11.
48. Ibid., p. 41.
49. Ibid., p. 65.
50. Ibid., pp. 118–19.
51. Ibid., p. 133.
52. Ibid., p. 157.

53. Ibid., p. 201.
54. Ibid., p. 442.
55. Ernest Hemingway, Introduction to *Men at War* (New York: Crown, 1942) xvi.
56. W. M. Frohock, 'John Dos Passos: of Time and Frustration, I' *South-West Review* (winter–spring 1948) 78.
57. *Three Soldiers*, p. 2.
58. Ibid., p. vi.

3 BROWNIAN MOTION: MANHATTAN TRANSFER

1. *One Man's Initiation*, p. 36.
2. Ibid., p. 4.
3. The epithet of Mason Wade in 'Novelist of America: John Dos Passos', *North American Review* (Dec 1937) 354.
4. 'Unanimisme', a term particularly associated with the fiction of Jules Romains, signified the use of a group or community in place of an individual protagonist. Dos Passos has denied that Romains influenced his technique: see 'Manhattan Transfer and the Service of Things' in *Themes and Directions in American Literature*, ed. R. B. Browne and D. Pizer (Lafayette; Purdue: University Press, 1969) p. 183. Perhaps 'unanimisme' was 'in the air', but the characters of *Manhattan Transfer* are carefully graded in the degrees of their realisation, and their separateness, not their unity is stressed.
5. 'July', *Transatlantic Review* II (Sep 1924) 154–79.
6. Ibid., p. 155.
7. Ibid., p. 166.
8. Ibid., p. 179.
9. Ibid., p. 164.
10. Ibid., p. 166.
11. Ibid., p. 168.
12. Ibid., p. 169.
13. Ibid., p. 170.
14. Ibid., p. 171.
15. Ibid., p. 67.
16. Ibid., p. 78.
17. Ibid., p. 81.
18. Ibid., p. 101.
19. Ibid., p. 106.
20. Ibid., p. 113.
21. Ibid., p. 114.
22. Ibid., p. 166.
23. Ibid., p. 165.
24. Ibid., p. 165.
25. Ibid., p. 218.
26. Ibid., p. 233.
27. Ibid., p. 232.

28. Ibid., p. 251.
29. Ibid., p. 282.
30. Ibid., p. 15.
31. Ibid., p. 40.
32. Maxwell Geismer, *Writers in Crisis – The American Novel 1925–1940* (New York: Hill and Wang, 1961) p. 124.
33. *Manhattan Transfer*, p. 330.
34. Ibid., p. 331.
35. Ibid., p. 337.
36. Ibid., p. 374.
37. Ibid., p. 342.
38. Ibid., p. 375.
39. Ibid., p. 378.
40. Malcolm Cowley, *After the Genteel Tradition* (Carbondale: Southern Illinois University Press, 1964) p. 137.
41. Blanche Houseman Gelfant, *The American City Novel* (Norman: Oklahoma University Press, 1954) p. 151.
42. *Manhattan Transfer*, p. 378.
43. Richard Hoggart, *The Uses of Literacy* (Pelican edition, 1958) p. 272.
44. Cowley's distinction, and the title of his chapter on Dos Passos in *After the Genteel Tradition*.
45. *Manhattan Transfer*, p. 132.
46. Ibid., p. 110.
47. Ibid., p. 251.
48. Ibid., p. 131.
49. Ibid., p. 157.
50. Ibid., p. 201.
51. Ibid., p. 231.
52. Ibid., p. 252.
53. Ibid., p. 320.
54. Ibid., p. 370.
55. Ibid., p. 374.
56. W. M. Frohock, *The Novel of Violence in America* (London: Arthur Barker, 1959) p. 37.
57. *Manhattan Transfer*, p. 3.
58. Ibid., p. 3.
59. Ibid., p. 4.
60. Ibid., p. 4.
61. Ibid., p. 3.
62. Ibid., p. 5.
63. Ibid., p. 10.
64. Ibid., p. 7.
65. Ibid., p. 26.
66. Gelfant, p. 149.
67. *Manhattan Transfer*, p. 12.
68. Ibid., p. 17.
69. Ibid., p. 23.
70. Geismar, p. 128.

71. 'Manhattan at Last!', *Saturday Review of Literature* (5 Dec 1925) 361.
72. Wade, p. 356.
73. E. D. Lowry, 'The Lively Art of Manhattan Transfer', *PMLA* 84 (Oct 1969) 1628–38.
74. *Manhattan Transfer*, p. 190.
75. Ibid., p. 51.
76. Charles Child Walcutt, *American Literary Naturalism, a Divided Stream* (Minneapolis: Minnesota University Press, 1956) p. 281.
77. *Manhattan Transfer*, p. 245.
78. Sanders, p. 180.
79. *Manhattan Transfer*, pp. 116–17.
80. Ibid., p. 25.
81. Ibid., p. 31.
82. John Dos Passos, 'Grosz Comes to America', *Esquire* VI (Sep 1936) 105, 128, 131.
83. *Manhattan Transfer*, p. 229.
84. Ibid., pp. 352–3.
85. Edmund Wilson, 'Dos Passos and the Social Revolution', in *The Shores of Light* (London: W. H. Allen, 1952) pp. 429–35.
86. Frohock, p. 41.
87. Auden, 'Song'.
88. Beach, p. 25.
89. Dos Passos, *Rosinante to the Road Again* (New York: George H. Doran, 1922) p. 93.
90. Walt Whitman, quoted in Lloyd Morris, *Incredible New York* (New York: Random House, 1951) p. 362.

4 AMERICA CAN BREAK YOUR HEART: 'USA'

1. Joseph Freeman, *American Testament* (London: Gollancz, 1938) p. 254.
2. In *American Social Fiction* (London: Oliver and Boyd, 1964) pp. 128–41.
3. John Dos Passos, *The Forty Second Parallel* (London: Constable, 1931) p. vii. All other references are to the Modern Library *USA*.
4. John Dos Passos, *The Forty Second Parallel* in *USA* (New York: Modern Library, 1939) p. 77.
5. Ibid., p. 80.
6. Ibid., p. 125.
7. Ibid., p. 128.
8. Ibid., pp. 138–9.
9. Ibid., pp. 150–1.
10. Ibid., p. 172.
11. Ibid., p. 174.
12. Ibid., p. 178.
13. Ibid., p. 193.
14. Ibid., p. 204.
15. Ibid., p. 204.
16. Ibid., p. 207. (Halley's comet is due in 1985–6.)

17. Ibid., p. 209.
18. Ibid., p. 211.
19. Ibid., p. 222.
20. Ibid., p. 225.
21. Ibid., p. 231.
22. Ibid., p. 235.
23. Ibid., p. 238.
24. Ibid., p. 243.
25. Ibid., p. 262.
26. Ibid., p. 263.
27. Ibid., p. 266.
28. In the light of Dos Passos' major emphasis on those who use words to deceive and who devalue language (Morehouse, Wilson) it is interesting to note the judgement of Philander Chase Knox on Andrew Carnegie, the subject of 'Prince of Peace': 'Now Mr Taft, all that old Scotchman is investing this money for is to have a funeral oration preached over him once a year at the anniversary of everything he has put a nickel into. He has bought up most of the orators of the world to talk from now until eternity'. Quoted in Mark Sullivan, *Our Times* (New York: Scribners,' 1932) Vol. IV, 158f.
29. As 'Mr Dooley' put it: '. . . th' poetic lie, th' business lie, th' lie imaginative, th' brassy lie, th' timid lie, th' white lie, th' pathriotic or red-white-an'-blue lie, th' lovin' lie, th' over-th' left, th' cross-me-heart, th' hope-to-die, histhry, political economy an' mathematics. They'll be a post gradvate coorse in perjury f'r th' more studyous an' whin th' hon-rary degrees is given out, we'll know what LL.D manes'.
30. *The Forty Second Parallel*, pp. 282–3.
31. Ibid., p. 310.
32. Ibid., p. 318.
33. Ibid., p. 325.
34. Ibid., p. 325.
35. Ibid., p. 336.
36. Ibid., p. 340.
37. Ibid., p. 344.
38. Ibid., p. 350.
39. Ibid., p. 350.
40. Ibid., p. 351.
41. Ibid., p. 354.
42. Ibid., p. 361.
43. Ibid., p. 368. In the first edition, 'a lost republic that had never existed'.
44. Ibid., p. 381.
45. Ibid., p. 405.
46. Ibid., p. 412.
47. T. K. Whipple, 'Dos Passos and the U.S.A.', *The Nation* (19 Feb 1938) 211.
48. Leon Trotsky, *Literature and Revolution* (Ann Arbor: University of Michigan Press, 1960) p. 218.
49. Lukacs, in *The Meaning of Contemporary Realism*, argues the former case; Lionel Trilling, in 'The America of John Dos Passos' (*Partisan*

Review IV, Apr 1938, 26–32), the latter. Trilling at least has noticed that the characters in *USA* occupy a relatively narrow social spectrum.

50. A good deal of the Camera Eye material on John Dos Passos Sr can be relocated in the form of straightforward reminiscence in the author's 'informal memoir', *The Best Times*.

51. Jean-Paul Sartre, 'A propos de John Dos Passos et de *1919*', *Nouvelle Revue Française* (Aug 1938) 294.

52. *One Man's Initiation*, p. 5. Dos Passos' use of the term does not carry the intensely bitter irony of Wilfred Owen.

53. *Three Soldiers*, pp. 28–9.

54. Ibid.

55. *1919*, in *USA* (New York: Modern Library, 1932) p. 96.

56. Sartre, p. 293.

57. *One Man's Initiation*, p. 2.

58. H. L. Mencken, *Selected Prejudices* (London: Cape Travellers' Library, 1926) p. 205.

59. *1919*, p. 246.

60. Ibid., p. 248.

61. Ibid., p. 249.

62. Stanley Cooperman, *World War 1 and the American Novel*, p. 143.

63. Marcus Cunliffe, *The Literature of the United States* (Pelican edition, 1961) pp. 282–3.

64. Sartre, p. 294.

65. *One Man's Initiation*, p. 18. (see also pp. 141–2.)

66. *The Best Times*, p. 42.

67. *1919*, p. 102.

68. Ibid., p. 189.

69. *1919*, p. 103.

70. Sartre, p. 296.

71. *One Man's Initiation*, p. 25.

72. *1919*, p. 190.

73. Alfred Kazin, *On Native Grounds* (London: Cape, 1943) p. 352.

74. John Aldridge, *After the Lost Generation* (New York Noonday Press, 1958) p. 65.

75. *1919*, p. 4.

76. Ibid., p. 45.

77. Sartre, p. 297.

78. *1919*, p. 201.

79. Cooperman, p. 143.

80. *1919*, p. 396.

81. Ibid., p. 218.

82. Ibid., p. 416.

83. Ibid., p. 440.

84. Sartre, p. 300.

85. 'Richard Gordon' in *To Have and Have Not* is scarcely a literal portrait of Dos Passos; but Hemingway certainly feared a libel suit. See Carlos Baker, *Ernest Hemingway* (London: Collins, 1969) pp. 359–60. For an entertaining graph of their relative positions see Herbert Solow's 'Substi-

tution at Left Tackle: Hemingway for Dos Passos', *Partisan Review* IV
Apr 1938) 62–4.

86. Daniel Aaron, *Writers on the Left* (New York: Harcourt Brace, 1961)
p. 348.
87. *One Man's Initiation*, p. 36.
88. Ibid., p. 154.
89. *1919*, p. 13.
90. Ibid., p. 104.
91. Ibid., 180.
92. Ibid., p. 147.
93. Aaron, p. 346.
94. Mencken, p. 223.
95. *1919*, p. 241.
96. Ibid., pp. 243–4.
97. Lionel Trilling, 'The America of John Dos Passos', *Partisan Review* IV.
98. *1919*, p. 247.
99. *1919*, p. 248.
100. Ibid., p. 247.
101. Clifton Fadiman, *Reading I've Liked* (London: Hamish Hamilton, 1946)
p. 138.
102. *1919*, p. 471.
103. Ibid., p. 472.
104. Milton Rugoff, 'Dos Passos, Novelist of our Time', *Sewanee Review*
(autumn 1941) 465–6.
105. Cooperman, p. 142.
106. Sartre, p. 299.
107. *1919*, p. 375.
108. Margaret Marshall, 'Writers in the Wilderness – II John Dos Passos', *The
Nation* CL (6 Jan 1940) 17.
109. Though both women share Morehouse's bed, details are carefully omitted;
and much of the unpleasantness of the relationship between the three
springs from the idea that they are not up to anything as straightforward and animal-clean as sex.
110. William Empson, 'Missing Dates'.
111. *1919*, pp. 417–18.
112. Sartre, pp. 292–3.
113. Leon Trotsky, 'Our Morals and Theirs', in *The Basic Writings of Trotsky*,
ed. Irving Howe (London: Mercury Books, 1964) p. 380.
114. *The Big Money* in *USA* (Modern Library, 1939) p. 8.
115. Ibid., pp. 12–13.
116. Ibid., p. 18.
117. Ernest Hemingway, *The First 49 Stories* (London: Cape, 1939) p. 137.
118. *The Big Money*, p. 37.
119. Thorstein Veblen, *The Theory of the Leisure Class* (New York, Modern
Library, 1961) p. 23.
120. *The Big Money*, p. 81.
121. Auden, 'Sir, No Man's Enemy'
122. *The Big Money*, p. 27.

123. Malcolm Cowley, 'The End of A Trilogy', *New Republic* (12 Aug 1936) 23.
124. Q. D. Leavis, 'Mr. Dos Passos Ends His Trilogy', *Scrutiny* v (Dec 1936) 295.
125. A sidelight: Dos Passos reports that once while Hemingway was resting up with a leg wound (he had shot himself trying to kill a shark) a package arrived from his mother with 'a chocolate cake, a roll of Mrs Hemingway's paintings of the Garden of the Gods which she suggested he might get hung at the Salon when he next went to Paris, and the gun with which his father had shot himself . . . Hem was the only man I ever knew who really hated his mother'. *The Best Times*, p. 210.
126. *The Big Money*, p. 117.
127. Ibid., p. 126. Camera Eye 45 seems to be connected with the feelings ex-Serviceman Dos Passos had when he met, in 1922, people like the Fitzgeralds who had stayed in the U.S. and whose behaviour struck him as bizarre. 'Their gambit was to put you in the wrong. You were backward in your ideas. You were inhibited about sex'. *The Best Times*, p. 128.
128. *The Big Money*, p. 151.
129. Ibid., p. 196.
130. Ibid., p. 197.
131. Ibid., pp. 238–9.
132. In *Twelve Great American Novels* (New York: New American Library, 1967) pp. 87–103.
133. Ibid., p. 102.
134. Ibid.
135. *The Big Money*, p. 164.
136. *Only Yesterday* was published in 1931; 'Echoes of the Jazz Age' in 1931; *Our Times* in 1932. No doubt after 1929 the gap looked wide.
137 John Dos Passos, 'Whom Can We Appeal To?', *New Masses* vi (Aug 1930) 8.
138. *The Big Money*, p. 293.
139. Ibid., p. 323 – and the phrase is echoed in 'Art and Isadora', p. 161.
140. Ibid., p. 66.
141. Ibid., p. 313.
142. Ibid., p. 25.
143. Ibid., p. 51.
144. Ibid., pp. 101–2.
145. Ibid., p. 17.
146. W. M. Frohock, 'John Dos Passos: Of Time and Frustration', *South-West Review* (winter–spring 1948) 75. Hemingway's hero, one recalls, is 'the man things are done to'.
147. *The Big Money*, p. 177.
148. Ibid., p. 277.
149. Ibid., p. 157.
150. Ibid., pp. 192–3.
151. Marshall, p. 17.
152. *The Best Times*, p. 172.
153. *The Big Money*, p. 446.
154. Ibid., p. 435.
155. Ibid., pp. 462–3.

156. Cowley, 'The End of a Trilogy', p. 24.
157. *The Big Money*, p. 464.
158. Ibid., p. 525.
159. Ibid., p. 560.
160. Trilling, 'The America of Dos Passos', p. 28.
161. *The Big Money*, p. 436.
162. Theodore Dreiser, *Tragic America* (London: Constable, 1932) p. 9.
163. John Ruskin, 'Ad Valorem'.

5　'REJOINING THE UNITED STATES' DISTRICT OF COLUMBIA AND THE LATER
　　FICTION

1. John Dos Passos, *The Theme is Freedom* (New York: Dodd, Mead, 1956)
　p. 103.
2. John Dos Passos, *Adventures of a Young Man* (London: Constable, 1939)
　p. 4.
3. Ibid., p. 21.
4. Malcolm Cowley, 'Disillusionment', *New Republic* xcix (14 June, 1939)
　p. 163.
5. *Adventures of a Young Man*, p. 38.
6. Ibid., p. 39.
7. Chester E. Eisinger, *Fiction of the Forties* (University of Chicago Press,
　1963) p. 122.
8. *Adventures of a Young Man*, p. 74.
9. Ibid., p. 156.
10. Ibid., p. 160.
11. Ibid., p. 172.
12. Ibid., p. 190.
13. Ibid., p. 238.
14. Ibid., p. 249.
15. Arthur Mizener. 'The Gullivers of Dos Passos' in *Dos Passos, the Critics
　and the Writer's Intention* (Carbondale: Southern Illinois University Press,
　1971).
16. *Adventures of a Young Man*, pp. 349–50.
17. Ibid., pp. 355–6.
18. John Dos Passos, *Number One* (London: Constable, 1944) p. 3.
19. Ibid., p. 21.
20. Ibid., p. 27.
21. Ibid., p. 55.
22. John Dos Passos, 'Carlo Tresca', *The Nation* (23 Jan 1943) 124.
23. *Number One*, p. 127.
24. Ibid., p. 149.
25. Ibid., p. 105.
26. Ibid., p. 197.
27. Ibid., p. 208.
28. Ibid., p. 212.
29. Louis D. Rubin, Jr, 'All the King's Meanings', *The Georgia Review* viii
　(winter 1954) 428.

30. Eisinger, p. 120.
31. Alfred Kazin, 'Where Now Voyager?', *New Republic* (15 Mar 1943) 353.
32. John Dos Passos, *The Grand Design* (London: John Lehmann) p. 23.
33. Ibid., p. 30.
34. Ibid., p. 33.
35. Malcolm Cowley, 'Washington Wasn't Like That', *New Republic* cxx (17 Jan 1949) 23.
36. *The Grand Design*, p. 206.
37. Ibid., p. 285.
38. Ibid., pp. 69–70.
39. Cowley, p. 23.
40. *The Grand Design*, pp. 234–5.
41. Ibid., p. 354.
42. Ibid., p. 86.
43. Ibid., p. 337.
44. Cited in A. Walton Litz (ed.), *Modern American Fiction* (Oxford: Galaxy Books, 1963) pp. 97f.
45. Maxwell Geismar, 'Dos Passos' New Novel of the New Deal Years', *New York Times Book Review* (2 Jan 1949) 4.
46. Andrew Hook, editor's introduction to *Dos Passos*, Twentieth Century Views (Englewood Cliffs: Prentice-Hall, 1974) p. 11.
47. *Number One*, p. 1.
48. Ibid., p. 280.
49. John Dos Passos, *The Fourteenth Chronicle*, ed. Townsend Ludington (London: Deutsch, 1974) p. 583.
50. A periodical to which Dos Passos had contributed an article in April 1942.
51. John Dos Passos, *Chosen Country* (Boston: Houghton Mifflin, 1951) p. 485.
52. For biographical information and analyses of the Dos Passos father–son relationship, see Martin Kallich, 'John Dos Passos: Liberty and the Father Image', *Antioch Review* x (spring 1950) 100–5, and Melvin Landsberg, 'J. R. Dos Passos: His Influence on the Novelist's Early Political Development', *American Quarterly* xvi (fall 1964) 473–85.
53. *Chosen Country*, 37.
54. John Dos Passos, *Most Likely to Succeed* (New York: Prentice-Hall, 1954) p. 3.
55. Ibid., p. 38.
56. Ibid., p. 36.
57. Ibid., pp. 84–5.
58. Ibid., p. 115.
59. Ibid., p. 228.
60. Ibid., p. 280.
61. Ibid., pp. 199–200.
62. John Dos Passos, *The Great Days* (London: Robert Hale, 1959) p. 3.
63. Ibid., p. 44.
64. Ibid., p. 280.
65. Ibid., p. 311.
66. Ibid., p. 66.
67. Ibid., p. 91.

68. Ibid., p. 44.
69. John Dos Passos, *Midcentury* (London, André Deutsch, 1961) p. 120.
70. Ibid., pp. 421–2.
71. Ibid., p. 496.
72. Brian Lee, 'History and Dos Passos', in *The American Novel and the 1920s* ed. N. Bradbury and D. Palmer (London: Edward Arnold, 1971) p. 199.
73. F. Scott-Fitzgerald, *The Crack-Up*, p. 181.
74. James T. Farrell, *Reflections at Fifty* (London: Neville Spearman, 1956) p. 65.
75. Ibid., p. 153.
76. *The Crack-Up*, pp. 77–8.

Selected Bibliography

John Dos Passos

NOVELS

One Man's Initiation: 1917, London, Allen and Unwin, 1920. Reprinted as *First Encounter* by the Philosophical Library, 1945, and by Cornell, 1969, under its original title.

Three Soldiers, New York, The Modern Library, 1932. Originally published by Doran in 1921.

Streets of Night, New York, George H. Doran, 1923.

Manhattan Transfer, Boston, Houghton Mifflin, 1925.

USA, New York, The Modern Library, 1939. A trilogy consisting of *The Forty Second Parallel* (1930); *1919* (1932); *The Big Money* (1936).

District of Columbia, Boston, Houghton Mifflin, 1952. A trilogy comprising *Adventures of a Young Man* (1939); *Number One* (1943); *The Grand Design* (1949).

Chosen Country, Boston, Houghton Mifflin, 1951.

Most Likely to Succeed, New York, Prentice-Hall, 1954.

The Great Days, New York, Sagamore Press, 1958.

Midcentury, Boston, Houghton Mifflin, 1961.

Other Books

A Pushcart at the Curb, New York, George H. Doran, 1922.

Rosinante to the Road Again, New York, George H. Doran, 1922.

The Garbage Man, A Parade with Shouting, New York, Harper and Brothers, 1926.

Facing the Chair: The Story of the Americanization of Two Foreignborn Workingmen, Boston, Sacco-Vanzetti Defense Committee, 1927.

Orient Express, New York, Harper and Brothers, 1927.

In All Countries, New York, Harcourt Brace, 1934.

Three Plays, New York, Harcourt Brace, 1934. Contains 'Airways, Inc.', 'Fortune Heights' and a revised version of 'The Garbage Man'.

Journeys Between Wars, New York, Harcourt Brace, 1938.

The Living Thoughts of Tom Paine, Living Thoughts Library, New York, Longmans Green, 1940.

The Ground We Stand On: Some Examples from the History of a Political Creed, New York, Harcourt Brace, 1941.

State of the Nation, Boston, Houghton Mifflin, 1944.

Tour of Duty, Boston, Houghton Mifflin, 1946.

The Prospect Before Us, Boston, Houghton Mifflin, 1950.

The Head and Heart of Thomas Jefferson, New Doubleday, 1954.

The Theme is Freedom, New York, Dodd, Mead, 1956.

The Men Who Made the Nation, New York, Doubleday, 1957.

Prospects of a Golden Age, Englewood Cliffs, Prentice-Hall, 1959.

Mr. Wilson's War, New York, Doubleday, 1962.

Brazil on the Move, New York, Doubleday, 1963.

Thomas Jefferson – The Making of a President, Boston, Houghton Mifflin, 1964.

Shackles of Power: Three Jeffersonian Decades, New York, Doubleday, 1966.

World in a Glass: A View of Our Century, Boston, Houghton Mifflin, 1966.

The Best Times: An Informal Memoir, New York, New American Library, 1966.

The Fourteenth Chronicle: Letters and Diaries of John Dos Passos, ed. Townsend Ludington, New York, Gambit, 1973.

Contributions to Periodicals

'The Almeh'. *Harvard Monthly* LVI, July 1913, 172–9.

'The Honor of a Klepht'. *Harvard Monthly* LVII, Feb 1914, 158–63.

'Malbrouck'. *Harvard Monthly* LIX, Mar 1915, 192–4.

'The Poet of Cordale'. *Harvard Monthly* LIX, Dec 1914, 77–84.

'Against American Literature'. *New Republic* VIII, 14 Oct 1916, 269–71.

'The New Masses I'd Like'. *New Masses* I, June 1926, 20.

'A Lost Generation'. *New Masses* II, Dec 1926, 26.

'Sacco and Vanzetti'. *New Masses* III, Nov 1927, 25.

'Towards a Revolutionary Theatre'. *New Masses* III, Dec 1927, 20.

'They Want Ritzy Art'. *New Masses* IV, June 1928, 13.

'Back to Red Hysteria'. *New Republic* LXIII, July 1930, 168–9.

'Intellectuals in America'. *New Masses* VI, Aug 1930, 8.

'Wanted: An Ivy Lee for Liberals'. *New Republic* LXIII, Aug 1930, 371–2.

'Whither the American Writer?' *Modern Quarterly* VI, summer 1932, 11–12.

'The Business of a Novelist'. *New Republic* LXXVIII, Apr 1934, 220.

'Grosz Comes to America'. *Esquire* VI, Sep 1936, 105, 128, 131.

'Death of José Robles'. *New Republic* XCIX, July 1939, 308–9.

'The Situation in American Writing'. *Partisan Review* VI, summer 1939, 26–7.

'To a Liberal in Office'. *Nation* CLIII, 6 Sep 1941, 195–7.

'There is Only One Freedom'. *'47* I, Apr 1947, 74–6, 78–80.
'U.S.A. Revisited'. *Atlantic Monthly* CCXIII, Apr 1964, 47–54.

SECONDARY SOURCES

I: Books

Belkind, Allen (ed.). *Dos Passos, the Critics and the Writer's Intention,* Carbondale, Southern Illinois University Press, 1971.

Brantley, John D. *The Fiction of John Passos,* The Hague, Mouton, 1968.

Davis, Robert Gorham. *John Dos Passos,* Minneapolis, Minnesota University Press, 1962 (pamphlet).

Hook, Andrew (ed.). *Dos Passos,* Twentieth Century Views, Englewood Cliffs, Prentice-Hall, 1974.

Wrenn, John H. *John Dos Passos,* New York, Twayne, 1961.

II: Essays and Critical Texts

Aaron, Daniel. 'The Adventures of John Dos Passos', in *Writers on the Left,* New York, Harcourt Brace, 1961.

Aldridge, John W. 'Dos Passos: The Energy of Despair', in *After the Lost Generation,* New York, McGraw, 1951.

Boynton, Percy F. 'John Dos Passos', in *America in Contemporary Fiction,* Chicago University Press, 1940; New York, Russell and Russell, 1963.

Cooperman, Stanley. 'The Aesthetic Rebellion', in *World War I and the American Novel,* Baltimore, Johns Hopkins, 1967.

Cowley, Malcolm. 'John Dos Passos: Poet Against the World', in *After the Genteel Tradition,* New York, Norton, 1937.

Eisinger, Chester. 'John Dos Passos and the Need for Rejection', in *Fiction of the Forties.* Chicago University Press, 1963.

Finkelstein, Sidney. *Existentialism and Alienation in American Literature,* New York, International Publishers, 1965.

Frohock, W. 'John Dos Passos: Of Time and Frustration', in *The Novel of Violence in America, 1920–1950,* New York, Criterion Books, 1960.

Geismar, Maxwell. 'John Dos Passos: Conversion of a Hero', in *Writers in Crisis,* Boston, Houghton Mifflin, 1942.

Geismar, Maxwell. 'John Dos Passos' in *American Moderns,* New York, Hill and Wang, 1958.

Gelfant, Blanche H. 'John Dos Passos: The Synoptic Novel', in *The American City Novel,* Norman, Oklahoma University Press, 1954.

Kazin, Alfred. *On Native Grounds,* New York, Reynal-Hitchcock, 1942; London, Cape, 1943.

Lee, Brian. 'History and John Dos Passos', in *The American Novel and the 1920s,* ed. N. Bradbury and D. Palmer, London, Edward Arnold, 1971.

Lydenberg, John. 'Dos Passos' *USA*: The Words of the Hollow Man', in *Essays on Determinism in American Literature*, ed. S. J. Krause, Kent State University Press, 1964.

McLuhan, Herbert Marshall. 'John Dos Passos: Technique v. Sensibility', in *Fifty Years of the American Novel 1900–1950*, ed. Harold C. Gardiner, New York, Scribner's, 1951.

Millgate, Michael. 'John Dos Passos', in *American Social Fiction: James to Cozzens*, Edinburgh, Oliver and Boyd, 1964.

Miziner, Arthur. 'The "Lost Generation" ', in *A Time of Harvest*, ed. Robert E. Spiller, New York, Hill and Wang, 1962.

Mizener, Arthur. 'The Big Money', in *Twelve Great American Novels*, New York, New American Library, 1967.

Mottram, Eric. 'The Hostile Environment and the Survival Artist' in *The American Novel and the 1920s*.

Pavese, Cesare. 'John Dos Passos and the American Novel', in *American Literature: Essays and Opinions*, Berkeley, California University Press, 1970.

Rideout, Walter B. *The Radical Novel in the United States 1900–1954*, Cambridge, Harvard University Press, 1956.

Sanders, David. '*Manhattan Transfer* and the Service of "Things" ', in *Themes and Directions in American Literature* ed. Ray B. Browne and Donald Pizer, Lafayette, Indiana, Purdue University Press, 1969.

Vidal, Gore. 'The Demotic Novel: John Dos Passos', in *Rocking the Boat*, London, Heinemann, 1963.

Walcutt, Charles C. 'Later Trends in Form: Steinbeck, Hemingway, Dos Passos', in *American Literary Naturalism, a Divided Stream*, Minneapolis, Minnesota University Press, 1956.

III: Articles in Periodicals and Reviews

Aaron, Daniel. 'The Riddle of John Dos Passos', *Harpers* ccxxiv, Mar 1962, 55–60.

Beach, Joseph Warran. 'Dos Passos, 1947', *Sewanee Review* lv, summer 1947, 406–18.

Bernardin, Charles W. 'John Dos Passos' Harvard Years', *New England Quarterly* xxvii, Mar 1954, 3–26.

Chamberlain, John. 'John Dos Passos', *Saturday Review of Literature* xx, 3 June 1939, 3–4, 15–16.

Chase, Richard. 'Chronicle of Dos Passos', *Commentary* xxxi, May 1961, 395–400.

Cooperman, Stanley. 'Christ in Khaki: Religion and Post W.W. I Literary Protest', *Western Humanities Review* xviii, autumn 1964, 361–72.

Cowley, Malcolm. 'The Poet and the World', *New Republic* lxx, 27 Apr 1932, 303–5.

Cowley, Malcolm. 'Reviewers on Parade', *New Republic* xciii, xciv, 2 Feb 1938, 371–2 and 9 Feb 1938, 23–4.

Diggins, John P. 'Dos Passos and Veblen's Villains', *Antioch Review* xxiii, winter 1963–4, 485–500.

Farrell, James T. 'Dos Passos and the Critics', *American Mercury* xlvii, Aug 1939, 389–94.

Farrell, James T. 'How Should We Rate Dos Passos?', *New Republic* cxxxviii, 28 Apr 1958, 17–18.

Footman, Robert H. 'John Dos Passos', *Sewanee Review* xlvii, July 1939, 365–82.

Gelfant, Blanche H. 'The Search for Identity in the Novels of John Dos Passos', *PMLA* lxxvi, Mar 1961, 133–49.

Goldman, Arnold. 'Dos Passos and his *USA*', *New Literary History* i, 1970, 471–83.

Hassan, Ihab. 'Love in the Modern American Novel: Expense of Spirit and Waste of Shame', *Western Humanities Review* xiv, spring 1961, 149–61.

Hicks, Granville. 'The Politics of John Dos Passos', *Antioch Review* x, spring 1950, 85–98.

Howe, Irving. 'John Dos Passos: The Loss of Passion', *Tomorrow* vii, Mar 1949, 54–7.

Kallich, Martin. 'John Dos Passos: Liberty and the Father Image', *Antioch Review* x, spring 1950, 100–5.

Kallich, Martin. 'John Dos Passos, Fellow Traveller: A Dossier with Commentary', *Twentieth Century Literature* i, Jan 1956, 173–90.

Knox, George. 'Dos Passos and Painting', *Texas Studies in Literature and Language* vi, spring 1964, 22–38.

Landsberg, Melvin. 'J. R. Dos Passos: His Influence on the Novelist's Early Political Development', *American Quarterly* xvi, autumn 1964, 473–85.

Lane, James B. '*Manhattan Transfer* as a Gateway to the 1920s', *Centennial Review* xvi, summer 1972, 293–311.

Leavis, F. R. 'A Serious Artist', *Scrutiny* i, Sep 1932, 173–9.

Lewis, Sinclair. 'Manhattan Transfer', *Saturday Review of Literature* ii, 5 Dec 1925, 361.

Lydenberg, John. 'Dos Passos and the Ruined Words', *The Pacific Spectator* v, summer 1951, 316–27.

Marshall, Margaret. 'Writers in the Wilderness. II: John Dos Passos', *Nation* cl, 6 Jan 1940, 15–18.

Mizener, Arthur. 'The Novel of Manners in America', *Kenyon Review* xii, winter 1950, 9–14.

Mizener, Arthur. 'The Gullivers of Dos Passos', *Saturday Review* xxxiv, 30 June 1951, 6, 7, 34–6.

Rugoff, Milton. 'Dos Passos, Novelist of Our Time', *Sewanee Review* XLIX, autumn 1941, 4 453–68.

Sanders, David. ' "Lies" and the System: Enduring Themes from Dos Passos' Early Novels', *South Atlantic Quarterly* LXV, spring 1966, 215–28.

Sanders, David. 'The "Anarchism" of John Dos Passos', *South Atlantic Quarterly* LX, winter 1961, 44–55.

Sartre, Jean-Paul. 'A Propos de John Dos Passos et de "1919" ', *Nouvelle Revue Française* LI, Aug 1938, 292–301.

Schwarz, Delmore. 'John Dos Passos and the Whole Truth', *Southern Review* IV, Oct 1938, 351–67.

Smith, James S. 'The Novelist of Discomfort: A Reconsideration of John Dos Passos', *College English* XIX, May 1958, 332–8.

Solow, Herbert. 'Substitution at Left Tackle: Hemingway for Dos Passos,' *Partisan Review* IV, Apr 1938, 62–4.

Stoltzfus, B. 'John Dos Passos and the French', *Comparative Literature* XV, spring 1963, 146–63.

Trilling, Lionel. 'The America of John Dos Passos'. *Partisan Review* IV, Apr 1938, 26–32.

Wade, Mason. 'Novelist of America', *North American Review* CCXLIV, Dec 1937, 349–67.

Ward, John William. 'Lindbergh, Dos Passos and History', *Carleton Miscellany* VI, summer 1965, 20–41.

Whipple, T. K. 'Dos Passos and the USA', *Nation* CXLVI, 19 Feb 1938.

Wilson, Edmund. 'Dos Passos and the Social Revolution', *New Republic* LVIII, 17 Apr 1929, 256–7.

IV: *Other Works Consulted*

Allen, Frederick Lewis. *Only Yesterday*, New York, Harper and Brothers, 1931.

Allen, Walter. *The Urgent West*, London, John Barker, 1969.

Baker, Carlos. *Ernest Hemingway: A Life Story*, London, Collins, 1969.

Bourne, Randolph. *War and the Intellectuals: Collected Essays, 1915–1919*, ed. Carl Resek, New York, Harper Torchbooks, 1964.

Cowley, Malcolm. *Exile's Return*, rev. ed., London, The Bodley Head, 1961.

Dreiser, Theodore. *Tragic America*, London, Constable, 1932.

Farrell, James T. *Reflections at Fifty*, London, Neville Spearman, 1956.

Fiedler, Leslie A. *Waiting For the End*, Pelican edition, 1967.

Fitzgerald, F. Scott. *The Crack-Up*, ed. Edmund Wilson, New York, New Directions, 1945.

Foner, Philip S. (ed.). *The Bolshevik Revolution: Its Impact on American Radicals, Liberals and Labour*, New York, International Publishers, 1967.

Freeman, Joseph. *American Testament*, London, Victor Gollancz, 1938.

Hemingway, Ernest. *A Moveable Feast*, New York, Scribner's, 1964.

Lasch, Christopher. *The New Radicalism in America, 1889–1963*, New York, Alfred A. Knopf, 1965.

Lukacs, George. *The Meaning of Contemporary Realism*, London, Merlin Press, 1969.

May, Henry F. *The End of American Innocence*, London, Cape, 1960.

Mencken, H. L. *Selected Prejudices*, 2 vols, Cape Traveller's Library, 1926, 1927.

Morris, Lloyd. *Incredible New York*, New York, Random House, 1951.

Reed, John. *Ten Days that Shook the World*, Penguin edition, 1966. Originally published in England by the Communist Party of Great Britain, 1926.

Russell, Francis. *Tragedy in Dedham*, London, Longmans Green, 1962.

Stearns, R. (ed.) *et al. Civilisation in the U.S.*, London, Cape, 1922.

Stevenson, Elizabeth. *Babbits and Bohemians: The American 1920s*, New York, Macmillan, 1967.

Sullivan, Mark. *Our Times*, 6 vols, New York, Scribner's, 1926–35.

Trilling, Lionel. *The Liberal Imagination*, London, Peregrine Books, 1970.

Veblen, Thorstein. *The Theory of the Leisure Class*, New York, Modern Library, 1934.

Wilson, Edmund. *Classics and Commercials: A Literary Chronicle of the 1940s*, London, W. H. Allen, 1950.

Wilson, Edmund. *The American Earthquake: A Documentary of the Jazz Age. The Great Depression, and the New Deal*, London, W. H. Allen, 1958.

Wilson, Edmund. *The Shores of Light: A Literary Chronicle of the 1920s and 1930s*, London, W. H. Allen, 1952.

Wilson, Edmund. *The Bit Between My Teeeth: A Literary Chronicle of 1950–1965* New York, Farrar, Strauss and Giroux, 1966.

Wilson, Edmund. *The Twenties*, ed. Leon Edel, London, Macmillan, 1975.

V: Bibliographies

Potter, Jack. *A Bibliography of John Dos Passos*, Chicago, Normandie Press, 1950.

Reinhart, Virginia S. 'John Dos Passos Bibliography: 1950–1966. *Twentieth Century Literature* xiii, 1967, 167–78.

Index